Joseph Hirst Lupton

Wakefield Worthies or Biographical Sketches of Men of Note

Joseph Hirst Lupton

Wakefield Worthies or Biographical Sketches of Men of Note

ISBN/EAN: 9783337025151

Printed in Europe, USA, Canada, Australia, Japan

Cover: Foto ©ninafisch / pixelio.de

More available books at **www.hansebooks.com**

WAKEFIELD WORTHIES;

OR,

BIOGRAPHICAL SKETCHES OF MEN OF NOTE

CONNECTED, BY BIRTH OR OTHERWISE, WITH

THE TOWN OF WAKEFIELD IN YORKSHIRE.

BY

THE REV. J. H. LUPTON, M.A.,

Fellow of St. John's College, Cambridge, and Second Classical Master in the City of London School.

"THERE ARE FEW INFLUENCES ON SOCIETY MORE WHOLESOME THAN THE FAME OF ITS WORTHIES."
DR. HAMILTON: *Lectures on Ecclesiastes.*

LONDON:

HAMILTON & CO., PATERNOSTER-ROW;
R. MICKLETHWAITE, WAKEFIELD.
1864.

TO

THE HON. AND REV. PHILIP YORKE SAVILE,

RECTOR OF METHLEY,

AND ONE OF THE GOVERNORS OF THAT

FREE GRAMMAR SCHOOL OF QUEEN ELIZABETH IN WAKEFIELD,

THE FOUNDATION OF WHICH

HIS ANCESTOR, SIR GEORGE SAVILE,

WAS CHIEFLY INSTRUMENTAL IN PROCURING,

THIS LITTLE VOLUME,

RELATING THE LIVES OF MANY FORMER SCHOLARS

OF THAT SCHOOL,

AND WRITTEN BY AN OLD PUPIL,

IS,

WITH PERMISSION, MOST RESPECTFULLY

DEDICATED.

PREFACE.

THIS little work had its origin in a series of short biographical sketches, contributed to the *Wakefield Journal and Examiner* during the course of 1859. As mere accident had suggested the subject, so, the author need hardly say, they were written without any view to future republication. That such has taken place at last, is due to the usual causes,—increase of materials, and the encouragement of friends. Such motives, it is true, would not be enough to justify a novice in undertaking a task requiring so much knowledge and research, as the complete history of an ancient town. But by confining himself almost entirely to the biographical portion of such a history, the author has endeavoured to lessen, though he cannot wholly remove, the charge of presumption. In one respect Wakefield is more unfortunate than its neighbours. Though not deficient in associations of more than local interest, it has not hitherto found a chronicler. Beyond a chapter in Dr. Whitaker's great work, and the writings of Sisson, Leatham, and Tyas, each illustrating some detached portion only of the past history of the town, little has been done in this field to make the way easy for fresh enquirers. This scarcity of pioneers, though likely to be most felt by the topographer, has not lessened the difficulties of the present work. As some compensation, it has lessened the danger of being led to take authorities at second hand. In quoting these so minutely, the author may be thought by some to have affected an unnecessary precision: but this is at all events the safer extreme on which to err. Even when every precaution is taken, the maxim of *suum cuique*, of the neglect of which Hunter so justly complains in the preface to his *South Yorkshire*, is not an over easy one to observe.

How far the author has acted wisely, in interspersing the *Lives* of his Worthies here and there with details of local history, the reader must judge. He has done so sparingly, and only from a desire to shew something of the soil, so to speak, from which they sprung; as a market-gardener brings his plants for sale, with a little of their native earth still adhering to the roots. From the same motive, the introductory sketch contained in the first fourteen pages was prefixed. Unfortunately, in this latter case, the subject was far too extensive for such narrow limits; and even after rewriting those pages (a circumstance which will explain one or two recent allusions found in them), the author fears that he has but indifferently succeeded in uniting brevity with completeness.

To a few friends, who have aided him with information and suggestions, he here returns his warmest thanks: more special acknowledgments will be found in the course of the work. Nor must he forget to pay this slight tribute to the patience and energy of his publisher, who has spared no pains that the *Wakefield Worthies*, such as they are, should at least lose nothing by their appearance in Wakefield typography. And so he commits this, his first attempt, to the world,— the little world of his native town. The labour spent on it has been no ungrateful one. It is well for one, "in populous city pent," to feel now and then beneath his feet, even in imagination, the soft, springy turf of the Wakefield Heath, and exchange the faint atmosphere of crowded streets for the freshening breezes of the Yorkshire dales. If, in turn, it contribute to the promotion of public spirit among his fellow-townsmen, of that *esprit de corps* of the right sort, which local history is designed to infuse, and, in short, of christian brotherhood in any form, the benefit will have been mutual.

London, May, 1864.

WAKEFIELD.

Respecting the early history of this town we have but little information. Its name, were the etymology certain, might afford us a slight clue; but on this point there is a difference of opinion. In Domesday Book, the earliest record where it occurs, it is spelt Wachefeld. This word, according to Whitaker, "probably denotes nothing more than the appellation of the first Saxon possessor, combined with that of the estate which he possessed. Nothing was more common," he adds, "at the time when the *villare* of this country was formed, than to denote whole townships by the terminating syllable *field*."[1] The analogy of Huddersfield (Oder's field), and other similar names, lends countenance to this; though no such name as Wac or Wache is to be found in the long list compiled by Sir Henry Ellis from the Domesday Survey.[2] In any case, the word is of Anglo-Saxon origin; the *c* of that language sometimes becoming represented by *k*, as here, and sometimes being softened into *tch*, as in the case of Wacenesfeld, afterwards Watchfield, in Berk-

---

(1) *Loidis and Elmete* (1816), p. 275.—Another derivation of the word will be discussed in the Appendix.

(2) A hundred years later, however, a Baldewinus Waac is mentioned by the chronicler Bromton. See *Historiæ Anglicanæ Scriptores X* (1652), p. 1158.

shire.[3] Whether Wakefield was an inhabited place, previous to the settlement of the Saxons in these parts, it is hard to say. A few inferences, drawn from the nature of the surrounding country, and the presence of the Romans in the neighbourhood, are all that on this head we have to offer.

That an extensive forest once overspread this region, a glance at a map of the country about Wakefield will testify. Within a compass of a few miles we meet with such names as Outwood, Whitwood, Woodlesford, Woodchurch; and others indicating the prevalence of particular trees, as Oakenshaw and Ackworth (from the oak), Alverthorpe (from the alder),[4] Birkinshaw (from the birch, or poplar),[5] Hollinthorpe (from the holly or holm-tree),[6] Hasle, Thornes, Thornhill, Elmley, and the like. The name of this last-mentioned place, to the south-west of Wakefield, suggests the probability of this whole district having been included in the great Elmet wood, a term which denoted "not only a large forest, but a great part of Yorkshire, called so from the grove of elms."[7] If this be so, then the history of our town, supposing there to have been any settlement on the spot in the early British period, must be traced in the history of this district of Elmet. Whether, before the establishment of the Roman

---

(3) See the Index to Kemble's *Codex Diplomaticus* (1848).

(4) In Anglo-Saxon *alr*, whence Alresford, Ellerton, &c.—See Ingram's *Saxon Chronicle* (1823), p. 425. The village is still commonly called "Allerthorpe;" and one of the Auditors of the Exchequer in 1370 was Laurence de Allerthorp. See Devon's *Issue Roll of Thomas de Brantingham* (1835), p. 143.

(5) "Birce, *populus*":—Wright's *Volume of Vocabularies* (privately printed, 1857), p. 285. Usually it means *birch*.

(6) A.S. *Holegn* or *holen*.

(7) Giles's note on Bede's *Ecclesiastical History*, ii. 14.

power in the island, any city, or centre of population, was to be found in the neighbourhood, depends on the question whether the Cair Loid Coit, which occurs in the list of British cities given by Nennius,[8] was Leeds. Thoresby,[9] observing a region called Loidis to be spoken of by Bede in connection with Elmet wood, argues in favour of this hypothesis; and his opinion has been seconded and enlarged upon by Mr. James.[10]

---

(8) Who Nennius was, or when he wrote, is uncertain. In Roberts's *Chronicle of the Kings of Britain* (1811), p. 76, the reader may see the tradition of his being the same as Nyniaw, king Caswallon's brother, and how he died of a wound inflicted by Cæsar's own hand in battle.

(9) *Ducatus;* Preface, p. ix.

(10) In an ingenious Paper, read at the meeting of the Archæological Association at Leeds in October, 1863, and printed in their *Journal* of March 31st, 1864.

As far as authorities go, the balance of opinion is in favour of Lincoln being the town referred to. So Usher (*Antiquitates*, 1687, p. 35); Stevenson (*Nennius*, 1838, in the Index); and others. Ingram (*Saxon Chronicle*, 1823, p. 448) proposes Ludlow, or Lytchett in Dorsetshire, to which last name the words of Nennius bear a resemblance in sound: Gunn (*Nennius*, 1819, p. 108) merely refers to Usher and Gale. The last-mentioned (*Historiæ . . . Scriptores XV.*, 1691, p. 135) hesitates between Lincoln and "Leodes in Elmeto;" though in a letter to Thoresby he gave a preference to the latter. I have only space to point to one or two arguments in favour of Lincoln, such as its great size and importance in early times, as evinced by the Domesday Survey; while there are no signs of Leeds having ever been a station of the Romans, though they undoubtedly had an encampment at Adle, not far off.—As regards the name of Leeds, it is probably of Saxon origin. Whitaker (*Loidis and Elmete*, p. 5) considers it as "merely the genitive case of the name borne by Loidi, the first Saxon possessor." Others (as in Gibson's *Camden*, 1772, vol. ii., p. 89) derive it from the Saxon *Leod*, "people" (as in *Ludlow*, &c.), implying it to have been a populous place in Saxon times. This view receives some slight confirmation from the fact of other places of the name being found in Germanic countries. In Domesday Book Leeds is spelt Ledes: and in Eastern Flanders, near Alost, is a town called Lede. See also the names Leden, Ledenford, &c., in the Index to Kemble's *Codex Diplomaticus* referred to above.

The Romans, during their occupation of the country, left traces of their presence in many parts round Wakefield, though no remains, as far as I am aware, have been discovered within the town. Legeolium (Castleford) was an undoubted Roman station, and Cambodunum (supposed to be Slack),[11] was another. The road connecting these, and passing through the encampment of which traces are to be seen at Kirklees, must have gone within no great distance of the present Wakefield. Agreeably with this, indications of such a road, between this town and Dewsbury on the west, remain in the names "Street," and "Streetside;" whilst signs of a like nature have been discovered in the neighbourhood of Altofts and Normanton on the east. In a letter which was published many years ago in a Pontefract newspaper,[12] Mr. Jesse Hartley stated that, "On the common of Birkwood, what (before the enclosure took place) was called Redhill, was the site of a Roman camp, close by the road leading to Stanley Ferry, and in the direct road from Castleford to the Roman fort at Almondbury. Around this camp were two or three lines of circumvallation thrown up; and the high part of the common was occupied by a many of what were called *Pit-audits*,[13] or *audins*, which had been worked as coal-pits by the Romans." A little distance north of the line which it is presumed this road joining Cambodunum with

---

(11) Reynolds (*Iter Britanniarum*, 1799, p. 193) judges it to be Ealand; Watson (see Crabtree's *History of Halifax*, 1836, p. 32) refers it to Longwood in the parish of Huddersfield.

(12) A copy of which was obligingly communicated to me by Mr T. H. Cromek, of Wakefield.

(13) i.e. *adits*, or passages;—a common term among miners.

Legeolium must have taken, namely, at Lingwell Gate, there have been dug up at intervals, ever since 1697, coins and coin-moulds, bearing the effigy of various Roman emperors. There is little doubt that Lingwell obtained its name from having been at some time a station of the second Cohort of the Lingones, the head-quarters of which were at *Olicana*, the modern Ilkley.[14] Whether the coins in question were the work of forgers, or only *pièces de nécessité*, such as Roman generals are known to have struck when in remote districts, is undecided.[15]

The space between the departure of the Romans from Britain, about the year 420, and the Norman Conquest, would be a blank in the history of Wakefield, but for a few faint, yet interesting, traces which remain of Saxon doings in the surrounding territory of Elmet. When the victory gained by Redwald, King of the East Angles, over Edilfrid, near the river Idle in Nottinghamshire,[16] placed Edwin on the throne of Northumbria, he proceeded to bring under his own dominion "the country for a little way about Winwidfield... anciently called Elmet... by the conquest of Cereticus, a British King, A.D. 620."[17] From

---

(14) "They were also at Ilkley, in Yorkshire, where Claudius Fronto their commander erected an altar to Verbeia; and they seem to be also mentioned in another inscription at the same place under Cecilius their commander, which shews them to have been here in the reign of Marcus Aurelius and Lucius Verus."— Horsley: *Britannia Romana* (1732), p. 90.

(15) Reade (*Numismatic Chronicle*, vol. i., p. 151) takes the former view; Knight (*Archæologia*, vol. xxiv., p. 349) the latter.

(16) Whence arose the saying "Amnis Idle Anglorum sanguine sorduit."—See Thorpe's edition of Florence of Winchester's Chronicle (1848), vol. i., p. 13, n. The date of the battle is variously given as 616, 617, and a still later year.

(17) *Camden's Britannia* by Gibson (1772), vol. ii., p. 90.

the fact that this district thus appears to have maintained its independence for nearly two hundred years, Mr. James draws several interesting conclusions; as, that this *Regiuncula* of Elmet "probably remained in inhabitants, religion, and manners, much the same from the time when the Romans quitted this country until the year 616;" and that it preserved the light of Christianity in the midst of the heathenism of the surrounding Saxon states.[18] Not long after his conquest of Elmet, Edwin himself became a christian, and was baptized at Easter, 627, by Paulinus, along with twelve thousand of his subjects.[19] The river Swale was one scene of that great missionary's labours; and, as Dewsbury was also a station of his, there is little doubt that he proceeded in like manner along the vale of the Calder. After reigning seventeen years, in 634, Edwin was defeated and slain by the unconverted

---

(18) *Journal of the Archæological Association* (1864), p. 34.—The argument by which Dr. Lappenberg (*History of England under the Saxon Kings*, translated by Thorpe, 1845, vol. i., p. 149), who is the authority quoted by James, shews this King of Elmet to have been a *British* King, is worth noticing. It rests on a passage of Bede (iv., 23), who speaks of Hereric (Edwin's nephew) being in exile under Cerdic, a king of the Britons, where he died of poison. Hence the inference is, that when Nennius (§ 63) says that Edwin "occupavit Elmet et expulit Certic, regem illius regionis," the allusion is to the Cerdic who poisoned Hereric; and that the now powerful Bretwalda took this step to avenge his nephew's murder. Otherwise, the name Cerdic might be Saxon, as well as British. In 494 a Certik and his son Kinerik landed, and after slaying the British chief Nathanliot, established a dynasty.—See Mayor's *Richard of Cirencester* (1863), vol. i., p. 25. A Ceretic, or Cerdic, was interpreter between Vortigern and Hengist; and in some MSS. of Nennius (§ 37), who relates this, the word *Elmet* is found as a gloss upon *Cerdic;* which confirms Lappenberg's opinion.

(19) Bede, ii. 14.

king of Mercia, the fierce Penda, aided by the Welch prince Ceadwalla.[20] This Battle was fought at Hatfelde, or Heathfield, the site of which has been much disputed.[21] Bede adds that a church which had been erected in *Campodonum*, where was also a royal residence, was at the same time destroyed by the pagans; but that the altar, being of stone, escaped, and was afterwards preserved in the monastery in Elmet wood, of which Thridwulf was abbot.[22] In 655 Oswi, the nephew and son-in-law of Edwin, avenged the death of his uncle, and also of his brother Oswald, who had been slain by Penda in 642, by signally defeating the Mercians near the river Winwaed; in which engagement their King and many of his allies were killed.[23] Thoresby's conjecture that Whinmore was the battle-field on this occasion, and the river Aire the Winwaed, has found little favour. "We shall probably discover the Winwaed of Bede," says Whitaker,[24] " a few miles to the southward, in the little river Went, which long since the Conquest is known to have been spelt Wynt." If this supposition be correct, then the tract of country between Wakefield and Doncaster is associated with the memory of each of the three great Northumbrian chieftains, Edwin, Oswald, and Oswi. For the Went, one feeder of which passes through Nostell Park, runs

---

(20) John of Bromton's Chronicle, as above, p. 784.

(21) Hunter *(South Yorkshire*, 1831, Pref. p. ix*)* places it near Doncaster.

(22) Where Campodonum was, and this monastery of Thridwulf, has been much debated. As the former is rendered in King Alfred's version of Bede by Donafelda, Gale supposed it to be Tanfield near Ripon.—See Smith's edition of Bede (1722). Hunter (as above, p. xiv) makes Campodonum to be Doncaster; an opinion for which he assigns many strong reasons.

(23) Bede : iii, 24.

(24) *Loidis and Elmete,* p. 4.

in an easterly direction till it falls into the Don ; and the name *Stagnum Sancti Oswaldi*, by which the pool at Nostell is described in a grant of Ocelin, "affords ground for presuming that, before the time of its refoundation (by Henry i.) Nostell was in some manner connected with the name and fame of Saint Oswald."[25]

Proceeding to the time of the Domesday Survey, we find the manor of Wakefield thus described :—

"In WACHEFELD cu'. ix. berew.' Sandala. Sorebi. Werla. fes!ei. Miclcie. Wadesuurde. Cru'betonestun. Langefelt. Stanesfelt. sunt ad gld. LX. carucate t'ræ. 7 iii. bouatæ. 7 iiicia pars uni' bouatæ. Hanc t'ram poss' arare xxx carucæ. Hoc Maner' fuit regis Edw' in d'nio. M'o in manu regis sunt ibi. iiiior. uill'i. 7 iii. pbri. 7 ii. æcclæ. 7 vii. sochem'. 7 xvi bord'. Simul hnt. vii. car'. silua pasc'. vi. lev' lg. 7 iiii. lev' lat. Totu' vi. lev' lg. 7 vi. lev' lat. T.R.E. LX. lib'. ual'. m'o. xv. lib'."[26]

"In *Wachefeld* (Wakefield) with nine berewicks, *Sandala* (Sandal), *Sorebi* (Sowerby), *Werla* (Warley), *Feslei* (Fixby),[27]

---

(25) Hunter : *South Yorkshire*, vol. ii., p. 205. "This strengthens the opinion," he adds, "that Nostel has a better claim than any other place can present, to be the *monasterium in sylvâ Elmeti* of which we have that interesting notice in Bede."— James places it at Tadcaster. Thoresby's conjecture, that it was at Halton, "rests solely," says Hunter, "upon an etymology extremely dubious. . . . Nostel appears to me to present more cogent probabilities." (p. 204).

(26) I quote from the folio edition of 1783.—A *carucate* was as much land as one plough *(charrue)* with its cattle could keep in tillage : at a rough estimate, about 100 acres. The *oxgang* was as much as a single pair of oxen could suffice for. The *villani* were an intermediate grade between serfs and *bordarii* or cottars. The *libra*, or pound weight, Troy, of silver, would represent at least £100 of our money. The value of the manor, it will be seen, had greatly fallen since Edward the Confessor's time ; probably in consequence of the devastation caused by William in the north of England in 1074. The value of Leeds, which appears to have escaped, rose in that period from six to seven pounds. The manor of Bradford, in King Edward's time, was estimated at four pounds.—See Kelham *(Domesday Book illustrated*, 1788*);* James *(History of Bradford*, 1841*);* and *Quarterly Review*, vol. liv., p. 325.

(27) This name, omitted by Bawdwen, I insert on the authority of Crabtree *(History of Halifax*, 1836, p. 469).

Miclei (Midgley), *Wadesuurde* (Wadsworth), *Crubetonestun* (Crosstone),[28] *Langfelt* (Langfield) and *Stansfelt* (Stansfield), there are sixty carucates and three oxgangs and the third part of an oxgang of land to be taxed: thirty ploughs may till these lands. This manor was in the demesne of King Edward. There are now there in the King's hand four villanes, and three priests, and two churches, and seven sokemen, and sixteen bordars. They together have seven ploughs. Wood pasture six miles long and four miles broad. The whole is six miles long and six miles broad. Value in the time of King Edward sixty pounds, at present fifteen pounds."[29]

From this it will be seen that the manor of Wakefield was very extensive. In population it was inferior to Leeds, which then boasted of a number of families of various classes, who made a total, according to Whitaker's computation,[30] of 270 souls.

From this point, it will be most convenient to trace separately, in very brief terms, the history of the Church and Manor.

---

(28) According to Crabtree (p. 527) this should be Crimsworth.

(29) *Translation of part of Domesday*, by the Rev. W. Bawdwen (1809), p. 15—Mr Bawdwen himself (as I am informed by Mr. T. N. Ince) was for some years curate of the Parish Church at Wakefield, whence he was promoted to the Vicarage of Hooton Pagnell. In the list of Vicars given in Hunter's *South Yorkshire* (ii., 146) he is said to have died in 1816. "He is to be ranked," says Hunter, "among those clergymen who have contributed to the topographical literature of England. He devoted a great portion of the leisure, which the duties of his parish allowed him, to the study of Domesday Book, a great part of which noble record he translated, with the intention of publishing the whole in an English version."

The neighbourhood of Wakefield has been prolific in antiquaries. Besides those to be alluded to hereafter, James Torre may be mentioned, who was born at Snydal. For a notice of his vast labours among the documents of York Minster, see Raine's *Fasti Eboracenses* (1863), Pref. p. ix.

(30) *Loidis and Elmete*, p. 5.

THE CHURCH.

The extract from Domesday Book has shewn that within the manor of Wakefield, in the Conqueror's time, there were two churches; and these, according to Whitaker,[31] "may without the slightest hesitation be assigned to Wakefield and Sandal" (the nearest *berewick*). The dedication of the Parish church to All Saints, or All Hallows, is a token of Saxon foundation ;[32] but Whitaker asserts that it was not one of the original Saxon churches, "of which," says he, "in the hundred of Morley there were only two ; namely, Morley itself, the hundred church, and Dewsbury." Between the years 1091 and 1097, William de Warren, second Earl of Surrey, gave this church to his father's monastery of Lewes in Sussex.[33] The prior and convent retained possession till 1325, when they made a grant of it, along with the church of Dewsbury, to Hugh Despenser the younger.[34] On the forfeiture of his estates, in 1326, Wakefield church most probably reverted to the crown ; and thus Edward iii. acquired the right, which we find him exercising in 1348, of bestowing it on his newly founded college of St. Stephen, Westminster. Hitherto the living had been a rectory, and a well-endowed one ; "yn so much," writes Leland,[35] "that one of the Erles Warines . . . did give the Personage to a sunne or nere Kinsman of his : and he made the most Parte

---

(31) *Ib.* p. 274.

(32) Churton's *Early English Church* (1840).

(33) Watson's *Memoirs of the Ancient Earls of Warren and Surrey* (1782), vol. i., p. 91.

(34) This fact, which had escaped Dr. Whitaker, was first pointed out by Hunter *(South Yorkshire,* vol. ii., p. 336, n.*)*

(35) *Itinerary* (1745), vol. i., p. 43.

of the House wher the Vicarage now is." Thomas Drayton, instituted June 21st, 1349, is the first on the list of Vicars.[36] With the Dean and Chapter of St. Stephen's the presentation remained till the dissolution of the monasteries, when it was resumed by the King; and no further alteration took place till 1860, when, by an exchange of benefices, it became vested in the Bishop of the diocese.

With regard to the fabric, the original structure was replaced, in 1329, by an entirely new building, containing three aisles. This appears from an entry in the Fabric Rolls of York Minster:—[37]

"Aug. 10, 1329. The feast of St. Laurence: the Archbishop (William de Melton) consecrated the church of Wakefield, and the great altar in honour of All Saints; the altar of the Virgin *ex parte australi;* the altar of St. Nicholas *ex parte boriali;* and that of St. Peter *in medietate ecclesiæ.*"

For some reason unknown, this building only remained till a little before the year 1470, when the present noble edifice was raised.[38] In the depression

---

(36) See Torre's *Catalogue*, quoted by Whitaker.

(37) *Surtees Society's Publications*, vol. 35, p. 236.

(38) *Loidis and Elmete*, p. 281.—Sisson says that the tower and spire of the second structure were left standing.

From its reference to the church in this its second stage, the following Will of Thomas Hankyn will be read with interest:—

"Octobr. penult. MCCCCLViij. Ego Thomas Hankyn de Wakefeld—sepeliendum in eccles. Omn. Sanctor. Lego fabricæ cancelli B. Mariæ predictæ ecclesiæ XLs, sub tali condicione, quod fiat usque ostium chori in longitudine: aliter lego nisi XXs. Lego Ricardo Hankyn, fratri meo, unum daykyr de overledder et unum daykyr de soleledder. Lego facturæ angeportæ ducentis a villa de Wakefeld ad les Outewode Xs." *(Testamenta Eboracensia,* vol. ii., p. 218; published by the Surtees Society*).*—The "dakir" is half a "last," and contains ten hides.

of the floor at the entrance of the chancel, the obliquity of the chancel itself, and other peculiarities, it bears traces of the symbolism prevalent at the time of its erection.[39] In 1724 the south front was entirely rebuilt, and a great part of the north side, together with the east end, towards the close of the century.[40] Finally, in 1859 and 1860, the old weatherbeaten tower was entirely cased in new stone, and the spire rebuilt; and soon, through the exertions of the Vicar and his willing coadjutors, we may hope to see the time-honoured fabric regain much of its ancient strength and beauty.

THE MANOR.

This wide domain, which includes the whole of the extensive parish of Halifax, with the exception of the townships of Elland-cum-Greetland and Southowram,[41] was in 1086, as we have seen from Domesday Book, the property of the Crown. The exact date at which it was thence granted to the Earls of Warren, is uncertain. As the first Earl, who married Gundred, the Conqueror's daughter, died in 1088, it is not likely that he had it with her, for a marriage portion. In any case the gift of the church to Lewes monastery, referred to above, shews that Wakefield was in the hands of William, the second earl, before the year

---

(39) This was pointed out to me by the kindness of the Vicar, the Rev. Canon Camidge.
(40) *Edinburgh Gazetteer* (1827).
(41) Crabtree's *History of Halifax*, p. 60.

1097. There is not space to follow the history of this powerful family. They have left traces of their ownership in the names of Warenne-gate, now Wrengate, and other localities; and appear, at times, to have exercised their rule with sufficient severity.[42] John, eighth and last Earl of Warren and Surrey, of that line, died without legitimate issue in 1347. He had led a turbulent life; and Sandal Castle is said to have been built by him as a stronghold wherein to keep Alice, wife of Thomas Earl of Lancaster, after forcibly carrying her away in 1317.[43] In 1316 he had procured a re-grant from the King to his children by Maud Neirford, his concubine: they all died before him; but she survived, and kept court at Wakefield, as Countess of Warren, till her death in 1359.[44] The manor then reverted to the crown, and was granted by Edward iii. to his son Edmund de Langley; Queen Philippa enjoying the profit during his minority.[45] The grandson of this Edmund was Richard, Duke of York, who was Slain at Sandal.[46] His son, on

---

(42) In Edward i.'s time a seneschal of theirs, Richard de Heydon, is found imprisoning the wife of a Rotherham tailor for a whole year, for bringing a law-suit against the Earl about a tenement in " Gresebrok." This same Richard, the account goes on to state, "cepit diabolicas oppressiones et innumerabiles, sicut patebit in rotulo de ministris"—*Rotuli Hundredorum* (1812), vol. i., p. 109.

(43) Kennett's MSS., vol. xxxviii, p. 87.

(44) Kennett, as above.—But Hunter *(South Yorkshire,* i. 110*)* says that the patent, conveying the manor to Edmund of Langley, was made out Aug. 6th, 1347, only 37 days after Earl Warren's death. Perhaps Maud de Neirford was allowed to hold some nominal state and dignity, till her death.

(45) Hunter, as above.

(46) In whose memory the beautiful Chapel on the Bridge is commonly said to have been built by Edward iv. But Scatcherd in his *Essay* (1843), brings conclusive arguments to show it

ascending the throne as Edward iv., brought the manor back to the crown; and so it remained till 1558, when it was annexed to the Duchy of Lancaster.[47] In the reign of Charles i., it was granted to Henry, Earl of Holland, on a rental of £303 11s. 0¼d.[48] That nobleman was beheaded in 1649; and in 1660 we find Sir Christopher Clapham holding the property by conveyance from his trustees.[49] The heirs of Sir Christopher sold it to Peregrine, third Duke of Leeds,[50] by whose successors it has since been inherited.

---

is of the time of Edward iii. He fixes on the year 1362. Wilson (see *Gentleman's Magazine* for 1863, p. 716) says it was built in 1357, and restored in 1460. After passing through strange vicissitudes, and being used (writes Leatham) as an Exchange, "as a warehouse, an old clothes shop, a flax-dresser's shop, a news-room, a cheese-cake house, a dwelling-house, and a corn-factor's office," it was restored in 1847 (unfortunately with too perishable stone), and re-converted to its proper use.

(47) Hardy's *Charters of the Duchy of Lancaster* (1845), p. 365.

(48) *Calendar of State Papers* (1860), p. 417.

(49) *Ib.*—But Whitaker (*Loidis and Elmete*, p. 278), says it passed through the family of the Earl of Warwick to Sir Gervase Clifton; by whose heirs it was sold to the Duke of Leeds.

(50) Crabtree, as above.

GEORGE A GREEN,

THE

PINDER OF WAKEFIELD.

This personage, who derived his name from being keeper of the *pound*, or pinfold for stray cattle, on the town green, appears to have early commenced his rebellion against established authority. The author of one of the popular lives of him, published in 1706, says that he was placed at school under a surly pedagogue, of which school George was captain; and being ordered to beg pardon of his master, he resolved to run away; previously taking his revenge for the whipping which he was to undergo, by thrusting his head between his master's legs, " and he cast him off from his shoulders with such a tumbling quail, as we call a back somerset, and left him lying flat upon his back, half-dead, in the midst of the school."[1] When he grew up, Robin Hood, who was always on the look-out for spirits of this kind, secured him as a follower by his usual method. " Wheresoever he hard of any that were of unusual strength and hardynes,"

---

(1) Quoted in Gutch's *Lytel Geste of Robin Hood* (1847), vol. i p. 39.

says the writer of an old MS. chronicle,[2] "he would disgyse him selfe, and rather than fayle, go lyke a beggar, to become acqueynted with them; and after he had tryed them with fighting, never give them over tyl he had used means to draw them to lyve after his fashion. After such manner he procured the pynder of Wakefyld to be one of his company." The encounter between them, in which, "with his back to a thorn, and his foot to a stone," George a Green came off victorious, is described in one of the Robin Hood ballads :—

> "In Wakefield there lives a jolly Pinder,
>   In Wakefield all on a green,
>   In Wakefield all on a green.
>
> "There is neither knight nor squire, said the Pinder,
>   Nor baron that is so bold,
>   Nor baron that is so bold,
> Dare make a trespass to the town of Wakefield,
>   But his pledge goes to the pinfold.
>
> "All this beheard three weighty yeomen;
>   'Twas Robin Hood, Scarlet, and John.
> With that they espied the jolly Pinder,
>   As he sat under a thorn, &c."

Semper viret might have been the motto of George a Green. In Drayton's *Polyolbion* he is mentioned as rendering Wakefield chiefly famous. "As good as George a Green" had become a proverb in the time of *Hudibras;* and it was his renown which procured Wakefield the honour of a visit from Drunken Barnaby :—[3]

---

(2) *Sloane* MSS :—thought to be of the date of 1600.—*Ibid.*, p. 379.

(3) In the Edition of 1778 this far from respectable character is said to have been one Barnaby Harrington, a native of Appleby; who graduated at Queen's Coll. Oxford, and ultimately settled down as a country farmer.

Hinc diverso cursu, sero
Quod audissem de Pindero
Wakefeeldensi, gloria mundi,
Ubi socii sunt jucundi,
Mecum statui peragrare,
Georgii fustem visitare.

Veni Wakefeild peramænum,
Ubi, quærens Georgium Grenum,
Non inveni, sed in lignum
Fixum reperi Georgii signum ;
Ubi allam bibi feram,
Donec Georgio fortior eram.

Turning thence, none could me hinder
To salute the Wakefield Pinder ;
Who indeed is the world's glory,
With his comrades never sorry.
This was the cause, lest you should miss it,
George's club I meant to visit.

Straight at Wakefield I was seen a ;
Where I sought for George a Green a ;
But could find no such a creature ;
Yet on a signe I saw his feature :
Where strength of ale had so stir'd me,
I grew stouter far than Geordie.

"That the figure of the Pinder," says Gutch, "was a popular sign elsewhere than at Wakefield; that it extended even to London, is proved by one of him which still does, or a short time ago did exist, at one of the oldest public-houses in Gray's Inn Lane. And the famous Bagnigge Wells, once a popular country excursion and resort for cockneys, but now in the heart of the town, had, over an ancient gate leading into the garden, a sculptured stone, with this inscription, 'This is Bagnigge House, neare the Pindar a Wakefeild. 1680;' proving the Pinder to be the older and better known of the two."

George a Green, as a contemporary of Robin Hood, "played his pranks" in Richard the First's time.

Passing on to the next reign, we find the miller of Wakefield serving to point a moral for Eustace, abbot of Haye in Normandy, who came over to this country in 1201, to preach the duty of extending the Sabbath from three o'clock on Saturday afternoon, to sunrise on Monday morning. "For this" (says Whitaker) "he pleaded the authority of an epistle written by Christ, and *found* on the altar of St. Simon at Golgotha." Roger de Hoveden[4] tells us, that on one occasion he related the following story in confirmation of his principles:—"At Wakefield also, one Saturday, while a miller was, after the ninth hour, attending to grinding his corn, there suddenly came forth, instead of flour, such a torrent of blood, that the vessel placed beneath was nearly filled with blood, and the mill-wheel stood immoveable, in spite of the strong rush of the water; and those who beheld it wondered thereat, saying 'Spare us, O Lord; spare thy people.'"

A little later on, in 1212, we meet with an indication of the state of things in King John's reign, in the following brief notice:—[5]

"Petrus de Wakefeld, qui vaticinabatur de morte Joannis regis, suspensus est una cum filio." . . . . . .
"Peter de Wakefeld was hanged, along with his son, for prophesying the death of King John."

No doubt, in his case, the wish was father to the thought. It is somewhat curious, however, to discover more than one instance of Wakefield men suffering

---

(4) Translated by Riley (Bohn's series, 1853). The old Chronicler himself was a Yorkshireman, probably of Hoveden, or Howden, in the East Riding; and wrote some time in Henry the Third's reign.

(5) Leland, *Collectanea*, vol. ii, p. 326.

for treasonable expressions, among the scanty records which remain. In the reign of Charles i. John Maud of this town was brought before the Star Chamber, on a charge of having said that "the king went to mass with the queen: he would be provided with powder and shot: another gunpowder blow, &c." There still exists a note of the proceedings in the handwriting of Laud, dated May 6, 1629.[6] And among the depositions taken at York Castle,[7] under date July 19, 1683, is a charge brought against Richard Barker, for that he on that day, at Wakefield, "begunne the Duke of Monmouth's health, and said hee was the king's own sonne, and that he hoped to see a change before twelve months should come about."

From the middle of the fourteenth century downwards, we meet with frequent mention of the old and influential family of Savile, in connection with Wakefield matters. Members of it resided at Stanley Hall, Howley, Methley, and other places in the immediate neighbourhood. "The family of Savile," says Cooper,[8] "was one of the most, if not the most illustrious in the West Riding of the County of York. Some writers have fancifully ascribed to it an Italian origin; but it probably had its rise at Silkston. It certainly flourished in those parts in the 13th century; and in the middle of the fourteenth century (1358) we find Margaret Savile prioress of Kirklees. In the same reign of Edward iii., the family divided itself into two

---

(6) *Calendar of State Papers* (1859).

(7) *Surtees Society's Publications* (1861).

(8) *Savile Correspondence:* being Letters to and from Henry Savile, Esq., envoy at Paris, and Vice-chamberlain to Charles ii. and James ii. (Camden Society's Publications) 1858.

main branches, in the persons of two brothers, John of Tankersley, and Henry of Bradley. The senior branch acquired its greatest renown in the person of George, first Marquess of Halifax. The junior branch is mentioned . . . as also of Copley and Methley, and having produced one of the most learned men of our country, Sir Henry Savile, the provost of Eton, and founder of the Savilian professorships of astronomy and geometry in the University of Oxford :[9] his brother, John Savile, a baron of the Exchequer (1598—1607) is now represented by the Earl of Mexborough."

Sisson, in his *Historic Sketch*, quotes, from the Surveys of Dugdale and others, the following inscription, as formerly to be seen in the East window of the Parish Church:—

---

(9) He was also one of the translators of the Bible, and editor of Chrysostom. As no anecdotes of such a man can be uninteresting, the reader will pardon the following, which relates to his great literary undertaking. It is from Peck's *Desiderata Curiosa* :—"I shall here take leave to set down one word or two more concerning Sir Henry Savil's cost and pains. For the first, it may be gathered from the *foot* of this *Herculean* labour, the paper; whereon he bestowed two thousand pounds, notwithstanding only one thousand copies were printed. For the second, he was so sedulous at his study, that his lady thereby thought herself neglected; and coming to him one day, as he was in his study, saluted him thus. 'Sir Henry, I would I were a book too, and then you would a little more respect me.' Whereto one, standing by, replied, 'Madam, you must then be an almanack, that he might change every year.' Whereat she was not a little displeased. The same, his lady, a little before Chrysostome was finished, (when Sir Henry lay sick) said, 'If Sir Harry died, she would burn Chrysostome, for killing her husband ;' which Mr. Bois hearing, answered, 'That so to do were a great pity.' To whom she replied, 'Why? who was Chrysostome?' To which he answered, 'One of the sweetest preachers since the Apostles' times.' Wherewith she was so satisfied, that she said 'she would not do it for all the world.'"

"Orate pro bono statu Johannis Savile, Mil. Senesch. Dominii de Wakefeld, et Aliciæ uxoris suæ, et omnium filiorum suorum. A.D. 1470."—An inscription (he adds) which goes far towards ascertaining the date of the present building.[10]

---

(10) A similar inference is drawn by Kennett from another inscription:—"At the east end of the south chappel or isle, adjoyning to the middle chancell or quire of the church of Wakefield, is this inscription under the arms of Pilkington:—
'This south chantery was founded by Sir John Pilkington, Knight, in the 15th year of the reign of King Edward the Fourth after the Conquest, by vertue of his majestie's letters patent, dated at Westminster the 20th day of December, A.D. 1475; and is maintained at the proper charge of Sir Lyon Pilkington of Stanley within this parish, Baronet, who is lineally descended from the abovesaid Sir John Pilkington." *(MSS. vol. 39.)*

Hence Kennett assigns the present structure to the beginning of Edward the Fourth's reign.

HENRY DE WAKEFELD.

Towards the latter part of the fourteenth century, there lived a man of some note, whom we must conclude, from his name, to have been an inhabitant of this town,[1] Henry de Wakefeld.

The earliest mention I can find of him is in 1362, when he was made prebend of St. Pancras, in the diocese of London. Six years afterwards he was raised to the treasurership of that diocese; and after being successively prebend of Gorwall and Overbury in the diocese of Hereford, of Stillington in that of York, and archdeacon of Northampton, he was chosen Bishop of Ely, on the death of John Barnet, in 1373. This choice received the royal assent on July 1st in that year, although the king had designed his own confessor, John Woodrove, for the vacant post. For some reason, however, the election was set aside, and by a Bull of Pope Gregory's, dated Aug. 13th 1373, Thomas Arundale, son of Robert Earl of Warren and Arundale, was appointed to the see.

---

(1) Though Fuller speaks of there being "three towns of that name within this county."—What has become of these terrestrial *parhelions*, or mock-Wakefields, I do not know.

On the death of William Linne, Bishop of Worcester, at the close of 1373, the monks there, with the king's approbation, nominated their Prior, Walter de Legh, to succeed him. This arrangement was also set aside; and by a papal Bull, dated Sep. 12th, 1375, Henry de Wakefeld was promoted to the see in question.

His name, to adopt Fuller's conceit, "is an episcopal one, which might mind him of his office, the diocese of Worcester being his *field*, and he by his place to *wake* or *watch* over it: nor hear I of any complaints to the contrary, but that he was very vigilant in his place. He was also for one year lord treasurer of England."[2] After enlarging and beautifying Worcester Cathedral, during his episcopate of twenty years, he died at Blockley, on his return from Parliament, March 11th, 1394, and "he lieth in his own church" (adds Fuller) *ingenti marmore contectus*, "and let none grudge him the greatness of his gravestone, if two feet larger than ordinary, who made the body of this his church two arches longer westward than he found it, besides a fair porch added thereunto."

This Henry de Wakefeld must be distinguished from another of the same name, who, previous to August 1376, was chantry priest of Blackrode in the parish of Bolton, Lancashire, on the foundation of Dame

---

(2) *Worthies of Yorkshire.* I was at first doubtful whether this statement were correct, inasmuch as Leland (*Collectanea*, vol. I.) speaks of Henry de Wakefeld as *thesaurarius domus regiæ*, "treasurer of the *king's household*," in 1373, when he was nominated to the Bishopric of Ely. It is clear however from Godwin (*Catalogue of English Bishops*) who quotes the Patent of 50 Edward iii., that in 1376 he was appointed to that high office, at the same time that Adam Houghton, another Bishop, was made Lord Chancellor.

Mabella, widow of Sir William de Bradeshaw. This appears by the following entry :—"1376. vii Id. Aug. Johēs le Arche cap. admissus fuit ad cantar. de Blakrode ad present. Dni Rogeri de Bradshagh patr. vac. per resign. Henr. de Wakefeld."[3]

As illustrative, in some degree, of the domestic life of the period, the reader will pardon the introduction here of a will made by one Richard Bate, tanner, of Wakefield, and proved May 2nd, 1401 :—[4]

"In Dei nomine, Amen. Die martis proximo post festum Sancti Marci Evangelistæ, Anno Domini MCCCC primo, Ego Ricardus Bate, coriarius, de Wakefeld, compos mentis meæ, facio testamentum meum in hunc modum. In primis commendo spiritum meum Deo omnipotenti, et Beatæ Mariæ, et omnibus sanctis, et corpus meum ad sepeliendum in cimiterio ecclesiæ Omnium Sanctorum de Wakefeld. Et lego pro mortuario meo unum equum cum cellâ et freno, et collobio duplici, et gladio ac peltâ, non plura. Et ad V cereos comburendos circa corpus meum in die sepulturæ meæ V libras ceræ. Et cuilibet capellano venienti ad dirige meum iij d. presbiterio vero parochiali iiij d. clĕrico vero ij d. Et cuidam capellano ydoneo celebraturo pro salute animæ meæ, per unum annum integrum immediate post decessum meum, C s. Et ad fabricam majoris ecclesiæ beati Petri Ebor. iiij d. Et summo altari ecclesiæ de Wakfeld ij s. Item beatæ Mariæ ejusdem ecclesiæ ij s. et lumini ejusdem vj d.

---

(3) *History of the Chantries in the County Palatine of Lancaster*, (Cheetham Society's Publications) 1862.

(4) *Testamenta Eboracensia, Part I.* (Surtees Society's Publications) 1836.

Item ad lumen Sanctæ Crucis vj d. Et ad fabricam ecclesiæ de Wakfeld xij d. Item ad emendacionem cimiterii murati noviter xij d. Et Ceciliæ matri meæ xl d. Item Margaretæ sorori meæ tantum. Item filiolæ meæ xij d. Et Willielmo Megson pauperi xl d. Item cuidam heremitæ, qui continue jacuit in lecto per quinquennium, ij s. Et cuidam mendicanti fere cæco, nomine Willielmo Parour, ij s. Item cuidam pauperi quondam probo, nomine Johanni de Thrustanland, xij d. Et Evotæ de Stanlay, quæ est cæca, xij d. Item Aliciæ [alii?] cæcæ mulieri nomine Sibillæ xij d. Et anachoritæ ejusdem villæ viij d. Item Johannæ filiæ Richardi vj d. Et Aliciæ Spynk vj d. Item Johanni Pollard de Wakfeld capellano xl d. Item Simoni Catenay de eadem xl d. Et cuidam Johanni de Southwod togam meam russetam non duplicatam. Item Willielmo Barbour aliam togam blodeam inveteratam, cum I par de liniis vestibus. Et in convocatione pauperum die sepulturæ meæ, et in expensis circa illos faciendis xiij s iiij d. Residuum vero omnium bonorum meorum dividetur in tribus partibus, videlicet una pars pro anima mea, et residuum Agneti uxori meæ, et pueris inter me et ipsam procreatis, ad dividendum inter se equaliter. Ita quod quilibet puerorum sit heres alterius, et post mortem illorum volo ut illius partis residuum ordinetur pro salute animæ meæ. Et Agnetem uxorem meam constituo principalem executorem, deinde Simonem Catnay conductorem, ac Johannem Polland [*sic*] de Wakfeld capellanum supervisorem."

"In the name of God, Amen. On the Tuesday next after the feast of St. Mark the Evangelist, A.D. 1401, I Richard Bate, tanner, of Wakefeld, being of sound mind, do make my will in manner following. *Imprimis* I commend my soul to Almighty God, and the Blessed Virgin, and all saints, and my body to be buried in the grave-yard of the Church of All Saints in Wakefeld. And I bequeath for my mortuary[5] one horse, along with a saddle[6] and bridle, and a double garment,[7] and a sword and buckler;—no more. And for 5 wax-candles to burn round my corpse on the day of my burial, 5 lbs. of wax.[8] And for any chantry-priest coming to say my *Dirige*, 3*d*; to the parish priest 4*d*; and to the clerk 2*d*. And to some suitable chantry-priest who shall celebrate mass for the repose of my soul, for one year complete, immediately after my decease, 100*s*. And towards the structure of the great Church of St. Peter at York, 4*d*. And to the high altar of Wakefeld Church 2*s*. *Item* to the Blessed Virgin in the same church 2*s*., and to the light (on the

---

(5) The mortuary, or "corpse present," usually consisted of a good horse, with his trappings; sometimes an ox instead. It became the property of the church or religious house where the deceased person was buried, but was redeemable. In the will of William Lord Morley (1379) it is directed, that "two of his best horses be disposed of for mortuaries, viz. his best black horse to the Augustine Friars at Norwich, and his palfrey, called Don, to the Rector of the Church of Halingburg." See Harris's *Testamenta Vetusta* (1826.)

(6) *Cella*, ephippium; Gall. *selle* (Du Cange.)

(7) *Colobium*, tunica absque manicis. (*id*) It was sometimes used as the name of a dress worn by monks.

(8) Compare the will of Robert Earl of Suffolk (1368): "And I will that five square tapers and four mortars, besides torches, shall burn about my corpse at my funeral."

"These burning lights," says Nicolas, "were placed round and upon the hearse during the performance of obsequies. The square tapers of yellow and white wax weighed sometimes 20lbs each. Mortars *(mortiers)* were more like lamps, and were broad and flat, of 10lbs. each."

altar) of the same, 6*d*. *Item* towards the light of the Holy Cross 6*d*. And towards the structure of Wakefield Church, 12*d*. *Item* for the improvement of the burial ground, newly walled in, 12*d*. And to Cecilia my mother 40*d*. *Item* to my sister Margaret, the same. *Item* to my little daughter 12d. And to William Megson, a poor man, 40d. *Item* to a hermit, who has lain 5 years in bed without intermission, 2*s*. And to a beggar nearly blind, by name William Parour, 2*s*. *Item* to a poor man, once respectable, by name John de Thrustanland, 12*d*. And to Evota de Stanlay [?] who is blind, 12*d*. *Item* to another blind woman named Sibyl, 12*d*. And to an anchorite [9] of the same town 8*d*. *Item* to Joan, Richard's daughter, 6*d*. And to Alice Spynk 6*d*. Item to John Pollard of Wakefield, chantry-priest, 40*d*. *Item* to Simon Catenay of the same, 40*d*. And to one John de Southwod my single russet gown. *Item* to William Barbour another gown, my old crimson [10] one, with one pair of linen vests. And (to be laid out) in the assembly of poor people on the day of my burial, and in expenses to be incurred about them, 13*s*. 4*d*. The residue of all my goods to be divided in three parts, to wit, one part for my soul, and the remainer to my wife Agnes, and the sons begotten between us, for them to share equally between them. In such wise that either of my sons

---

(9) Leland, in Hen. viii.'s time, speaks of there being a chapel in the town, " where was wont to be *anachoreta in mediâ urbe.*"

(10) So Cardinal Beaufort, in his will (1446) bequeaths to the Queen, *lectum blodium de panno aureo de Damasco*, which was a bed of crimson colour, worked with cloth of gold of a damask pattern. The word *blodius* is a barbarous term, to express "blood-red" or "crimson." See Nicolas.

be the other's heir;[11] and after their death I will that the residue of that portion be disposed of for the welfare of my soul. And I appoint my wife Agnes executrix in chief; next Simon Catnay as director,[12] and John Polland of Wakfeld, chantry-priest, as overseer."

Richard Bate, honest man, had probably little suspicion that his will would ever be discussed by his fellow-townsmen, some hundreds of years after his death. But there is no telling what the stream of time may throw up as waifs upon its banks.

---

(11) In assuming two sons only to be referred to, I may probably be wrong : but the passage is otherwise obscure to me.

(12) *Conductor*, actor, curator ; nostris etiam *conduiseur* (Du Cange, *addenda*).

RICHARD FLEMING.

Nearly contemporary with Henry de Wakefeld lived Richard Fleming, the founder of Lincoln College, Oxford. He was born of a good family at Crofton near Wakefield. From school he passed to University College, Oxford; of which University in 1407 he was chosen a Proctor. The times were then troubled and Oxford no place of repose. Wickliffe's opinions were fast making head, in spite of the persecution which "King Bolingbroke's" writ for the execution of Sawtrey, in 1401, had let loose. They were formally condemned at Oxford, in the synod presided over by Arundel in 1408; and before that time, the occupant of the see which Fleming was subsequently to fill, was putting into operation, at his palace of Woburn, the cell in his prison called *Little-Ease*. Fleming at first was a warm supporter of the Reformer; "but his zeal" (says Zouch, charitably or uncharitably) "being extinguished by offers of high preferment, he became a violent adversary." After being successively prebend of Newbold and of Langtoft, and rector of Boston in Lincolnshire, he was raised to the see of Lincoln by a papal Bull dated Nov. 20th, 1419; succeeding the Cardinal Philip de Repingdon. Four years later, in 1424, he was dispatched as an envoy to the council of Sens. By the eloquence and ability which he there displayed, he so won the good opinion of Pope Martin v., that he was translated by him to the Archbishopric of York, then vacant through the death of Henry Bowet. This proceeding was not only resisted by the Dean and Chapter, who had fixed upon John Kemp, Bishop of London, but gave great offence to the King's Council. They (as Henry vi. was then in his minority) not only seized on the temporalities of the see of Lincoln, which had just been vacated by Fleming, but compelled him to relinquish all pretensions to the archbishopric. The Royal letter, dated from Westminster, May 24th, 1424, thus instructs the Lord Chancellor:—

"Whereas we are credibly informed that the Holy Father the Pope has translated the honourable Father in God Richard, late Bishop of Lincoln, from the cathedral see of Lincoln to the metropolitan church of York, lately vacant by the death of the very reverend Father in God, Henry, the last Archbishop there; and that to such translation the said Richard, late Bishop of Lincoln, consents,—wherefore the said Church of Lincoln is void, by which voidance the temporalities of the said Church of Lincoln appertain to us;—we will, of the advice and assent of our council, and command you to make and address our several writs to the escheators where those temporalities be, commanding them to seize into our hands the same temporalities."

As a punishment for accepting such promotion without the royal approbation, he was obliged to agree to certain humiliating conditions proposed by the council; in return for which they agreed to reappoint him to the see of Lincoln, to obtain a pardon for him in the next Parliament, and to procure his restoration to the Royal favour. The temporalities of his see were then restored to him, Aug. 3rd, 1426. The Pope, to escape the mortification of seeming to acquiesce in what was done against his will, issued a Bull, in which he translated Fleming again to the diocese of Lincoln, by the title of Richard, Archbishop of York. He died at Sleaford, Jan. 25th, 1431; and was buried in a chapel he had built near the north door of his Cathedral, his brother Robert, Dean of Lincoln, reposing hard by.

He is chiefly remembered as the founder of Lincoln College, which was established by him in 1427, and enriched with many illuminated and other costly books by Robert Fleming, who, as Protonotary of the Holy See, had had abundant means of collecting them. The college, like its founder, is an example of the uncertainty of all human designs; for it was established for the purpose "of educating able men to oppose the doctrines of the Reformation, as defended by John Wickliffe;" and Richard Fleming, who in early life was a supporter of those doctrines, ended by disinterring the bones of the Reformer, after they had lain forty years at Lutterworth in his Diocese, and committing them to the flames, as the Council of Sens had ordered. The ashes were thrown into the Swift, a tributary of the Avon; and thus

" The Avon to the Severn ran,
   The Severn to the sea ;
So Wycliffe's dust was borne abroad
   As wide as waters be. "

He has left behind him a work in one volume on

English Etymology, and an edition of his speeches before the Council of Sens.[1]

Within thirty years from the death of Bishop Fleming was fought the battle of Wakefield, Dec. 30th, 1460.[2] The events which preceded it, and the particulars of the engagement itself, have been so fully discussed by Tyas and others, that it is unnecessary here to recapitulate them. After merely observing, therefore, that Queen Margaret, dissatisfied with the Act of Settlement, which appointed the Duke of York heir to the throne on the King's death, was marching southward with an army of 18,000 or 20,000 men, and that the Duke of York rashly ventured out from his Castle of Sandal to meet her, though at the head of some 5,000 men only,—I will content myself with referring the reader to the well-known passage in Shakespere's *Henry the Sixth*, and quote instead a few extracts that may be less familiar.

With regard to the precise spot on which the battle was fought, Brooke *(Fields of Battle*, 1857*)* writes:—

"Looking from Sandal Castle Hill, a flat plain appears, of considerable extent, cultivated as meadow fields, extending from the Castle to the river Calder. Those meadows are at present called "the Pugnays." They are designated "the Pukenills" on the Manor Court Rolls, which are still in existence, and of a date

---

(1) See Zouch's works, vol. ii.; Tanner, *Bibliotheca Britannica*; Le Neve, *Fasti Anglicani*; and Godwin, *de Præsulibus*.

(2) In some accounts, Dec. 31st. But John Hardyng, a contemporary chronicler, says it was the *fifth* daye of Christmasse."

prior to the fourteenth century. Adjoining the tract of meadow land, and in the extreme northwestward, bounded by the river Calder, is Porto-Bello, a mansion erected by Samuel Holdsworth, Esq., and now occupied by William Shaw, Esq.[3] The battle was fought upon that spot, upon part of the meadow-land before mentioned, and upon the tract of ground formerly part of Wakefield Green, extending from thence across the turnpike road in a north-easterly direction. The Green must have been at that time a large open tract of ground, but it has long been enclosed, and its position appears to have been on the southward side of, and about half a mile from, the bridge. Its site is crossed by the modern turnpike road from Wakefield to Barnsley; and part of it has acquired the name of the Fall Ings, according to tradition, from the great numbers who fell there in the battle.

"In digging the foundations of Porto Bello house, and in forming the sunk fence there, human bones, broken swords, spurs, and other relics were discovered, which were considered fully confirmatory of that locality having been the scene of the conflict."

The planting of an ambuscade in the woods adjoining the Castle by Queen Margaret's party, the Duke's impatience of waiting for the Earl of March's reinforcements, his death, and the murder of the young Earl of Rutland, are described in the following stanzas from a now almost forgotten poem, Drayton's *Miseries of Queene Margarite*:—

> "The vexed Queene, whose very soul forgot
> That such a thing as patience it had knowne,...

---

(3) It is now (1863) occupied by Lieut.-Colonel Holdsworth.

> " She downe to Sandall doth the Duke pursue,
>   With all the power her friends could her provide,
> Led by those Lords that had beene ever true,
>   And had stood fast upon King Henry's side;
> With that most valient and selected crue
>   This brav'st of queenes so well her businesse plide,
> That, comming soone in Sandal's lofty sight,
> Into the field she dares him forth to fight......
>
> " But in her host she having those that were
>   Expert in all the stratagems of warre,
> To fight with him doe cause her to forbeare,
>   Till from his Castle she had got him farre;
> Whilst, in an ambush, she had placed there
>   Wiltshire and Clifford with their strengthes, to barre
> Him from his home, in offering to retire,
> Or wound his back even as they would desire.
>
> " When to't they fell, upon an easie plaine
>   At the hill foote, where furiously they fought
> Upon both sides, where there were many slaine;
>   But, for the Queene four to his one had brought,
> The Duke of Yorke, for all his pride, was faine
>   Back to recoyle, where he was finely caught;
> For Wilt and Clifford, that in ambush were,
> The van thus routed, overthrew the reare.
>
> " Where Yorke himselfe, who proudly but of late
>   With no lesse hope than of a kingdom fed,
> Upon this field before his castle gate,
>   Mangled with wounds, on his own earth lay dead;
> Upon whose body Clifford downe him sate,
>   Stabbing the corpes, and, cutting off his head,
> Crown'd it with paper, and (to wreake his teene)
> Presents it so to the victorious Queene...
>
> " Some clime up rocks; through hedges others runne,
>   Their foes so roughly execute their rage;
> Where th' Earle of Rutland, the Duke's youngest sonne,
>   Then in his childhood, and of tender age,
> Comming in hope to see the battaile wonne,
>   Clifford, whose wrath no rigour could asswage,
> Takes, and whilst there he doth for mercy kneele,
> In his soft bosom sheathes his sharpened steele."

These quotations, it is to be feared, may be thought over long already; but I insert the following, as an interesting specimen of early French. It is an Epitaph for the Duke of York, published, with a translation, by Wright *(Political Poems,*[4] *1861)* from a MS. in the Harleian collection :—

> "A remembrer à tous ceurs de noblesse
> Que ycy gist la fleur de gentillesse,
> Le puissant duc d' York, Rychart ot nom,
> Prince royal, preudomme de renom,
> Saige, vaillant, vertueux en sa vie,
> Qui bien ama loyaulté sans envie,
> Droyt heritier, prouvé en mainte terre,
> Des couronnez de France, et d' Engleterre.
> Ou parlement tenu à Vestmestre,
> Bien fut congneu et trouvé vray heir estre.
> Sy fut roygent et gouverneur de France,
> Normandie il garda d'encombrance,
> Sur Pontaysse la ryviere passa,
> Le roy Francoyez et son doulfin chassa.
> En Erllande mist tel gouvernement,
> Tout le pais rygla paisiblemeut.
> D' Engleterre fut long temps proltetur,
> Le peuple ama, et fut leur deffendeur.
> Noble lygne ot d' enfans, que Dieu garde.
> Dont l' aysné fylz est nomé Edouarde,
> Qui est vray roy, et son droit conquessta,
> Par grant labeur qu' il en prinst l'aqueta,
> Il est regnant solitaire ou jour d' uy,
> Dieu et ses sainz sy le gardent d' envy !
> Ce noble duc á Wacquefylde mourut,
> Doux paix traitant force sur luy courut,
> L' an soixnte, le xxxe de Decembre,
> Cinquante ans ot d' age, comme on remembre,
> En priant Dieu et la tresbelle Dame
> Qu' en Paradiz puist reposser son ame !
>   Amen.   *Chester le Ht.*"

"Let it be remembered by all noble hearts
that here lies the flower of gentility,
the powerful Duke of York; Richard was his name,
a royal prince, a gentleman of renown,
wise, valiant, virtuous in his life,

---

(4) Where is also given a short Latin poem *de bello apud Wacfeld habito*, by John de Whethamstede, monk of St. Alban's.

who loved well loyalty without envy;
the right heir, proved in many a land,
of the crowns of France and England.
In the parliament held at Westminster
he was fully acknowledged and found to be the righteous heir.
And he was regent and governour of France,
Normandy he guarded from danger,
he passed the river at Pontoise,
and drove away the French king and his dauphin.
In Ireland he established such government,
that he ruled all the country peaceably.
Of England he was long protector,
he loved the people and was their defender.
He had a noble lineage of children, whom may God have in his keeping!
The eldest of whom is named Edward,
who is true king, and conquered his right,
he purchased it by great labour which he bestowed upon it;
he is reigning singly at the present day,
God and his saints preserve him from injury!
This noble Duke died at Wakefield;
while treating of sweet peace, force rushed upon him,
the year sixty, the 30th of December;
he was fifty years of age, as people remember;
praying God, and the very fair Lady,
that his soul may repose in Paradise!
    Amen. *Chester the Herald.*"

On the accession of Edward the Fourth, a petition was drawn up by the House of Commons to the king, for forfeiture of estates of those abetting the Duke of Somerset in the late encounter; including, among others, "John Preston, late of Wakefeld," and "Richard Litestr', the yonger, late of Wakefeld, yoman." As a contrast to Drayton, it may be worth while to present a few lines from the preamble to this curious document :—[5]

---

(5) *Rotuli Parliamentorum,* anno 1461.—The disturbed state of the country about this period can hardly be better evinced, than by the various petitions there preserved. As an instance, may be taken one from John Asheton, Knt., of Holley, in the township of Morley, in 1472; where he complains of being forcibly carried off from his house, in the night-time, by armed men, and lodged in "Pountfrette Castle."

"Whereuppon" (it sets forth) "at Wakefeld in the shire of York, the seid Duc of Somerset, falsely and traiterously the same noble Prynce Duc of York, on Teuisday the 30th day of Decembr' last passed, horribly, cruelly, and tyrannously murdred; and also the worthy and good Lordes Edmund Erle of Ruthland, brother of our seid Soverayne Lord, and Richard Erle of Salesbury; and not content therewith, of their insaciable malice, after that they were dede, mayde them to be heded with abhomynable cruelte and horrible despite, ayenst all humanite and nature of Nobles."

JOHN FORMAN.

It is pleasant to see how, in times of warlike commotion, the quiet paths of scholarship are not always forsaken. Some men are as undisturbed by the tumult, as the deaf and dumb soldier, by whom General Brook was shot at the siege of Lichfield. Such a one was Sir Thomas Browne. In the height of the civil war, "he was tranquilly preparing his *Pseudodoxia Epidemica;* as if errors about basilisks and griffins were the paramount and fatal epidemic of the time."[6] And such a one, in his degree, (if we may again compare great things with small) was John Forman, a native of Rothwell, near Wakefield; who, in the year after the battle fought at this town, endowed Magdalen College, Oxford, with a fellowship. The holder of it was to be one of his own kindred, or, in default of that, one born

---

(6) *Edinburgh Review,* Oct. 1836.

in or near to the parishes of Rothwell and Ruston, near Wakefield; of the first of which places he was a native, and of the second, vicar. In January 1502 he founded a school at the Ruston (Royston?) above-mentioned.[7]

---

(7) Wood: *History and Antiquities of Oxford;* Zouch's Works, vol. ii.

SIR RICHARD LYSTER.

For one filling the office of Lord Chief Justice of King's Bench in Henry the Eighth's reign, the life of the above-mentioned person was a somewhat uneventful one. True that, as Lord Campbell remarks,[1] "Chief Justices occasionally had been quite obscure till they were elevated to the bench; and then, confining themselves to the routine discharge of their official duties, were known only to have decided such questions as 'whether beasts of the plough, taken in *vetito namio*, may be replevied.'" Yet we might have expected that one in such a position at the middle of the sixteenth century, could hardly fail to be connected with some of the memorable events of that period. But Sir Richard Lyster appears to have had the art of keeping aloof from troubled waters.

He was of an old Wakefield family; his grandfather, Thomas Lyster, being settled there in Henry the Sixth's reign. His father, John Lyster, married one of the Beaumonts of Whitley in Yorkshire. Their son Richard, with whom we are now concerned, being destined for the legal profession, was entered at the

---

(1) *Lives of the Chief Justices of England* (1849.) Pref. p. vi.

Middle Temple; where he was made Reader in 1516, Double Reader in 1522, and Treasurer the following year. After filling in succession the offices of Solicitor General, and (as there is every reason to believe) Attorney General, he was raised to the Bench, May 12th, 1529, as Chief Baron of the Exchequer. On his elevation he was knighted, and afterwards appointed one of the commissioners for trying Fisher, Bishop of Rochester, and Sir Thomas More. After continuing as head of the Exchequer for sixteen years, he was promoted to the rank of Chief Justice of King's Bench, Nov. 9th, 1546. His predecessor in that office, Sir Edward Montagu, had apparently found his task too irksome, and so resigned it for the post of Chief Justice of Common Pleas, "which," says Campbell, "though lower in rank, was quieter."—"He might feel some mortification," the same writer adds, "when he saw Richard Lyster, whom he had lately snubbed at the bar, take precedence of him in judicial processions, as Lord Chief Justice of the King's Bench."—In his new capacity Lyster attested the submission of Thomas, Duke of Norfolk, whom it was one of the king's last acts to commit to the Tower, along with his son, the Earl of Surrey; the nominal charge being that the latter had presumed to quarter the royal arms upon his shield. This was on Jan. 12th, 1547. A fortnight afterwards the king died. On the accession of Edward vi., Sir Richard was re-appointed; and we find him addressing a body of new serjeants, on their inauguration at Lincoln's Inn, "in a godly, thowghe sumwhate prolix and long declaration of their duties," as Dugdale calls it. He held office till 1552, when he resigned; and spent the remainder of his life at Southampton. Leland, who visited the town, has left a short notice of his residence :—"The house that Master Lighster, chiefe Barne of the King's Escheker, dwellyth yn, is very fair." He died there, March 14th, 1553, and was buried in the Church of St. Michael.

If he shunned notoriety in his lifetime, it has certainly not pursued him after his death. For many years his very monument in St. Michael's was believed to indicate the resting-place of another person,—Lord Chancellor Wriothesley, Earl of Southampton. This is so stated in the *Southampton Guide-book*, published in 1781. When or how such a notion first got about, does not appear: that it was unknown in 1719 is clear from the description of the tomb left us in a manuscript collection of notes on Hampshire churches,[2] taken in that year. The writer, speaking of St. Michael's, says, "In the aforesaid dormitory, against the south part, lyes on a handsome stone tomb the figure of a Judge on his back, dress'd in scarlet; a collar of S.S.[3] round his breast, a Judge's cap on his head, and a book in his right hand. On a sort of cornice, supported by three pillars, this remnant of an inscription :—

ET. DICTO. ELIZABETH. HOC. IN. VIDVETATE. SVA. CVZAVIT *(sic).* 18 DIE. MARCIE. 1567."

---

(2) Quoted by Sir F. Madden, in his *Remarks, &c.* (on this monument) before the meeting of the Archæological Institute at Winchester, Sep. 1845.

(3) "This has been from great antiquity the decoration of the Chief Justices. Dugdale says it is derived from the name of Saint Simplicius, a christian Judge, who suffered martyrdom under the emperor Dioclesian :—Geminæ vero S.S. indicabant Sancti Simplicii nomen. (Or. Jur. xxxv.)"—Campbell's *Lives.*

"This evidence," says Madden, "is valuable, because it proves that, with the exception of the disappearance of the colour from the robes, the monument remains now in precisely the same state as it was in the year 1719. The whole is of white freestone, and of tolerable execution. Under the canopy of the tomb, and against the wall which separates the north from the middle chancel, is sculptured a coat of arms, quarterly; namely, 1 and 4, on a cross 5 mullets between 4 birds; 2 and 3, a lion rampant, within an orle of crescents. Above the shield is the date 1567, and below are the initials R. L."

The Elizabeth mentioned in the inscription was his second wife. Her maiden name was Stoke. For his first wife he married Jane, daughter of Sir Ralph Shirley of Wistneston, Sussex, and widow of Sir John Dawtrey of Petworth. Her portrait, by Holbein, is in her Majesty's collection.[4]

Of the general state of the town during Henry viii.'s reign, we are enabled to gather a few particulars, chiefly from the description left by Leland,[5] who visited it about 1540. As the passage is interesting, I will quote it at length:—

"*Wakefeld* upon *Calder* ys a very quik (*i.e.* busy) market Toune, and meately (moderately) large; well

---

(4) Foss's *Judges of England* (1857), vol. v.; from which most of my information on this subject is derived.

(5) John Leland was appointed King's Antiquary in 1533, and set out, by royal commission, on his tour of research in 1536. He returned in 1542, after traversing most parts of the kingdom.

servid of Flesch and Fische, both from the Se and by Ryvers, whereof divers be thereaboute at hande. So that al Vitaile is very good chepe there. A right honest man shall fare wel for 2 Pens a meale. In the toune is but one chefe Chirche. There is a chapel beside, where was wont to be *Anachoreta in media urbe* .... There is also a Chapel of our Lady on *Calder* Bridge, wont to be celebratid (frequented) *a peregrinis*. A forow lenght (furlong), or more, oute of the Toune, be seene Dikes and Bulwarkes, and *monticulus egestæ terræ, indicium turris specularis*.[6] Whereby apperith that ther hath bene a Castel. The *Guarines*, Earles of Surrey, as I reede, were ons lordes of this Toune. It standith now al by clothyng."[7]

---

(6) The origin of this mound, dear to the memories of all Wakefield children as Low-hill, has never, I believe, been satisfactorily explained. Leatham (n. to *Sandal in the olden time*) says that "it may have a Roman origin, but at present it bears the marks of a Danish mount, surrounded with a double ditch." The former opinion is countenanced by the resemblance which the spot bears to the "Castle-hills," formerly existing near North Allerton, and engraved in Ingledew's *History*, which proved, on excavation, to be Roman. In a document of the 17th century, referring to Grammar School property, the name is spelt Lawhill: but the conjecture based on this, that it was a sort of Tynwald, is very precarious. In Leland it is spelt Lo-hill; which agrees with the popular pronunciation. In either case, the origin of the name is probably the same. *Lowe* (more commonly *hlæw* or *hlaw*) in Anglo-Saxon denoted a mound, or barrow: thus the modern Hounslow was *Hundes-hlaw*, "the dogs' hill;" Ludlow was *Leod-* (or *Lude-*) *hlaw*, "people's hill;" &c. See Bosworth's *Dictionary of Anglo-Saxon* (1838). Hence the mound in question was most probably called simply "Lowe" or "Hlaw" by our Saxon forefathers; and when this word ceased to be significant of the meaning to a later generation, and was taken for a proper name, the descriptive termination *hill* was added. A familiar example of this process is to be found in the name *Wansbeckwater*.——See further an article in the *Saturday Review*, Nov. 14th, 1863.

(7) *Itinerary* (1745), vol. vii.

We shall get a better notion of the probable size of the town, by comparing this with the descriptions of Leeds and Bradford, which follow :—

"*Bradeforde*, a praty quik Market Toune, *dimidio, aut eo amplius, minus* Wachefelda. It hath one Paroche Chirche, and a chapel of St. Sitha. It standith much by clothing, &c."

"*Ledis*, 2 miles lower then *Christal* (Kirkstall) Abbay on *Aire* Ryver, is a praty market, having one Paroche Chirche, reasonably well buildid, and as large as *Bradeford*, but not so quik as it. The Toun standith most by clothing."

From this it appears that Leeds and Bradford were about equal in size, and Wakefield greater by at least a third. Now in 1602, when an assessment, for the support of maimed soldiers, was made by the Justices of the West Riding on its various parishes, Bradford was rated at 9d per week, Halifax at 8d, and Wakefield and Leeds at 10d each. If James,[8] from whom I quote this table, be right in computing the population of Halifax at that date as 2,500, then Wakefield, at the same period, may be supposed to have contained rather more than 3,000 inhabitants. On this supposition, the population of Wakefield, in Leland's time, would be somewhat less than 3,000; and that of Leeds and Bradford, less than 2,000 each. The town, as Leland elsewhere informs us, was built chiefly of timber, with some stone houses intermixed; and extended in length east and west. Probably therefore it consisted of little more than Westgate, Warrengate,

---

(8) *History of Bradford*, p. iii.

and Kirkgate; the "chapel of the anchorite" being thought by some to have lain in the direction of the present Northgate.

That Wakefield had early acquired a reputation for coal, as well as its cloth manufacture, (which we should infer from Leland's mention of the "plenty of se cole" in its neighbourhood,) appears from an entry in the fabric rolls of York Minster:[9]—

"Tertius compotus magistri Thomæ Marsar . . . custodis fabricæ, a 29 Nov. 1527 usque 28 Nov. 1528.

"Expensæ minutæ—pro diversis saccis carbonum de Waikfeld, et saccis carbonum vocatorum charcool, et chawders carbonum de Newcastell, £5 5s. 8d."

The first express mention of a colliery, which I can find, is in 1624, when a lease of certain coal mines near Wakefield was granted by William Rolfe, vintner, of London, to Lancelot Gledhill and Thomas Brackenbury.[10]

That the good qualities of the Calder for dyeing purposes were also early known, may be presumed from a stray notice we find of "protection being given to Robert Knollys of Wakefield, *dyer*, on his going to the wars in the retinue of Richard Tempest, squire of the body."[11] This was in 1513.

But the Calder was useful for other purposes than dyeing. The fish which it contained, along with the game to be found in the Old and New Parks, and the malt liquor from the barley grown in abundance round

---

(9) *Surtees Society's Publications*, vol. 35.

(10) *Calendar of State Papers* (1859)

(11) *Letters and Papers of the time of Henry* viii., catalogued by J. S. Brewer (1862).

about, doubtless contributed to that "chepeness of vitaile," which enabled Leland (right honest man) to "fare wel for 2 Pens a meale." Those were indeed the palmy days of "merrie Wakefield." Sir William Brereton, who passed through the town nearly a century later, in 1635, speaks equally well of its hospitality, though he had to pay much dearer for it. "We lodged at Wakefield at the Bull," is his memorandum, dated June 11th, "where we paid 5s. for supper and breakfast: it is an honest and excellent house."[12]

As regards the local government, a lease was granted to Sir Richard Tempest, in 1514, "of the farm of the town of Wakefield, with the office of bailiff there, the bakehouse and fishery therein, all meadows called Wilbigh, Dibford, and Erlesing, parcel of the township of Wakefeld, the mills of Wakefeld and Horbury, le New Milne super le dam, and the fisheries there, with timber for repairs from the old and new park, at an annual rent of £89 16s. 7½d., on surrender by Richard Peke (since the death of Thomas Grice) of patent 9 Nov. 16 Hen. vii., by which the said premises were leased to Peke and Grice for 20 years."[13]

---

(12) *Travels in Holland, &c.*, by Sir W. Brereton, (Cheetham Society's Publications) 1844.

Whilst on this subject, it may amuse the reader to be informed, that to Queen Margaret's approval of its good fare in 1460, Wakefield owes the privilege of bearing on its coat of arms the royal emblem of France. A friend has pointed out to me no less an authority for this than M. Soyer, who, in his *Shilling Cookery Book*, under the heading "Wakefield Beef Steak," writes:—"This dish proves that the inhabitants of Wakefield have not lost the culinary reputation they formerly possessed, and which they first acquired some four hundred years since, when the French Queen and her suite came to reside there, and allowed them to quarter the *fleur-de-lis* in the arms of the town."

(13) *Letters and Papers, &c.*, as above.

The Chantry on the bridge was served by Richard Coke (or Cyke) during the early part of the reign; and on his death, in 1514, by Thomas Spenke. The Vicar [14] of Wakefield from 1502 to 1546 was Thomas Knolles, a man of coniderable eminence; "being," according to Dodd,[15] "one of the most celebrated preachers of his time." He was a native of Westgate, in Yorkshire, and was educated at Magdalen College, Oxford, of which in 1527, he rose to be president. In 1507 he was made sub-dean of York, and held this office till 1529, when he was appointed prebendary of Absthorpe (or Aplethorpe) in the same church. "He gave way to fate," adds Wood,[16] "the 9th of May, 1546, and was buried near to the grave of his father and mother, in the south ally, adjoining to All-hallows Church in Wakefield." The following inscription was said by Whitaker to be the oldest memorial of a vicar of the church extant in his time:—

"HIC IACET THOMAS KNOLLIS SACRÆ THEOLOGIÆ PROFESSOR, COLLEGII MAGDALENÆ OXONIENSIS PRÆSES, ECCLESIÆ DE WAKEFIELD VICARIVS, QVI QVIDEM THOMAS OBIIT IX. DIE MAII M° CCCCCXXXXVII. CVIVS ANIME PROPICIETVR DEVS AMEN. AC ECIAM ORATE PRO EIVS ANIMA ET PRO ANIMABVS PARENTVM SVORVM VT PER GRACIAM DEI . . . ."

---

(14) The living ceased to be a rectory in 1349.
(15) *Church History of England* (1737) vol. I.
(16) *Athenæ Oxonienses*, under the year 1518.

ROBERT WAKEFIELD.

Contemporary, or nearly so, with Thomas Knolles was Robert Wakefield. This learned Hebrew scholar was born of good parentage at Wakefield: but in what year I am ignorant. The date given by Zouch,[1] 1536, is clearly wrong. After studying at Cambridge, he travelled over most parts of Europe, and acquired such a knowledge of the Latin, Greek, Hebrew, Syriac, and Chaldee tongues, as marked him out for "the prime linguist of his time."[2] On his return to England, he was appointed chaplain to the king, and soon rose high in the royal favour. When Henry re-endowed Christ Church, Oxford, in 1532, Robert Wakefield was presented to the twelfth canonry on that foundation. The part taken by him in the ensuing dissolution of the monasteries, is variously represented, according to the opinions and prepossessions of the writers. With regard to the great abbey of Ramsey, in Cambridgeshire, for example, which was suppressed in 1536, Pits[3] speaks of him as having not only been a consenting party, but as having stolen not a few books

---

(1) *Works*, by Wrangham (1820), vol. ii.
(2) Wood: *History, &c. of Oxford* (1786)
(3) *Relationes Historicæ* (1619)

from its library, Lawrence Holbeck's Hebrew Lexicon among the number. Wood, on the other hand, declares that "in one thing he is to be commended, and that is this; that he *carefully preserved* divers books of Greek and Hebrew at the dissolution of the religious houses, and especially some of those in the library of Ramsey Abbey, composed by Laurence Holbeck, monk of that place, in the reign of Henry v." A curious instance of the different constructions that may be put upon the same act. Anyhow, he was made to suffer in turn; for his Chaldee Lexicon, a work on which he had bestowed great labour, along with several other books, was stolen from his house at Margate, (or, as others may denominate it, *carefully preserved*) by one Richard Collier, vicar of Sittingborn, formerly a Carthusian monk.[4]

He died in London, Oct. 8th, 1537; leaving behind him, according to Leland, the surname of Polypus, for his "witty and crafty behaviour," and the reputation of having been the first to introduce the study of Hebrew, and its kindred tongues, into the English universities.[5]

---

(4) Tanner, *Bibliotheca Britannica* (1748).

(5) "Primus omnium in Angliam Chaldæum, Hebræum, Arabicumque invexit, et illa publicè in utrâque academiâ docuit:"— *From his inaugural address in* 1524. His brother, or near kinsman, Thomas, began to lecture on Hebrew, at Cambridge, in 1540. Several works of his still remain, some published by Wynkyn de Worde.

THOMAS ROBERTSON.

Thomas Knolles was succeeded in the vicarage of Wakefield by Thomas Robertson, who is chiefly to be remembered as one of the compilers of our Liturgy. He was born either in or near Wakefield, and, after entering at Queen's College, Oxford, removed to Magdalen, of which he ultimately became a Fellow, and master of the school adjoining. "In this capacity he shewed," says Fuller, "an admirable faculty in teaching of youth; for every boy can teach a *man*, but it must be a masterpiece of industry and discretion to descend to the capacity of children."[1] In 1525 he took his degree of M.A., and for the next few years was employed in the composition of grammatical treatises, which were then much needed. They were dedicated by him to his patron, John Longland, Bishop of Lincoln; and gained him a great reputation for sound scholarship. The list of his preferments is a long one; but they need not be here enumerated. In June, 1546, he renewed his connection with his native town; being then instituted to the vicarage, on the presentation of the Dean and Convent of St. Mary and St. Stephen, Westminster. He was at the same time treasurer of

---

(1) *Worthies of England.*

Sarum, archdeacon of Leicester, and prebend *any* of Croperdy, in the diocese of Lincoln. In 1548 he was one of the twelve "learned and discreet bishops and divines," appointed by the king as coadjutors with Cranmer, "to draw an order of divine worship, having respect to the pure religion of Christ taught in the Scripture, and to the practice of the primitive church." The "Order for the Communion" was published in 1548, and the "Book of Common Prayer" in the year following. In the old editions of Sparrow's *Rationale*, Robertson is depicted as sitting at table in consultation with the rest; but he seems to have taken no active part, at least after the first stage of their proceedings. "He was a friend to the Reformers," writes Dodd, "as far as concerned discipline; but drew back when they began to pare to the quick." And to the same effect the author of the article in the *Biographie Universelle*:—"Sous Edouard vi. il fut de la commission chargée de rédiger le livre de la Prière Commune; mais il ne paraît pas qu' il y ait travaillé. Il était assez d'accord avec les nouveaux réformateurs sur l'article de la discipline ecclésiastique. On le trouvait très-accommadant en fait de doctrine; mais il finit par se décider absolument pour le catholicisme, quelque temps avant sa mort, arrivée sous le régne de Jacques Ier."[2]

After Edward's death, he seems to have withdrawn from all connection with the Reformers; for in 1557 he was promoted by Mary to the deanery of Durham;

---

(2) As James i. did not begin to reign till 1603, this would make Robertson about 100 years old. There is no evidence, as far as I am aware, of his surviving much beyond 1560.

and "being greatly in respect," says Wood, "for his piety and learning, the Queen would have had him take a bishoprick, but he modestly refused it."

On Elizabeth's accession, he was ejected from the deanery of Durham, about the latter end of 1559; and soon after resigned the archdeaconry of Leicester, to prevent a like fate. He had an opportunity of returning to the first of these offices, had he been willing to take the oath of supremacy, owing to the promotion of his successor, Dr. Horne, to the see of Winchester. But this he declined to do. What became of him afterwards is uncertain. Strype says that he began to propagate his opinions against the Reformation, and was overlooked; but others think he was taken into custody. The exact year of his death is not known; but it was probably about 1560.

Besides his grammatical works, he was the author of "Resolutions of some Questions concerning the Sacraments," which will be found among the documents quoted at the end of Burnet's *History of the Reformation*.[3]

---

(3) For further particulars the reader is referred to Wood's *Athenæ Oxonienses;* Bale's *Scriptores Illustres* (1557,) vol ii ; Le Neve's *Fasti* (1854), vol. ii ; and the Lives of the Compilers of the Liturgy, prefixed to Sparrow's *Rationale.*

SIR MARTIN FROBISHER.

The common accounts of this brave seaman represent him as having been born near Doncaster; to which it is sometimes added that he was of humble parentage. Probably neither statement is correct. A Francis Furbisher, or Frobisher, was Recorder of Doncaster about the middle of the sixteenth century; "a right worshipful esquyer and just justicer," as he is called by Bosvile. He was buried there June 4th, 1563. The names of others of the family appear in the early registers of Doncaster; and hence it has been concluded that Sir Martin was a native of those parts. But Hunter,[1] after discussing this opinion, adds that "there seems to be no reason for depriving the little village of Altofts, near Wakefield, of the honour of having produced this truly eminent man." This judgment is confirmed by some genealogical memoranda, attached to Frobisher's will, and now in possession of Mr. Frobisher, of Crofton.[2] From this source it appears, that the earliest of the race, whose name has been preserved, was a John Frobisher, Esq., of Flint-

---

(1) *South Yorkshire* (1828) vol. i.
(2) For a copy of which I am indebted to the kindness of Mr. Cromek.

shire, in North Wales. In the sixth generation from him we come to a John Frobisher, Esq., of Altofts, who married Joan, daughter of Sir William Scargill, of Thorp Stapleton, near Leeds. According to the *Visitation* of 1563, which Hunter quotes, Francis, the Recorder, was grandson of this John Frobisher; but the pedigree above mentioned makes him to have been great-grandson. They, and the intermediate members, are all there described as of Altofts. Passing downwards, we come to another Francis, great-grandson of the above-named Recorder of Doncaster, who is described as of Fenningley, and married Cressee, daughter of Mr. Rogers, of Everton, in Nottinghamshire. The second of their three sons was Martin, the subject of this sketch.

There is no certain evidence, after all, as to where Sir Martin was born: but that he was a native of Altofts is rendered probable from the fact, that several generations of the family, as we have seen, were settled there; and from the baptism of a Margaret Frobisher, believed to be his sister, being registered in the parish church of Normanton, Feb. 10th, 1541; and lastly, from the fact, "that he was seized in Free farm of the Lordship of Altofts, where he built a house near the Park," and directed by will that his funeral should be solemnized there.

An apology is due to the reader for detaining him thus long with genealogical matters. But it was necessary to "try the previous question," so to speak, as to whether we could claim Sir Martin Frobisher for one of our Worthies, or no.

To enter into any long account of one, whose name

and actions are so familiar to his countrymen, would be superfluous. He was the first Englishman who attempted to solve the problem, which has of late years attracted so much attention, of finding a north-west passage to China and India. "Certaine learned Ingenies of the time," writes an old Chronicler,[3] "inflamed with an honest desire of discovering the more distant regions of the earth, and the secrets of the ocean, incited certaine well-moneyed men, who were no lesse inflamed with the desire of getting more, to make discovery, if, in the north parts of America, there were any way, by which men might sayle to the rich country of Cathay; and so, by a mutual commerce, to joyne the riches of the East and Occident together." The project is said to have been in Frobisher's mind for fifteen years, before he found means to execute it. At last, by the help of Ambrose Dudley, Earl of Warwick, and others, he succeeded in fitting out what looks but a tiny fleet for such an undertaking; namely, two little barks of 25 tons burden each, and a pinnace of 10 tons. With these he set sail from Deptford, June 8th, 1576; and after passing the Shetlands, being in 61° of latitude, discovered land bearing W.N.W. This was one of the islands north of Hudson's straits. The ice prevented them from disembarking; but he named the east point of it *Queen Elizabeth's Foreland*, which name it still bears. On the eleventh of August, being then in latitude 63° 8', he entered the strait, which has ever since being known as Frobisher's Strait. A week later,

---

(3) *The true and royall History of the famous Empresse Elizabeth*, 1625.

the party landed, and took formal possession of the country in the name of the Queen of England. The men being ordered, in token of such possession, to bring away something of what each might find, one of them "brought a piece of black stone, much like a sea-coal, but very weighty. Having, at his return, distributed fragments of it among his friends, one of the adventurers' wives threw a fragment into the fire, which being taken out again, and quenched in vinegar, glistered like gold; and being tried by refiners in London, was found to contain a rich quantity of that metal. From this essay, the nation dreaming of nothing but mountains of gold, great numbers earnestly pressed, and soon fitted out, Captain Frobisher, to undertake a second voyage the very next spring."[4] This time he started under the immediate patronage of the Queen, who lent him a ship of 200 tons, named the Aid. "On Munday morning, the 27th of May," he writes in his Journal, "aboord the Ayde, we received all the Communion by the minister of Gravesend; and prepared us as good Christians towards God, and resolute men for all fortunes."[5] In this expedition of 1557 we need not follow the adventurers; nor in a third one undertaken a year after. Their object was now not to discover the north-west passage, but to obtain supplies of this so-thought precious ore. The stones proved worthless: and, "when neither gold, silver, nor any other metall could be drawne from them," says the chronicler above-mentioned, "we saw them throwne awaye to repayre the highwayes."

---

(4) *Biographia Britannica.*
(5) Quoted in the *Biographia* from Hakluyt's *Collection of Voyages.*

After this, we hear no more of Frobisher till 1585, when he commanded the Aid in Sir Francis Drake's expedition to the West Indies. On the invasion of the Spanish Armada he had command of the largest crew afloat, in one of the largest vessels, the Triumph. For his conduct on that occasion he was knighted on board his own ship, the Ark, by the Lord High Admiral, July 26th, 1588. He subsequently led a squadron, to keep in check the Spanish coast; and in 1594, being sent with four men of war to the assistance of Henry iv. of France, who was fighting against a body of Leaguers and Spaniards then holding part of Bretagne, he was shot by a ball in the hip, in an assault upon Croyzon, near Brest, on the 7th of November. "The wound was not mortal in itself," says Fuller,[6] "but swords and guns have not made more mortal wounds, than probes in the hands of careless and skill-less chirurgeons, as here it came to pass. The chirurgeon took out only the bullet, and left the bumbast (wadding) about it behind, wherewith the sore festered, and the worthy Knight died at Plymouth, anno 1594."

He married Dorothy, daughter of the Right Honorable Lord Wentworth, of the South, and widow of Sir Wm. Widmerpoole, Kt., who survived him, and was afterwards married to Sir John Savile. Having no issue, he left all his estate, including "the manors of Warmfield-cum-Heath, and Whitwood, with several other lands and leases of very considerable yearly revenue," to his nephew Captain Peter Frobisher. By him it was lavished away; and Hopkinson[7] says that he died

---

(6) *Worthies of England*.
(7) Quoted by Hunter, as above.

very necessitous and obscurely, in or about London. Sir Martin's will was made at sea, and is dated Aug. 4th, 1594. In it he directs that his body shall be buried where God pleases; "but my will and myndd is, that the solemnizacon of my funeralls shall be kept at the p'ish church of Normanton, and at my house called Frobisher Hall, in Altofts, in the countie of York."

He died at Plymouth, as above said, on the 22nd of November; and the place "where it pleased God his body should be buried," was St. Giles's, Cripplegate.

Two years before Frobisher's death, the Wakefield Grammar School was founded; a school which, had it produced no other scholars than Bentley and Bingham, could not be said to have existed in vain. It was established at the suit of the inhabitants, "for teaching children and youth belonging to the parish of Wakefield in good learning;" and by a charter of Queen Elizabeth, dated Sept. 19th, 1592, George Savile, Esq. and thirteen other persons were incorporated as governors.

The property of the school was subsequently increased by various bequests; the most considerable being those of Cave and Storie. The former, Thomas Cave, of Wakefield, chapman, gave in 1602 one half of the rectory or parsonage of Warmfield, for the foundation of two scholarships at Clare Hall, Cambridge, to be given to candidates from Wakefield school. The latter, John Storie, of Hasleborrow, in Derbyshire, merchant, by his will dated April 29th,

1674, "devised his copyhold and freehold within the county of York, for maintaining and bringing up three boys, the children of parents not able to bring them up, at one of the universities of Cambridge or Oxford, for three years; such boys to be chosen out of those poor children that he had lately settled lands upon, for their teaching at the petty school, until they should be fit to go to the free school at Wakefield."[1]

George Savile, Esq., died in London, Jany. 3rd, 1595, but his fostering care of the Grammar School was continued by William Savile, Esq., who was the first Spokesman elected by the Governors. One or two of his donations may perhaps raise a passing smile. Along with other things, he "did give the great deske in the myddle of the schole, and a plate dyall which standith in the courte, and the Queen's arms in a frame which be in the upper end thereof. . . . He also did give the great large Dictionary, made by Bishop

---

(1) See *Reports of the Commissioners for Charities* (1827) vol. 17; and Kennett's MSS., vol. 39.

The regulations above-mentioned have never been observed. "By indentures of the 25th and 26th May, 1674, and surrender, John Storie conveyed a house and 9 acres of freehold land at Ardsley, and surrendered 1 acre 2 roods of copyhold land in Sandal, to the Governors of the Free Grammar School, in trust, for teaching twelve children at a petty school until they should be fit to go to the Free Grammar School: the children to be chosen (1) out of Northgate, (2) out of Kirkgate, and (3) out of Westgate."— *Report*, as above.

From the Ardsley property never falling in, no such preparatory school was established. But in 1707 the Governors of the Wakefield Charities, out of their general funds, erected a school in Westgate, since known as the Green-coat School, "for teaching the poor children of the town in reading, writing, and arithmetic." Of the good done by this unpretending, but truly useful school, the author (whose father was for many years its hard-working master) has had abundant evidence.

Cowper, called in Latine *Thesaurus linguæ Romanæ*, &c. . . . item, one bedstead of waynscott carved and wrought, made at the charges of the governours standing in the master's chamber." [2]

---

(2) Extracted by Kennett from the Register-book of the Grammar School, July 24th, 1724.

The "Queen's arms in a frame" may still be seen on the outer wall of the old School, near the south-east corner.

JEREMIAH WHITAKER.

Among the earliest pupils of this school was Jeremiah Whitaker, who was born at Wakefield in 1599. He was one who, from his earliest years, showed a marked predilection for the calling he was afterwards to follow. "While he was a Grammar-scholar," writes Simeon Ash,[1] "though his father endeavoured often and earnestly to divert his thoughts from the ministery, yet he was unmovable in his desires to be a minister. I have many times heard him speak these words: 'I had much rather be a preacher of the gospel than an emperor.'" At the age of sixteen he entered as a sizar at Sidney Sussex College, Cambridge; and was thus for some time a fellow-collegian with Oliver Cromwell, who was born in the same year as himself, and went up to the same college at the age of seventeen. Taking his Bachelor's degree in 1619, he went to Oakham, where he had been appointed master of the School. Four years after, he married Chephtzibah, daughter of Master William Peachey, minister in that town; and at the end of seven years more, succeeded to

---

(1) *Living loves between Christ and dying Christians;* a funeral sermon on the death of Jeremiah Whitaker, preached June 6th, 1654.

the pastoral charge of Stretton in the same county. In this office he continued thirteen years. On the ejection of Thomas Paske from the rectory of St. Mary Magdalene, Bermondsey, in 1644, Whitaker was chosen in his stead. At this point let Fuller continue the story:—" He well discharged his duty, being a man made up of piety to God, pity to poor men, and patience in himself. He had much use of the last, being visited with many and most acute diseases. I see God's love or hatred cannot be conjectured, much less concluded, from outward accidents; this merciful man meeting with merciless afflictions. Sure I am, this good Jeremiah was tormented with gout, stone, and one ulcer in his bladder, another in his kidneys; all which he endured with admirable and exemplary patience: though God of his goodness grant that (if it may stand with his will) no cause be given that so sad a copy be transcribed. Thus God, for reasons best known unto himself, sent many and the most cruel Bayliffes to arrest him, to pay his debt to nature, though he was ready willingly to tender the same at their single summons. His liberality knew no bottom but an empty purse; so bountiful he was to all in want."[2]

When the Assembly of Divines was convened at Westminster, by an Order of the two Houses, dated June 12th, 1643, Whitaker was elected a member, and in 1647 filled the office of Moderator. In the same year also he was chosen by the House of Lords, along with Dr. Thomas Goodwin, to examine and superintend the Assembly's publications. Besides these labours, he

---

(2) *Worthies of England.*

preached, during his residence in London, four sermons weekly; and, for private reading, went through all the Epistles once a week in the original tongue. He was moreover a good Oriental scholar, and "well acquainted both with the Schoolmen and the Fathers; a good disputant, judicious in cases of conscience, and second to none in acquaintance with the Holy Scripture."[3]

The last years of his life were disturbed by acute bodily suffering. In the *Sloane Collection* is a letter of his, addressed to Cromwell, in which he excuses himself from delivering a certain religious treatise in person, "being confined to my chamber under extreme tormenting pains of the stone, which forceth me to cry and sorrow night and day." He died June 1st, 1654, in the 56th year of his age; and was buried in the chancel of St. Mary Magdalene's, near the remains of Elton, another famous Puritan divine. The inscription on his monument may be seen in Stowe's *Survey of London*. In lieu of it, we will conclude this account with an extract or two from the elegies, printed at the end of the third edition of Ashe's *Funeral Sermon*. Some of them are curious, as specimens of the quaint and far-fetched style of expression then prevailing. One writer, for instance, says that he is not dead, but

"Heaven's Whit-acre onely, newly mowne."

The grief of another finds its simile in—

"A Thames and Medway from our heads arise,
Their streams our tears, their channels are our eyes;
Our many losses call for tears not fewer,
The brest a bason makes the eye an ewer."

---

(3) Simeon Ashe, as above.—See also Brook's *Lives of the Puritans* (1813).

A third has recourse to an anagram; and reads in Jeremiah Whitaker, "I have hit everi mark," whilst another again ends with—

> "A chariot and an horseman we have lost,
> In whose each single prayer incampt an host.
> How have I heard him on some solemn day,
> When doubtful war could make all London pray,
> Mount up to Heaven with armed crys and tears,
> And rout, as far as York, the Cavileers.
> Have you not seen an early-rising lark
> Spring from her turf, making the sunne her mark,
> Shooting herself aloft, yet higher, higher,
> Till she had sung herself into heaven's quire?
> Thus would he rise in prayer, and in a trice
> His soul became a bird of Paradise:
> And if our faint devotions prayers be,
> What can we call this less than extasie?"

JOSEPH NAYLOR.

As Thomas Paske had been ejected from his rectory at Bermondsey by the Puritans, to make room for Whitaker; so the latter's son William, who succeeded him there, was ejected in his turn after the Restoration, in 1662. The same event restored another Wakefield man, Joseph Naylor, to preferments of which he had been deprived. This Joseph Naylor was born in 1594, and became Fellow of Sidney Sussex College; so that he too was probably, for a short space, contemporary there with Cromwell.[1] In 1632 he was made archdeacon of Northumberland, and four years later, prebendary of Durham. From the rectory of Sedgefield, to which he had been presented in 1634, he was expelled by the Puritans; but restored to it, as has been intimated, on the accession of Charles ii. He wrote

---

(1) Oliver Cromwell was admitted April 23rd, 1616, and probably returned no more after July in the year following. In the Admission-book of Sidney Sussex College, between the entry of Cromwell's name and the next, some one of later date has crowded in the words:—"*Hic fuit grandis ille Impostor, Carnifex perditissimus, qui, pientissimo Rege Carolo Primo nefariâ cæde sublato, ipsum vsurpavit Thronum, et Tria Regna per quinque ferme annorum spatium, sub Protectoris nomine, indomitâ tyrannide vexavit.*"—See Carlyle's *Cromwell's Letters and Speeches*, (1850) vol. i.

Additions to the Life of Bishop Morton, whose chaplain he had been; and, dying in 1667, was buried in the chancel of Sedgefield Church.[2]

---

(2) See Hutchinson's *History and Antiquities of Durham*, vol. ii.

LADY BOLLES.

Before quitting the reign of Elizabeth, to which Whitaker and Naylor by birth belong, we must not forget to mention one, who was long connected with Wakefield, by her residence at Heath Hall, and whom many a Wakefield youth has had cause to remember with gratitude, Lady Bolles.

"The right worshipful Dame Mary Bolles" was born about 1579; being one of the daughters of William Witham, Esq., of Ledston, and, after her brother Henry's death, co-heiress of his estates. For her first husband, she was married to Thomas Jobson, Esq., of Cudworth, by whom she had two children, Thomas and Elizabeth; and for her second, to Thomas Bolles,[1] Esq., of Osbarstone, or Osberton, in Nottinghamshire, by whom she had other two children, Anne and Mary. "She was a lady in her own right," says Hunter,[2] "that is, a baronetess, so created by Charles the First; a rare, if not a solitary instance. She lived in much

---

(1) The name is variously spelt.—For an instance of the extent to which such variation sometimes prevails, see Eastwood's *History of the Parish of Ecclesfield* (1862) p. 425, where the name Shiercliffe is spelt, "on documental authority," in no less than 56 different ways.

(2) *Antiquarian notices of Lupset, &c.* (1851) printed privately.

honour, wealth, and prosperity, to a good old age; dying at the Hall, on the 5th May, 1662." The inscription on her monument in Ledsham Church, where she was not buried till the sixteenth of June, is given in Thoresby.

By her will dated May 4th, 1662, she gives the sum of £500, the interest thereof to be applied by "the minister of Wakefield for the time being, and three individual trustees," to binding young men as apprentices. Some of the provisions of her will betray a certain oddity of character. Thus for the entertainment of guests at the Hall, during the six weeks that elapsed before her funeral, she sets apart £120. "And to this end," she continues, " I give all my fat beeves and fat sheep to be disposed of, at the discretion of my executors, whom I charge to perform it nobly, and really to bestow this my gift in good provision; two hogsheads of wine or more, as they shall see cause, and that several hogsheads of beer be taken care for (there being no convenience to brew). And, my bedding being plundered from me, I desire that the chambers may be well furnished with beds borrowed for the time, for the entertaining of such as shall be thought fit lodgers." For the purchase of mourning apparel she assigns £700, and £400 for funeral expenses. Every poor person present at her interment is to receive sixpence, if above sixteen years of age; if under, threepence.[3] "This part of the will," writes the Rev. B. Forster to B. Gough, Esq., in 1766,[4] " was fulfilled;

---

(3) Hunter, as above.
(4) Nichols' *Literary Illustrations* (1828) vol. v.

some others were not to the satisfaction of the *menu peuple:* Lady Bolles therefore long walked in Heath Grove, till at length she was conjured down into a hole of the river, near Heath Hall, called to this day Lady Bolles' Pit. The spell however was not so powerful, but what she still rises and makes a fuss now and then."

In seriousness, she must have been no ordinary person, to have obtained such a hold on the minds of the neighbouring villagers, that her memory is still fresh there, after the lapse of two hundred years.

HUGH PAULIN CRESSY.

Early in the seventeenth century we come to one, who was in many respects a remarkable man, Hugh Paulin Cressy. He was born at Wakefield in 1605, being descended, on the father's side, from an old and respectable family settled at Holme, near Hodsack, in Nottinghamshire. His father,[5] Hugh, was a barrister of Lincoln's Inn; his mother, Margery, was daughter of Dr. Thomas D'Oylie, a London physician. After remaining at the Grammar School, under Mr. Philip Isaac, till the age of fourteen, he proceeded to Oxford, where he obtained his Bachelor's degree in 1623. Three years afterwards he was elected Fellow of Merton College; and after proceeding to the degree of Master of Arts, and taking Holy Orders, he became domestic chaplain to Thomas Lord Wentworth, afterwards Earl of Strafford. In this capacity he attracted the favourable notice of archbishop Laud, who, not aware of his being in the Lord-Deputy's household at the time, thus writes to Earl Strafford concerning him :—

---

(5) In 1614 one Hugh Cressy, whom I presume to have been this one, was Spokesman of the Governors of the Grammar School.

"I have only one thing more to trouble your lordship with at this time, and that is concerning one Mr. Cressy, a divine, who is lately arrived in Ireland. I have received good testimony of his sufficiency as a younger man, and had thought to have recommended him to your lordship a good while since, but that other businesses have caused me to slip it. I pray you, when he comes in your way, will you be pleased to take notice of him from me? And as he shall approve himself by his good carriage, so let him stand or fall in your lordship's estimation."[1] This letter which was dated July 10th, 1634, met with a courteous reply; but it does not appear to have procured any preferment for Cressy, as we find him accompanying Lucius Viscount Falkland into Ireland, in 1638, in the capacity of chaplain. From his return to England in the year following, to the latter end of 1642, we hear no more of him; but at length, through the interest of Lord Falkland, then one of the Secretaries of State, he was made Canon of Windsor. The letters patent are dated Dec. 27th, 1642, but he was never installed. In fact, owing to the disturbed state of the times, there appears to have been no installation from this period till after the Restoration.[2] The same cause rendered the Deanery of Leighlin, in Ireland, conferred upon him about this time, an equally barren honour. The battle of Newbury impairing his prospects still further, by depriving him of his friend and patron Lord Falkland, he was glad to have an opportunity of leaving England.

---

(1) Quoted in Wood's *Athenæ Oxonienses*, from which also the foregoing particulars are taken.

(2) Le Neve, *Fasti, &c.*, vol. iii.

"It was in the moneth of June," he writes, "in the yeare of our Lord, 1644, that those most unnatural and bloody dissensions in Greate Britaine . . . . constreined mee (not so much to avoyde my personall danger, as out of the horrour to be a spectatour of such inhumane Tragedies as were everywhere dayly acted) to recreate myselfe with a voluntary exile."[3] As travelling tutor to Charles Berkeley, afterwards Earl of Falmouth, Cressy went on to the Continent; and at length, his allegiance to the Church of England having been for some time growing weaker and weaker, he recanted, and made profession of the Roman Catholic faith, in presence of the Inquisition, in 1646. This was followed by the publication at Paris, next year, of his "*Exomologesis, or a faithful narrative of the occasion and motives for his conversion.*" His intention now was to enter the English College of Carthusians, at Newport, in Flanders; but from this he was dissuaded by the knowledge that but little leisure would be there allowed him for the use of his pen. Ultimately, he entered the college of English Benedictines, at Douay, Queen Henrietta Maria having given him 100 crowns to defray the expenses of his journey. Here he changed his name from Hugh Paulin to Serenus; and for seven years, or more, was occupied in composing various religious treatises.[4] Of these the most important is his *Church History of Brittany*, published at Rouen, in 1668. He had intended to continue this work down to the dissolution of the monasteries by

---

(3) *Exomologesis*, p. 8.
(4) A list of them is to be found in Sir James Ware's *History and Antiquities of Ireland*, continued by Harris (1764) p. 356.

Henry viii. ; but the first volume was all that saw the light. Dodd informs us that a considerable portion of the manuscript for the second volume was preserved in the college at Douay, its publication being stopped "upon account of some nice controversies between the see of Rome and some of our English kings, which might give offence." It is supposed to have perished in the devastations of the French Revolution.

His *Exomologesis,* or Account of his Conversion, is the one of his books which would probably be read with most interest now. It was highly applauded by the members of his adopted communion ; it procured him distinguished antagonists ; and " a new edition of it," says Charles Butler, "with a succinct view of the controversy between Cressy and his two great opponents, would form an interesting manual of Catholic controversy."[5] The two opponents alluded to were Bishop Stillingfleet and Lord Clarendon. The tone of it is temperate for the age. At times the author speaks his mind pretty freely, as when he talks of "the accursed idol of schisme," which "that sacrilegious tyrant King Henry the viii. dedicated," or when he asks, "how could that infernall monster of schisme proove her originall better, than by being the designe of that Prince so abandoned to all impiety as that he made choice to establish this his darling by sacriledge and murder?"[6] But it is pleasant to find him on kindly terms with such men as Hammond and Chillingworth. With reference to the latter, he speaks of

---

(5) *Historical Memoirs of the Catholics, &c.,* (1822) vol. iv.
(6) Dedication p. iii.

"the inwardness which I had for many years with that worthy person" . . . . "the mutual friendship betweene us, the great obligations I have to cherrish his memory, and the high esteeme of his excellent partes, &c."[7] The book leaves an impression of one who had grown weary of the distractions which tore his native church and country; who transferred the dislike he felt to the personal character of Luther and Calvin, to the church which he chose to consider as of their foundation; and who would not

. . . . "rather bear those ills he had,
Than fly to others that he knew not of."

What remains of Cressy's life may be soon told. After leaving Douay, he became a member of the Mission in England; and on the marriage of Charles ii. with the Infanta Katharine, was appointed chaplain to the Queen. He died on the 10th of August, 1674, at the house of Richard Caryl, Esq., and was buried in the church of East Grinstead, in Sussex.

---

(7) *Exomologesis*, p. 141.

BARNABAS OLEY.

Contemporary, or nearly so, with Hugh Cressy was Barnabas Heyolt, or Oley. He was born at Kirkthorpe, near Wakefield, of which place his father was vicar; and after being educated at the Grammar School, which he entered in 1607,[1] proceeded to Clare Hall, Cambridge, probably as Cave's Exhibitioner. Here be became Fellow and Tutor, and subsequently President, of his college; and, after filling in addition the offices of Taxor and Proctor in the University, was presented to the vicarage of Great Grantsden, in Huntingdonshire. He was a zealous royalist; and when, in 1642, the two Universities sent their plate to be converted into money for the King's use at Nottingham, he was entrusted with the guidance of the party from Cambridge. This task his knowledge of the country enabled him to discharge with safety and expedition. But though he baffled Cromwell's soldiers on this occasion, he was made to pay the penalty of

---

(1) Zouch, (*Walton's Lives*, 1807, *p.* 320, *n.*) who says that he was taught by Mr Jeremy Gibson.—Gibson was only temporarily head master, holding that office from June 4th to July 20th, 1607. He was succeeded by Robert Saunders, M.A., Senior Fellow of King's College, Cambridge, who also resigned before the year was out.—(*Register-book of the school.*)

his successful enterprise two years later, when he was ejected from his Fellowship, by the Earl of Manchester, Maior-General of the Parliamentarians. "He was at this time plundered of all his property," says Zouch, "and so much harrassed and menaced by the rebels, as to be under the necessity of leaving his vicarage. To avoid discovery he frequently changed his habit. For seven years he wandered about, having scarce wherewith to support himself. He fled for safety to the town of Wakefield, and we find him at one time in Pontefract Castle, along with some other loyal and worthy clergymen, preaching to the soldiers of the garrison, and encouraging them to defend the place against the King's enemies."[2] At length times changed. In 1659 he was enabled to return to Grantsden, and the year following was collated to the third prebend in the diocese of Worcester."[3] In November, 1679, he was raised to the archdeaconry of Ely, which he resigned the year after. He died Feb. 20th, 1686.[4]

Beyond the prefaces to Herbert's *Priest to the Temple*, and to Dr. Thomas Jackson's works, which he edited, he does not appear to have left any published writings. To his parish in Huntingdonshire, of which he had charge for fifty-three years, he was a liberal benefactor, and also to his college, the buildings of which had

---

(2) *Walton's Lives*, as above. See also Walker's *Sufferings of the Clergy*, part ii.

(3) Le Neve, *Fasti Anglicani*.

(4) "I'm told that this day your friend Mr. Barnabas Oley is to be buryed. His parishioners are already extremely sensible of their loss of that reverend and eminently worthy good man."— Letter of R. Burton to Dean Granville, dated St. John's, Feb. 27th, 1686. (*Surtees Society's Publications, vol.* 37.)

become dilapidated. "He may be truly termed *Master of the Fabric,*" writes Fuller,[5] "so industrious and judicious was he in overseeing the same." His native parish of Warmfield had its share in his bounty, the vicarage receiving from him a considerable augmentation; to which however were attached three rather whimsical conditions :—first, that the vicar should not smoke tobacco; secondly, that he should not wear a periwig; and thirdly, that he should not go often to the town of Wakefield.[6]

The period over which Oley's prolonged life extended was so eventful a one in the history of the country, that it will be well to pause here, and notice how Wakefield was affected by the commotions of the civil wars. The King's cause was espoused by most of the leading men in Yorkshire; the Fairfaxes of Denton and Nunappleton being those of most note on the opposite side. In 1643 this town was held by a Royalist garrison, consisting of more than 3,000 foot, under command of Sir Francis Mackworth, and about seven troops of horse, led by General Goring.[7] On the evening of Saturday, May 20th, a party of some 1500

---

(5) *History of the University of Cambridge.*

(6) Kennett, *Register and Chronicle* (1728), vol. i.

(7) *Antiquarian notices of Lupset, the Heath, &c.* The author follows Nathaniel Johnston's account, that Goring and the other officers were drinking at Heath Hall, on the Saturday afternoon, and so allowed themselves to be surprised and beaten by a greatly inferior force.

men, drawn from the garrisons in Leeds, Bradford, and elsewhere, was led by Sir Thomas Fairfax to attack Wakefield. "Howley was the rendevouz, where they all met . . about twelve o'clock at night: about two next morning they marcht away, and coming to Stanley, where two of the enemy's troops lay, with some dragooners that quarter was beaten up, and about one and twenty prisoners taken. About four o'clock in the morning we came before Wakefield, where, after some of their horse were beaten into the town, the foot, with unspeakable courage, beat the enemies from the hedges, which they had lined with musketiers, into the town, and assaulted it in two places, Wrengate and Northgate; and after an hour and a half fight we recovered one of their peeces, and turned it upon them, and entered the town at both places, at one and the same time."[8] General Goring, Sir Thomas Bland, and other officers of note, were taken prisoners, along with about 1500 common soldiers; a number as great as that of the whole attacking force. This was on Whit-Sunday. The Saturday following, it was resolved in Parliament, "that a public thanksgiving should be given, in all the churches and chapels of London, &c., for the great and good success it had pleased God to give the forces

---

(8) Official dispatch, quoted by Tyas, *Battles of Wakefield* (1861), where see a fuller and more particular account.—The occurrences in the neighbourhood, which preceded this event, are related in a scarce and curious little quarto, entitled *The Rider of the White Horse, and his Army; their late good success in Yorreshiere, &c.* (Lond. 1643). A copy is in the Grenville Library of the British Museum.

under the command of the Lord Fairfax, at the taking in of Wakefield."[9]

Two years afterwards, Sandal Castle, which was garrisoned by Colonel Bonivant for the King, surrendered to Colonel Overton, having stood a siege of three weeks. By an order of the House of Commons, dated April 30th, 1646,[10] it was dismantled; and now, "from the destroying hand of man, and the mouldering effects of time, the fortress has disappeared, and a diminutive ruin marks the place where it stood. No lofty gateway, no grim and massive keep, with frowning battlements, overlooks the vale below; no remains of banqueting hall, where the feudal noble displayed his little less than regal splendour, are to be seen: all gone—all vanished.

> 'No ivied arch—no pillar lone,
> Pleads haughtily for glories gone.'

Some small fragments of grouted work, from which the outside facing of hewn stone has been stripped, remain, serving to shew the thickness of the walls; while the whole space of ground on which the castle stood is covered with hillocks of rubbish."[11]

Some idea of the confusion, into which these civil discords threw the ordinary affairs of the town, may be formed from the following affidavit respecting the Grammar School property, dated Feb. 14th, 1653.[12]—"Whereas, in the late unnatural warrs, the counting-

---

(9) *Journals of the House of Commons*, vol. iv.

(10) *Journals*, as above.

(11) *Battles and Battle-fields of Yorkshire*, by William Grainge (1854).—For a poetical description of the ruined castle, see W. H. Leatham's *Sandal in the Olden Time* (1841).

(12) Quoted in Kennett's MSS., vol. 39.

house over the Church Porch in Wakefeild aforesaid, where the Evidences and rights of the Free Grammar Schole were preserved, was broken up by the soldiers and some malevolent hands: We, the then present schoolmaster and only surviving Governour (whose names are subscribed), at our first coming into the said chamber after the said breeking of it up, did find severall of the Schoole's Donations (by Benefactors), scattered up and down the said chamber or counting-house, defaced, and the seale plucked off (though some nevertheless we found intire); and, by the examinations of the present Governours, some are supposed to be taken away: Therefore doe enter this evidence in this Book of Graunts for the said School at the request of all the present Governours joyned with us, and are ready to attest the same when we are thereunto called: And allso do hartily desire (it tending to a publick good) that our ancient accounts may be examined, whereby all due rents may be clearly discovered; and after such discovery, that all the Rights due to the said School (so cleared) may be confirmed in some court of Record unto the said School in as good state and tenure as if the said writings and Deeds of gift had not been defaced nor taken away; which we conceive would be a just and merciful act, and much conducing to the encouragement of the present and future Governours of the said Free School, in the discharging of their duties for so publick a good.

Robt. Doughty, Schoolmaster.
William Waler."[13]

---

(13) As there may be no occasion to speak particularly of the

Even after the Restoration, it was many years before tranquility and good order were restored to the West Riding. In the *Depositions from the Castle of York, relating to offences committed in the Northern counties during the 17th century*,[14] the enthusiast for the good old times will find matter enough to temper his ad-

---

Grammar School again, my reader (at least if an old schoolfellow) will excuse the introduction of another extract or two from the same source, which will enable him to compare himself with his predecessors in the reign of William and Mary. On a complaint being made to the Governors, that for some time past "severall laudable customes had been omitted, relating to the good order and government of the Free School," the following instructions were issued, June 11th, 1695 :—

"*Of the Monitor of the Free Schole and his duty.*

"That there be a monitor for each end of the Schole, and their office to continue for a week, to be chosen out of one of the three first Formes in each end.

"*Their office on Sundayes.*

"To see how the Boys behave themselves at Church, and to note down the absent; to goe out once or oftener in Sermon-time, to see if there be no idle persons about the Schole, breaking the windows, &c.

"*On Schole-dayes.*

"To call the boys into the Schole at the usual times, morning and afternoon, and more especially if the master be not there : to take care the boys keep every one their proper place; that they make no noise in the Schole; and this as well in the absence as presence of the master.

"To note down all offenders, *viz.* such as swear, curse, use filthy and obscene words, give bad names, fight, game for money, break the schole windows, teare the schole-bookes, speak English [!], come late, or are absent.

"To lay up the Schole-books carefully, and to see that the doors be duly locked.

"Not to permit more to go out than two at a time; and none to go into the town and churchyard in Schole hours."

Some short *memoranda* were also furnished at the same time, for the use of the master; of which the only noticeable one is, that he should "have a chapter read in the morning, in English, and another at one o'clock afternoon, by a boy at the lower end."

(14) Published by the Surtees Society, 1861.

miration. Among the many cases of fanaticism, political hatred, and general insecurity of life and property, which are there and elsewhere to be met with, we will only stay to notice one or two of those which concern Wakefield and its neighbourhood. As an instance of party spirit, we find a certificate drawn up by Sir Richard Mauleverer, and eight other gentlemen of Yorkshire, dated Jan. 22nd, 1662, to the effect that "William Browne, postmaster of Wakefeild during the Rebellion, and still allowed to carry letters for his own friends, &c., was in arms against the king; that he disperses intelligence for fanatics and malcontents, and is unworthy of this trust; and that John Naylor, who was in arms for the king, and now carries letters for his good subjects, should be the sole person employed."[15]

The frequency of trials for witchcraft, throughout this period, bears sad testimony to the superstition which prevailed. Take, for example, the following statement, made at the trial of Jennet and George Benton, June 7th, 1656:[16]—"Richard Jackson of Wakefeild sayth that, he beinge tennant to Mr. Stringer of Sharlston, for a farme called by the name of Bunny Hall, nyare Wakefeild, one Jennet Benton, and George

---

(15) *Calendar of State Papers*, (1861).—If this were the Browne mentioned in the following passage of Boothroyd, he deserved to feel the turn of fortune :—"On Easter Sunday, during the second siege of the (Pontefract) castle, the Governour solicits Col. Forbes to permit him to buy some wine in the town, for the sacrament. Col. Forbes readily granted a protection to any person the governour might send; but the men on duty refused permission; and one Browne of Wakefield observed, that 'if it was for their damnation, they should have it, but not for their salvation.'"—*History of Pontefract* (1807), p. 188.

(16) *Depositions, &c.*, as above.

Benton her sonne, pretended to have a highway thorough the grounds belonginge to the said farme; which one Daniel Craven, servant to the informant, and by his mayster's appoyntement, did indevor to hinder. Upon which the said George Benton did cast a stone at him, the said Craven, wherewith he cut his overlipp, and broake two teeth out of his chaps. Soe, an action being brought against the said Benton for the trespass, it was submitted unto by him, and indevors used to end the difference, which was composed, and satisfaction given unto the said Craven. After which, the said Jennet Benton and her sonne did say that it should be a deare day's worke unto the said Richard Jackson, to him or to his, before the yeare went out. Since which time his wife haith had her hearinge taken from her; a child strangely taken with fitts in the night-time; himself alsoe, beinge formerly of helthfull body, have been suddenly taken without any probable reason to be given, or naturall cause appearinge, being sometimes in such extremity that he conceived himselfe drawne in peices at the hart, backe, and shoulders. And, in the beginninge of these fits, the first night, he heard a greate noyse of musicke and dancinge about him. The next night, about twelve of the clocke, he was taken with another fitt, and in the midst of it, he conceved there was a noyse like ringinge of small bells, with singinge and dancinge; upon which he called of his wife, and asked her if she heard it not, and soe of his man, who answered they did not. He asked them againe and againe if they heard it not; at last he, and his wife, and servant, all heard it give three hevie groones: at that instant doggs did howle and yell at the windows, as though they would have puld them in peeces. He had also a great many swine which broake thorrow two barn dores. Also the dores in the howse at that time clapt to and fro; the boxes and trunks, as they conceived, were removed; and severall aparitions, like blacke doggs and catts were seene in the house. And he saith that, since the time the said Jennet and George Benton threatened him, he hath lost eighteen horses and meares. And he conceives he hath had all this loss, by the use and practise of some witchcraft or sorcerie by the said Gennet and George Benton."

Clipping and deteriorating the coin, too, was an offence very common in the West Riding during Charles the Second's reign; so much so, that "there was hardly a single silversmith, who had not trafficked in such iniquitous bargains and devices." In these malpractices Dewsbury, "at that time" (says the editor of the *Depositions* above-cited) "one of the most disreputable villages in Yorkshire," held a bad pre-eminence. To it belonged the notorious Daniel Awty, whose character may be judged of from the following declaration, made at his trial, June 16th, 1675.[17] "Mr. William Frier, of Leeds, saith that, being in the company of Richard Oldroyd, of Water Yate in Dewsbery, he told this informant that, if he would at any time procure him moneys, he would clipp it upon reasonable tearms. And further said that there was a neighbour, one Daniel Awty, could doe it better than himselfe, and that he had sold severall peices of bullion to the goldsmith of Leeds,

---

(17) *Depositions, &c.*, p. 216.

which was betwixte Daniel Awty and himselfe. He had fourty pounds in the hands of Mr. Peoples of Dewsbery, clerk of the peace, which was granted him at Knaesborough Sessions, for his good service formerly done for the country, which said summe Richard Oldroyd told him, if he would intrust him with it, he would clipp it upon reasonable tearms, and that two shillings in the pound he could easily take off. And the aforesaid Richard Oldroyd invited him to come to Dewsbery, for he had a chamber that was very convenient for discovering the Ratchdale clothiers in Lancashire, which trade from thence to Wakefield weekely,[18] for the taking of theire moneys from them as they returned from theire markett, and that, what prises he gott from them, he would be very civill in his requitall."

Of the highwaymen, whose depredations many besides the "Ratchdale clothiers" had to mourn, none

---

(18) The cloth trade of Wakefield has been before noticed. In 1628 we find the town described by the Justices of the West Riding as "the greatest market and principal place of resort of all sorts of traffickers for cloth." This occurs in their report to the Council of a petition presented by the clothiers for a continuance of hot-press boards and papers, which they preferred to the cold-press.—See *Calendar of State Papers*, (1859).

For want of a fitter place, I will here subjoin another item of trading intelligence, which may chance to interest a stray reader. In 1632, the Justices of the Peace for the county of York, "having informed themselves in what towns in the hundred of Agbrigg tobacco might be most conveniently vented by retail," wrote to the officers of Wakefield, Almondbury, and Huddersfield, the towns they thought fittest for the purpose, and forwarded the certificates received from them to the Council. The Constables of Wakefield certify, "that four named persons, three being described as grocers, may be permitted to sell tobacco by retail, with two innkeepers and two alehouse-keepers."—*Calendar of State Papers* (1862), p. 391.

signalised himself more than John Nevinson. "It was related of him," says Macaulay,[19] "that he levied a quarterly tribute on all the northern drovers, and, in return, not only spared them himself, but protected them against all other thieves; that he demanded purses in the most courteous manner, and that he gave largely to the poor what he had taken from the rich." The "Claude Duval of the North," as he has been called,

> "He maintained himself like a gentleman;
> Besides, he was good to the poor;
> He rode about like a bold hero,
> And he gained himself favour therefore."

His exploits are too well known to need repeating here. After a long career of adventures and escapes, he was arrested while sleeping in an inn at Sandal, March 1684, and executed at York the following May.[20]

If the civil affairs of the country were in a disordered state, throughout this period of the seventeenth century, equally so were the religious. Allusion has been already made to the sufferings of the clergy during the Protectorate, in the cases of Nayler and Oley; and the hardships endured by the Puritan ministers who had superseded them, when the tide turned at the Restoration, have of late been brought forward with sufficient prominence. From the list given by Calamy,[21] it appears that several of those, whom the

---

(19) *History of England*, vol. i., p. 380.—Macaulay calls him William Nevinson.

(20) *Depositions, &c.*, p. 259.—The inn referred to was, if report speak true, the present "Sandal Three Houses."

(21) *Account of the Ejected Ministers* (1713), vol. ii.—A counter list of "Beneficed ministers in London, turned out by Sectaries," may be seen in a volume of curious broadsides, of dates 1644 to 1646, now in the British Museum. Walker's more complete account has lately been abridged by the Rev. Robert Whittaker.

Act of 1662 disqualified for retaining their preferments, were connected with Wakefield; among them, Edward Hill, Rector of Crofton, and Timothy Wood, of Sandal Magna. Jeremiah Marsden, of Ardsley, who was charged with participation in the Yorkshire plot, and inclined to Fifth-monarchy principles, died in Newgate. Scargil, of Chapelthorpe, after resigning like the rest, subsequently conformed. The only man of any note among them, however, seems to have heen Joshua Kirby, who, though not a native of Wakefield, yet, from his long residence in it, may claim a place in our list.

JOSHUA KIRBY

was born in London in 1617, and educated at Oxford. On the establishment of Lady Camden's Lectureship at Wakefield, in 1650, the Mercers' Company, who were the trustees, appointed him as the first Lecturer. In honour of his benefactress, he named the first child born to him, after this appointment, Camdena. "He was a solid, substantial preacher," says Calamy, "and a great scripturist. . . . . He had something of singularity in his sentiments and in his common practice; but there was no danger attending it. His garb was wonderful plain, and he required the same of all under his charge. He was a man of great courage and resolution, and inflexible when he had once fixed his principles." He was several times in danger for his loyalty, being imprisoned on one occasion for praying publicly for Charles i., and on another for sharing in the insurrection of Sir George Booth. On this last charge he was incarcerated in Lambeth. Being silenced by the Act of Uniformity, he established a lecture in his own house, for which contumacy he was committed to York Castle.[1] The charge against him is thus recorded in the *Depositions* before quoted.

---

(1) Among the indictments preferred for holding conventicles, to be found in the *Depositions*, is one dated Jan. 17th, 1678, against John Loxley, Samuel Thornes, and Richard Dawson, for being guilty of that offence at Wakefield.

"March 1663. Joshua Kirkby, of Wakefield, clerke, formerly lecturer there, haveing not subscribed the declaracion mentioned in the Act of Uniformity of publicke praiers, and is not licensed to preach by the archbishopp of this province, nor hath read the thirty-nine articles of religion mentioned in the statute of the 13th Elizabeth, nor read the booke of Comon Praiers, as by law is required, and dyvers tymes since his disability hath preached in his owen house on his usuall lecture-day: Committed by Jo. Armitage, Bart., Richard Tanckard, Kt., Thomas Stringer, Esq., Francis Whyte, Esq."

He died at Wakefield, June 12th, 1676, "and was buried in his own garden, because he was excommunicated."

But perhaps no phenomenon of these troubled times strikes us as stranger or sadder than the rapid upgrowth of fanatical sects, especially of those called Quakers. Familiarised with the image of quietness and retiring simplicity which the name now conveys to us, it is hard to realise the turbulent character of the sect in its infancy. They had a part in most of the plots that were going on.[2] They walked about the

---

(2) How rife sedition was in the neighbourhood of Wakefield, in the early part of Charles the Second's reign, may be inferred from the following memoranda in the *Calendar of State Papers* (1861 and 1862)—"July 7th, 1662. The King to the Duke of Buckingham. Sends a letter to inform him of factious meetings about Leeds and Wakefield, where Noste and Marsden, under the profession of godly preachers, possess the minds of the seduced auditors, who flock to them from all parts, with dislike to the present government."—"1663. Dec. 16th. Questions to be demanded of Captain or Cornet Carey, as to whether he was in

streets naked. "In all the great towns Quakers go naked on market-days through the town, crying 'Woe to Yorkshire,' and declare strange doctrine against the government;"[3] so that an order had to be passed at the General Sessions held at Wakefield for checking their proceedings. "They railed at the judges sitting upon the bench, calling them scarlet-coloured beasts. The justices of the peace they styled 'justices *so-called*,' and said there would be Quakers in England when there should be no justices of the peace. They made it a constant practice to enter into the churches with their hats on, during divine service, and to rail openly and exclaim aloud against the ministers with reproachful words, calling them liars, deluders of the people, Baal's priests, Babylon's merchants selling beastly ware, and bidding them come down from the high places."[4]

As the neighbourhood of Wakefield had the honour, such as it is, of producing one of the most remarkable of them, a short account of him will properly find its place here.

Yorkshire in October, at Haigh Hall near Wakefield and Gildersome near Leeds; whether he conversed with John or William Dickinson, or Jeremy Marsden; whether he took a message to defer the insurrection, because of some dissenting; or whether he assured them that many who came with the general out of Scotland, would join in the plot."

(3) *Calendar of State Papers* (1860).

(4) From a pamphlet by Francis Higginson, vicar of Kirkby Stephen, quoted in the *Depositions*.

JAMES NAYLER,

"The Grand Quaker of England," as he is styled in one of the biographies of him,[1] was born at Ardislaw, or Ardsley, near Wakefield, in 1618. He was brought up as a husbandman, and, marrying about the year 1640, removed to Wakefield. The civil war breaking out shortly after, he enlisted in Fairfax's army, and afterwards became a quarter-master under Lambert. At the end of some eight years' service, being disabled by sickness, he returned to Wakefield; and here, on the occasion of George Fox's visit in 1651, he eagerly embraced the doctrines of Quakerism. Hitherto he had been an Independent, and, it was said, had been expelled from a congregation of that body at Horbury, of which Christopher Marshall[2] was the leader, for unbecoming conduct. Shortly afterwards he commenced his travels; and in 1652 we find him indicted at the quarter-sessions at Appleby for blasphemy, and sentenced to twenty weeks' imprisonment. On his

---

(1) *A true Relation of the Life, &c., of James Nayler* (1656).

(2) A true bill was found against this Christopher Marshall, at York, for saying in his pulpit at Horbury, on August 1st, 1666, that "Those that have taken the Protestacon, and, after, come to the Common Prayer of the Church, are perjured persons before God and man."—*Depositions, &c.*, p. 85. n.

liberation he continued travelling about the north of England, for the spread of his doctrines, and at length, in 1654, made his way to London. Here his preaching had the effect of breaking up a congregation of Friends formed by Edward Burrough and Francis Howgil, two of his fellow-prisoners at Appleby, and drawing "some inconsiderate women" after himself. The profane titles by which his followers now began to salute him need not be quoted: even his apologist describes their language as "impious adulation."[3] Passing over intermediate events, we will come to his entry into Bristol in 1655, and let a more vigorous pen describe it:—

"In the month of October, 1655, there was seen a strange sight at Bristol in the West. A procession of eight persons; one a man on horseback, riding single; the others, men and women, partly riding double, partly on foot, in the muddiest highway, in the wettest weather; singing—all but the single-rider, at whose bridle splash and walk two women—'Hosannah! Holy, Holy, Lord God of Sabaoth!' and other things, 'in a buzzing tone,' which the impartial hearer could not make out. The single-rider is a raw-boned male figure, 'with lank hair reaching below his cheeks,' hat drawn close over his brows, 'nose slightly rising in the middle,' of abstruse 'down look,' and large dangerous jaws strictly closed: he sings not; sits there covered, and is sung to by the others bare. Amid pouring deluges, and mud knee-deep, 'so that the rain ran in at their necks, and they

---

(3) *A refutation of some of the more modern representations, &c., with a Life of James Nayler*, by Joseph Gurney Bevan (1800)

vented it at their hose and breeches,'—a spectacle to the West of England and Posterity. Singing as above. Answering no question but in song. From Bedminster to Ratcliff Gate, along the streets to the High Cross at Bristol. At the High Cross they are laid hold of by the authorities; turn out to be James Nayler and company :—James Nayler from Andersloe or Ardsley in Yorkshire; heretofore a trooper under Lambert, now a Quaker and something more. Infatuated Nayler and Company; given up to enthusiasm—to Animal Magnetism—to Chaos and Bedlam in one shape or other! who will need to be coerced by the Major-Generals, I think : to be forwarded to London, and there sifted and cross-questioned. Is not the spiritualism of England developing itself in strange forms?"[4]

For this proceeding Nayler was examined before a committee of Parliament; and on the receipt of their report, the House, after almost interminable discussions, decided on Dec. 8th, 1656-7, "that James Nayler upon the whole matter-of-fact is guilty of horrid blasphemy;" also, "that James Nayler is a grand impostor and seducer of the people." A motion that

---

[4] Carlyle : *Letters and Speeches of Oliver Cromwell* (1850), vol. iv. The description of Nayler's personal appearance, which Carlyle partially quotes, is contained in *The Grand Impostor examined, or the Life, Tryall, &c. of James Nayler, the seduced and seducing Quaker*, (1656) :—"He is a man of ruddy complexion, brown hair and slank, hanging a little below his jawbones ; of an indifferent height ; not very long-visaged, nor very round ; close shaven ; a sad down-look, and melancholy countenance ; a little band, close to his coller, with no band-strings ; his hat hanging over his brows ; his nose neither high nor low, but rising a little in the middle."

he should be put to death being lost by a division of 82 against 96, it was resolved "that he should be set on the pillory, with his head in the pillory, in the Palace Yard, Westminster, during the space of two hours, and whipped through the streets from Westminster to the Old Exchange, &c., and that at the Old Exchange his tongue be bored through with a hot iron, and that he be there also stigmatized in the forehead with the letter B." He was afterwards to be whipped through the streets of Bristol, and then imprisoned in Bridewell till released by Parliament.

This sentence was carried into effect. Nayler did not long survive his imprisonment, dying in October, 1660. During his confinement he seems to have repented of some of his extravagances, writing in one of the pamphlets then published by him,—" Dear brethren, my heart is broken this day for the offence that I have occasioned to God's truth and people, and especially to you, who in dear love followed me, seeking me in faithfulness to God."[5]

---

(5) Bevan's *Life of James Nayler*, as above. For more on the subject, see, on the one side, Kennett's *Register and Chronicle*, (1728), vol. i.; and, on the other, *James Nailer, the Quaker's great Apostle . . . . published by an impartial hand, &c.*, (1719).

CHARLES HOOLE.

A few years before Nayler there was born at Wakefield one of a very opposite character, whose reputation, considerable in its time, was acquired in the peaceful walks of the scholastic profession. Charles Hoole, "the most celebrated grammarian of his age," as he has been called,[1] after being educated at the Grammar School under the care of Robert Doughty,[2] proceeded to Lincoln College, Oxford, in 1628. Here he was distinguished as a good Hebraist and classical scholar, and, after graduating at the usual time, was ordained, and went into Lincolnshire. In 1642, he was presented to the rectory of Ponton Magna in that county, but deprived of it afterwards by sequestration, his royalist principles making him obnoxious to the dominant faction. By the interest of his kinsman, Dr. Robert Sanderson, he was elected head-master of the Free School, at Rotherham, which office also he

---

(1) *Lectures delivered at Literary and Mechanics' Institutions*, by W. H. Leatham, (1845).

(2) "That able schoolmaster, whom I heartily reverence as my master," as Hoole writes of him in one of his books, was elected May 6th, 1623 ; John Wilcocke, B.A., of Benet College, Cambridge, being appointed usher in the same year.—*Register-book of the School.*

does not appear to have long held. Removing to London, he established a private school near Aldersgate, and afterwards one near the Royal Exchange, in Lothbury. He was an able and successful teacher. To his method of teaching he alludes in the advertisement to one of his works, dated June 3rd, 1659:—
"And this I dare thus publickly aver upon trial, that whereas (especially since I have got those Helps printed), I am constant to my rule, (which of late I have observed to be injoyned by Christopher Helvicus)[3] *never to whip a boy for his Book*, or, (as my Tutor once advised me), *not to punish a child for his Intellectuals*, though I seldom let voluntary misdemeanors in point of manners go unpunished (especially where I meet with a stubborn spirit), I rarely have a child come to me that doth not studiously attend his learning, and after a while make a show of profit."

On the Restoration, he was instituted to the rectory of Stock, or Haverstock, near Chelmsford; and in the following year, 1661, collated to a Prebend in the diocese of Lincoln, of which his kinsman, Dr. Sanderson, was now Bishop. He died at Stock, March 7th, 1667, in the 57th year of his age, and was buried in the chancel of the church there.

Of his works, original and translated, a catalogue of twenty-four is given in Wood;[4] the principal being an edition of the Greek Testament, of Terence's Plays, and a translation of the *Visible World* of Commenius.

---

(3) Author of *Hebrææ linguæ Synopsis* (1612), *Historical and Chronological Theatre*, &c.

(4) *Athenæ Oxonienses*, vol. iii.

JOSEPH MOXON

was born at Wakefield, Aug. 8th, 1627; but with the particulars of his early life I am unacquainted. He was an excellent practical mathematician, and his works are often referred to in Johnson's Dictionary as authorities for terms of art. In the construction of navigators' maps and charts, and of terrestrial and other globes, he particularly excelled; carrying the art to a higher degree of perfection than any of his countrymen had yet attained.[1] In 1667 he made the drawings for a plan which was then started of uniting the Thames and Severn by a canal. "A new cut was to be made," writes Andrew Yarranton,[2] "from Lechlode along near Criclett into Avon, and so down Avon to Bath, and so for Bristoll. And a map was drawn for Mr Mathews by Mr. Moxon, to demonstrate the thing. Many Lords and Gentlemen were ingaged in it; amongst which were the Duke of Albemarle, and the Earl of Pembroke. But some foolish discourse at Coffee-houses laid asleep that design, as being a thing impossible and impracticable."

---

(1) A fishmonger named William Saunders had introduced many improvements into the art. See also the advertisement for Rowley's globes, in the *Spectator*, No. 552. (Quoted in Granger's *Biographical Dictionary*).

(2) *England's improvement by sea and land*, (1677), p. 64.

In 1667 he commenced the publication, in monthly parts, of one of his most important works, *Mechanick Exercises, or the Doctrine of Handy-work.* Of the merit of the portion relating to typography a competent authority speaks with approbation:—"Though it may yield in extent and practical value to those of Fournier, it must be remembered that the pursuits of Mr Moxon were those of general science; while Fournier was by birth, education, and profession, a letter-founder. Moxon was the first of English letter-cutters who reduced to rule the art which before him had been practised but by guess; and left to succeeding artists examples that they might follow: by nice and accurate divisions he adjusted the size, situation, and form of the several parts and members of letter, and the proportion which every part bore to the whole."[3]

In the *Mechanick Exercises* above-mentioned there is a curious account of the customs observed in a printing-house of that period. The printing-house itself is called a *Chapel*, probably (as is suggested[4]) on account of the learned works in Divinity which used to issue from it. In the *Chapel* certain laws and usages are prescribed, any breach of which is visited by a penalty called a *solace*. Such violations are, swearing in the *Chapel*, fighting in the *Chapel*, being drunk, or resorting to abusive language in *Chapel*, leaving a candle burning there at night, letting the composing-stick drop, &c. The *solaces* are to be bought off, for the good of the *Chapel*, at prices

---

(3) *Encyclopædia of Literary and Typographical Anecdote,* by C. H. Timperley, (1842), p. 514.

(4) *Encyclopædia,* &c., as above.

varying from 1*d* to 12*d*. If a workman prove refractory, his companions *solace* him, by laying him on his face athwart the correcting-stone, while one of the number, with a paper-board, gives him £10 *and a purse*, that is, eleven blows behind. Every workman on his first arrival, has to pay 2*s* 6*d* as his *bienvenue*, —and so on.

Besides the *Mechanick Exercises*, Moxon wrote several other works; among them a treatise on *Mechanick Dyalling*, a translation of Barozzio's *Complete Architect*, and a *Compendium Euclidis*, from the Dutch; all which he published at the Sign of the Atlas, on Ludgate Hill. In 1678 he was elected a Fellow of the Royal Society, and also appointed hydrographer to Charles ii. He died in 1700.

WILLIAM PINDAR AND RICHARD THOMPSON.

About the year 1650, or a little earlier, were born two natives of Wakefield, of whom, from the similarity of their early life, and of the causes which gave them a brief celebrity, it will be most convenient thus to make mention together.

The first of these, a son of Nicholas Pindar, was educated, like his companion, at the Grammar School, and afterwards was apprenticed for a short time (as Thompson also was[1]) to an oil-drawer in the town. Proceeding subsequently to University College, Oxford, he graduated there in 1667, and obtained a Fellowship. Having taken Orders, he was made rector of St. Ebbe's, Oxfordshire; but only held this office for a little while, resigning it on being appointed chaplain to Ford, Lord Grey, of Werke, in which capacity he died. "He was a very ready disputant," says Wood, "and a noted preacher; and might, if life had been spared, have been very serviceable to the Church of England." What chiefly brought him into notice was the publication of a sermon,[2] preached in the autumn

---

(1) Wood: *Athenæ Oxonienses*, vol. iv.
(2) "*A Sermon of Divine Providence, in the special preservation*

of 1678. The minds of the people were then in a ferment about the existence of some Popish plot; and when Oates and Bedloe began to spread abroad their pretended disclosures, some, who had listened to Pindar's sermon, called to mind expressions in it which now seemed to have been prophetical. Such passages are, "A flourishing nation may sometimes be ruined by rebels from within" (p. 21): "Upon what slender and secret hinges have the fates of whole nations turned" (p. 25): "Sedition is commonly the work of mean varlets; a Massaniello and a Wat Tyler can give sufficient disturbance to a lawful government" (p. 33): and the like.

He died on the eve of the so-called plot, Sep. 23rd, 1678, and was buried at Gosfield, in Essex, where Lord Grey had a seat.

The same political events brought Richard Thompson into notice. At the time of the Informations he was vicar of St. Mary Redcliffe, Bristol; and having expressed himself a zealous upholder of the Church of England, both there, and at his former cure of Bedminster, "the faction aspersed him," says Wood, "with the name of papist; and more particularly for this reason, when he said in his prayer or sermon in the church of St Thomas, in Bristol, Jan. 30th, 1679, that there was no popish but a presbyterian plot. About which time, shewing himself a great stickler against petitions to His Majesty for the sitting of a parliament,

---

of Government and Kingdoms, on Ps. cxxvii, 1. By William Pindar .... *Published on the discovery of the late Plot, &c.,*" (1679).—Wood says it was published in Nov. 1678, with the date as above.

which the faction with all their might drove on, he was brought into trouble for so doing; and when the parliament sate, he was, among those many that were against petitioning, brought on his knees in the House of Commons and blasted for a papist." To clear himself from this imputation, he published in 1681 a pamphlet, with the title "*The visor pluckt off from Richard Thompson, of Bristol, Clerk. In a plain and true character of him.*" From this we can obtain a sketch of his life, as related by himself.—" Richard Thompson," he writes, "was descended of honest Protestant parentage both by father's and mother's side; and whilst he was yet but very green in years, he was sent by them from Wakefield School, in Yorkshire, about the year 1663, unto University College, in Oxford, and thereof he was a member and a scholar in the old foundation, by the space of six or seven years. Before he had fully compleated his exercise for his Master's degree (which he afterwards went to compleat at Cambridge,[3] forasmuch as he took himself unjustly put by a Fellowship in Univ. Coll. Oxon.) he entered into Deacon's Orders, Dr. Fuller, Bishop of Lincoln, ordaining him in St. Margaret's Church, Westminster, about the year 1668," &c. After serving some years as curate at Brington, in Northamptonshire, of which Dr. Pierce, President of Magdalene College, Cambridge, was rector, he accompanied the latter, on his promotion to the deanery of Sarum, and received from him in 1676 a prebend in that church. In consideration of the persecution he had met with, Charles ii.

---

(3) He entered at Magdalene College, and took his degree of M.A. in 1670, D.D. 1684.—*Graduati Cantabrigienses.*

conferred upon him a prebendal stall in the church of Bristol, in 1683, and in the year following raised him to the Deanery. He died Nov. 29th, 1685, and was buried in the south aisle of his Cathedral.

In the pamphlet before-mentioned he speaks out manfully for himself:—"Besides, even his enemies that now persecute him cannot deny, but, though he be very young, yet he leadeth a most strict and severe life, and someway answerable to his high character and calling. He hath a cloud of friends to attest that he hath been always most industrious to serve the King and the Church of England, notwithstanding the many difficulties which he had to wrestle with . . . . . For example, it is notoriously known there (in Bristol), that, in less than two years space, he proselyted many Anabaptists and Quakers, baptizing them publicly . . . . Lastly, forasmuch as his present circumstances do require it, he may dare to boast farther, that, as no young man was ever more persecuted by the Church of England's enemies within that city, so hath no young man ever been more beloved there among her's and our gracious sovereign's most obedient subjects and friends."

Beyond a sermon, and a short *Vindication of the Church of England's Catechism*, he does not appear to have left any other published writings.

JOHN RADCLIFFE

was born at Wakefield in the year 1650,[1] in the house, if tradition speaks true, now occupied by Mr. Charles Hicks.[2] His father, George Radcliffe, was a man of strong republican principles; and when Mr. John Somester had been "outed" from his post of Governor of the Wakefield House of Correction, "for his good affection to his Majesty," in 1647, the former was appointed to supersede him, and retained the office till Somester's recall in 1661.[3] The elder Radcliffe was possessed of some property, which he had increased by his marriage with a daughter of Mr. Loader; but having a large family, he was unwilling to bring up any of his sons for a learned profession. As John, however, "showed a towardly disposition," he was sent to the Grammar School, then "as famous as any whatsoever in these Kingdoms, except those of Westminster, Winchester, and Eton."[4] At the age of

---

(1) Sisson says 1653, but this is incorrect. He was *baptized* Jan. 23rd, 1653.

(2) Leatham: *Lectures, &c.*, as above, p. 142.

(3) From a note contributed to the *Wakefield Journal and Examiner* of Nov. 11th, 1859, by Mr. T. N. Ince, of Wakefield.

(4) *Some Memoirs of the Life of John Radcliffe, M.D.* (1715) p. 4.—In Ingledew's *History, &c. of Northallerton*, (1858), p. 83, he is stated to have received a portion of his education at that

fifteen he entered University College, Oxford, graduating there in 1669. After taking his degree he was elected senior scholar of his College; but as there appeared no immediate prospect of a Fellowship, he became a candidate for one at Lincoln College, and was successful. For the next few years he applied himself to the study of botany, chemistry, and anatomy, in which he is said to have received great assistance from his mother, now a widow. He never was much indebted to books, and possessed so few himself, that when the Master of Trinity, Dr. Bathurst, asked him one day, "Where was his study?" he answered, pointing to a few phials, a skeleton, and a herbal, "Sir, this is Radcliffe's library."[5] On taking his degree of Bachelor of Medicine in 1675, he began to practise; and soon distinguished himself by the

---

place. "I truly thought," writes Archbishop Sharp to Thoresby, Sep. 7th, 1708, "that our famous Dr. Radcliffe had been bred at Wakefield School, as Dr. Bentley was, but this account of Mr. Nelson's [author of *Fasts and Festivals*] says otherwise." He was probably at Northallerton first.

(5) An expression which savours of a time posterior to the erection of "Radcliffe's Library" at Oxford.—Another anecdote told of him by Leatham, with respect to his fondness for the bottle, is referred by Rogers (*Table Talk*, p. 23) to Dr. Fordyce: —"Dr. Fordyce sometimes drank a good deal at dinner. He was summoned one evening to see a lady patient, when he was more than half-seas over, and conscious that he was so. Feeling her pulse, and finding himself unable to count its beats, he muttered 'Drunk,— —!' Next morning, recollecting the circumstance, he was greatly vexed; and just as he was thinking what explanation of his behaviour he should offer to the lady, a letter from her was put into his hand. 'She too well knew,' said the letter, 'that he had discovered the unfortunate condition in which she was when he last visited her; and she intreated him to keep the matter secret in consideration of the enclosed,'—a hundred-pound bank note."

boldness of his innovations on established modes of treatment. In the case of small pox, for example, which was then very prevalent in Oxford, whilst his fellow-practitioners reduced the patient's strength by low diet, and excluded every breath of air from him, Radcliffe prescribed nourishing food, and flung door and window open. Such contempt of authority naturally made him many enemies; physicians of the old school styling his cures "guess-work," and he in return designating them "old nurses." But the apothecaries of the town were soon glad to have his name on their lists for prescriptions; and a cure of Lady Spencer, of Yarntown, completely established his reputation. He remained in Oxford till 1682, when he took his degree of M.D., and shortly afterwards removed to London, settling in Bow Street, Covent Garden. Here his talents had a wide field for their exercise. The two physicians of most eminence at that day were Dr. Lower and Dr. Short, of whom the former was growing unpopular from his Whig principles, whilst the latter died in 1685. Radcliffe had thus full scope, and was soon reaping a golden harvest. Twenty guineas a day is said to have been his average remuneration before he had been a year in London. Many persons would even feign illness, that they might have a chance of enjoying the wit and vivacity of his conversation; a mode of appreciation which, when discovered, he did not fail to resent.

When the Prince of Orange landed in 1688, he was joined by Prince George of Denmark, while the Princess Anne retired to Nottingham, to await the turn of affairs. Hither Radcliffe was pressed to accompany her; the birth of a child—the future Duke of Gloucester—being expected shortly; but he too was probably watching the turn affairs would take, and declined to compromise himself by becoming an adherent of either party. According to Miss Strickland,[6] "he really was a Jacobite; he attended the Revolutionary sovereigns very unwillingly, and studied to plague them with vexatious repartees. Nevertheless they all insisted on receiving his medical assistance." Whatever his political bias may have been, he soon rose to high favour with William iii., who perceived his superiority to Bidloe, the physician whom he had brought with him; and his successful treatment of two favourites of the King, Bentinck, afterwards Earl of Portland, and Zulestein, afterwards Earl of Rochford, brought Radcliffe an offer of being appointed one of the royal physicians, with a stipend greater by £200 a year than any of the others received. This proffered honour he declined; conjecturing probably that he should always be consulted on emergencies. Nor was he mistaken. In the latter part of 1689 he was the means of relieving the king from an attack of rheumatism, which had baffled the efforts of his other physicians, and thus enabled him to take the command in the battle of the Boyne. In 1691 the little Duke of Gloucester, then in his third year, was seized with such incessant fainting fits that his life was despaired of. Radcliffe succeeded in restoring him so effectually, that he was never subject to the same disorder again.

---

(6) *Lives of the Queens of England* (1852), vol. vii.

For this service he was presented with a thousand guineas by Queen Mary, who liked the child, though not on the best terms with its mother. Three years afterwards Mary herself was seized with a distemper, on the very nature of which her medical attendants could not agree. It was measles, it was scarlatina, it was scarlet fever, it was spotted fever, it was erysipelas; and their prescriptions were as ineffectual as might have been expected from such divided opinions. "But Radcliffe," says Macaulay,[7] "uttered the more alarming words, small-pox;" and such it proved to be. All he could do was to alleviate her sufferings in some slight degree; and her death, which shortly ensued, is a sad memorial of the state of diagnostic science in those days.

Some few months afterwards he had the misfortune to lose the favour of the Princess Anne, from his too great addiction to the bottle. Twice she sent to request his immediate attendance at the Palace: but the first messenger got no answer; and when the

---

(7) *History of England*, vol. iv. p. 530.—To the same effect the *Memoirs* above cited. Miss Strickland, on the contrary, says that Radcliffe mistook measles for small-pox; but yet that the real mischief arose from the Queen's "high-fed condition and luxurious habits," for which he was not responsible. Burnet's opinion is very unfavourable to him, and expressed in striking language :—"I will say no more of the physician's part, but that it was universally condemned; so that the Queen's death was imputed to the unskilfulness and wilfulness of Dr. Radcliffe, an impious and vicious man, who hated the Queen much, but virtue and religion more. He was a professed Jacobite; and was by many thought a very bad physician, but others cried him up in the highest degree imaginable. He was called for, and it appeared but too evidently his opinion was depended on. Other physicians were called, when it was too late."—*MS.* quoted by Miss Strickland.

second urged the importance of his mistress's illness more forcibly, Radcliffe, unwilling to leave his company, exclaimed "that her Highness's distemper was nothing but the vapours; and that she was in as good a state of health as any woman breathing, could she but give in to the belief of it." This affront the Princess never forgave; and when, a little while afterwards, the delinquent would have entered the Palace, to repair to her presence, he was stopped with the words "that the Princess had no further need of a physician who would not obey her orders; and that she had made choice of Dr. Gibbons to succeed him in the cure of her health." In the king's esteem he still stood high; and when the Duke of Albemarle was seized with a dangerous attack of fever during the campaign of 1695, he could not rest till Radcliffe was sent for. On the recovery of his favourite, he rewarded the physician's skill with a present of £1200, and an offer of a baronetcy, which last honour was declined.[8] Not even William's regard for him, however, could hold out against the bluntness of language in which he indulged. One day, towards the end of 1697, he was summoned to Kensington, when the king was lying prostrate under an attack of his old enemy, dropsy. He was asked his opinion of the

---

(8) Radcliffe appears to have claimed descent from a titled family. In *Dr. Radcliffe's Life and Letters*, &c., (1716), p. 3, it is stated that "The Heralds denied Radcliffe's title to bear arms as a descendant from the Radcliffes of Dilston, in the County of Northumberland, the chiefs of which family had been Knights, Barons, and Earls, from Henry the Fourth's time. But the late Earl of Derwentwater, Sir Francis Radcliffe, acknowledged him for a kinsman, and suffered him to wear a bend ingrailed sable on a field argent, on his coach."

case; and is reported to have made answer, "Why truly I would not have your Majesty's two legs for your three kingdoms!" This freedom of speech was, as might have been expected, much resented; and not all that the Duke of Albemarle could do was sufficient to restore him to the royal favour.

In a sort of rough humour, of which the above is a specimen not the most favourable, Radcliffe certainly abounded; and of it many anecdotes are preserved. On one occasion, a young practitioner from Oxford, Dr. Edward Hans, a man of some ability and more ambition, was endeavouring to push himself into notice by a device in which he showed himself in advance of his age. He would send his footman out, with orders to stop all the carriages he met, and enquire, with the air of a stranger, if they belonged to Dr. Hans. Coming into Garraway's one day, where Radcliffe happened to be sitting with some of his friends, the man began asking, with assumed anxiety, whether Dr. Hans were there. "Dr. Hans is not here: who wants him?" asks Radcliffe. "Such and such a lord," was the answer. "No, no! friend, you are mistaken," was the rejoinder: "the Doctor wants those lords."— Some time before, when Radcliffe was living next to Sir Godfrey Kneller, the king's portrait-painter, he had one day been admiring his neighbour's garden, which was separated from his own only by a wall. This wall he asked permission to break through, so as to enjoy access, by a doorway, to both gardens alike. The courteous owner granted his request; but when Radcliffe's servants began to abuse the privilege, and Sir Godfrey's garden was becoming trodden down and destroyed, the latter, finding all polite intimations unheeded, was forced to send word that he must brick up the doorway, if his complaints were any longer ineffectual. To this Radcliffe answered "That Sir Godfrey might even do what he thought fit, in relation to the door, so that he did but refrain from *painting* it." "Did my very good friend Dr. Radcliffe say so?" cried the other to his servant, who had delivered his message with some hesitation; "go you back to him, and after presenting my service to him, tell him that I can take anything from him but *physic.*"

Sometimes he found his sallies returned with still ampler interest. A paviour, after long and fruitless attempts to obtain payment of his bill from him—for Radcliffe is said to have been slow in discharging tradesmen's accounts[9]—caught him one day, when getting out of his chariot at the door of his house in Bloomsbury, and set upon him for his money. "Why, you rascal," said the Doctor, "do you pretend to be paid for such a piece of work? why, you have spoiled my pavement, and then covered it over with earth to hide your bad work." "Doctor," said the paviour, "mine is not the only bad work that the earth hides." "You dog, you!" cried the other, "are you a wit? you must be poor: come in!"—and paid him.

---

(9) "He owned he was avaricious, even to spunging whenever he any way could, at a tavern reckoning, a sixpence or a shilling among the rest of the company, under pretence of 'hating (as he ever did) to change a guinea, because (said he) it slips away so fast.' He could never be brought to pay bills without much following and importunity; nor then, if there appeared any chance of wearying them out."—*Richardsoniana, or occasional Reflections &c., by the late Jonathan Richardson, Esq.* (1776); whence also the anecdote which follows is taken.

Upon Anne's accession, Radcliffe's staunch friend, Albemarle, made great efforts to procure his restoration to the favour which he had forfeited. But it was in vain. Though suffering at times severely from the gout, she resolutely refused to have his assistance called in. "He would send her word again," she said, "that her ailment was nothing but the vapours." However he was often consulted privately; and it was through his advice some time later that the Queen was saved from the brink of the grave at Windsor. It was his misfortune, that he incurred equal obloquy by attending, and by neglecting, his royal patients. In Queen Mary's case he had been blamed on the former score; in Queen Anne's he was to be still more so on the latter. When this sovereign was seized with her last illness, in 1714, the thoughts of a disputed succession made men watch every turn of the disorder with more than usual eagerness. And in proportion as the suddenness of her death disappointed the schemes of the Jacobites and others, was their anger against all whom they considered instrumental in hastening it. On the 5th of August, Sir John Pakington moved in the House that a vote of censure should be passed on Radcliffe, for his culpable neglect in not attending the Queen's illness. As Radcliffe (who had been elected in the previous year a member for Buckingham) was not in his seat at the time, the matter dropped. But outside the House there was still a loud outcry against him. It was alleged that the Duke of Ormond had sent Mr. Lowman in all haste, with one of the Queen's coaches, to fetch him. He himself declared that no one but Lady

Masham had sent for him, and that, only two hours before the Queen died. Though suffering severely from gout, which rendered him unfit to leave his house at Casehalton, he yet returned answer, "That his duty to Her Majesty would oblige him to attend her, had he proper orders for so doing; but he judged, as matters at that juncture stood between him and the Queen, who had taken an antipathy against him, that his presence would be of more disservice to Her Majesty than use; and that, since Her Majesty's case was desperate, and her distemper incurable, he could not at all think it proper to give her any disturbance in her last moments, which were so very near at hand; but rather an act of duty and compassion to let Her Majesty die as easily as was possible." In a letter also, dated August 3rd, he writes, "God knows that my will to do Her Majesty any service has ever got the start of my ability; and I have nothing that gives me greater anxiety than the death of that glorious princess." The state of apprehension in which he was kept for some time, through the clamour that was raised against him, may be judged of from the following letter which he received shortly after the Queen's death:[10]—

"Doctor,

"Tho' I am no Friend of yours, but, on the contrary, one that could wish you Destruction in a legal way, for not preventing the death of our most excellent Queen, when you had it in your power to save her; yet I have such an aversion to the taking away men's Lives unfairly, as to acquaint you, that, if you go to meet the Gentleman you have appointed to dine with at the Grey Hound in Croydon, on Thursday next, you will be most certainly

---

(10) *Life and Letters*, &c., as above, p. 78.

murther'd. I am one of the persons engaged in the conspiracy, with twelve more, who are resolved to sacrifice you to the Ghost of her late Majesty, that cries aloud for your Blood; therefore neither stir out of doors on that day, nor any other, nor think of exchanging your present abode for your house at Hammersmith, since there and everywhere else we shall be in quest of you. I am touched with Remorse, and give you this Notice; but take care of yourself, lest I repent of it, and give proofs of so doing, by having it in my power to destroy you, who am

"Your sworn enemy
"N. G."

But Radcliffe was soon to be beyond the reach of his enemies. His convivial habits had fostered the gout; and on the 1st of November, just three months after the death of Queen Anne, the physician himself was laid low. His body lay in state till the 27th of the same month, and was then removed to Oxford, and buried in St. Mary's on the 3rd of December following.

His bequests, which were very large, cannot all be enumerated here. The most important was a legacy of £40,000, to be paid in ten years, for founding a library in Oxford, along with an annuity of £150 per annum for a librarian, and of £100 for the purchase of books. The first payment was to commence on the demise of his two sisters, to whom he left annuities of £1,000 and £500 respectively. Besides this, he bequeathed £600 per annum for the foundation of two "Travelling Masterships" in his University; £600 per annum to St. Bartholomew's Hospital, for mending their diet and purchasing linen; and a sum of £5000 towards completing the front of University College.

The foundation-stone of the noble library in Oxford which bears his name, was laid on the 16th of July, 1737, and the work was completed in 1747.

Radcliffe's character was one of those about which very opposite opinions are sure to be expressed. Self-reliant in action, and often rough and caustic in speech, he could hardly fail to make himself enemies. We have seen what Bishop Burnet thought of him: and to the same effect is another contemporary description[11]: —"The common opinion procured him such vast practice, and consequently riches, and puffed him up to that degree of surly pride, that he often disdained to consult with other physicians, and on many occasions refused to attend persons of the highest quality." On the other hand, he is admitted to have possessed "rare skill in diagnostics;"[12] and, in private life, his rough exterior often covered much real kindness and generosity. When, on one occasion, in 1705, his country house had been broken into, and valuables to the amount of £150 carried off, the culprit escaped undetected; but by and bye came a letter from one Jonathan Savil, who was in prison for another offence, confessing himself the guilty person, and begging Radcliffe's intercession on his behalf. The letter was brought to him while sitting with some friends in a tavern in Fleet street; and when its contents were made known, the company not unreasonably expected a severe reply. But Radcliffe merely bade the messenger return for an answer in two days, and then, taking Lord Granville (who was with him) into another room, professed himself so delighted at being made assured of the innocence of another person, whom he had suspected, that he must beg his lordship to use

---

(11) *Political State of Great Britain,* for 1714.
(12) Macaulay, as above.

his interest in the man's behalf. Savil's punishment was by this means commuted to transportation; and in time, becoming established as a small tradesman in Virginia, he made his benefactor such returns in native produce, as more than compensated for the loss he had sustained.

Radcliffe was never married. In 1693 he had thought of changing his condition, but his destined bride proved unfaithful, and married her father's clerk. In 1709 he made a second attempt, but with no better success; and in the *Tatler* of July 21st and 28th may be read Steel's caricature of the great physician, who, when now in his 60th year, was altering his equipages, and assuming the airs of youth, to please a young and high-born damsel who cared nought for him. Something of the testiness of an old bachelor might be pardoned in him after this double disappointment, and anecdotes of such are not wanting. We will conclude this account, however, with a letter which shows him in a kindlier aspect, and which contains moreover some of his latest words. It was found in his closet after his decease, and was directed thus[18]:—

" *To my dear Sister Mrs. Millicent Radcliffe.*

"Oct. 22. 1714.

"My dear, dear Milly,

"When this shall come to your hands, you will know that the writer of it is no longer in the Land of the Living, where he has sojourned by the mercies of God to an advanced age; and from whence, though an unworthy sinner, he has made his retreat in full

---

(13) *Life and Letters, &c.;* Appendix, p. 97.

confidence of Salvation, by the precious blood of his and all mankind's gracious Redeemer.

"You will find by my Will, that I have taken better care of you than perhaps you might expect from my former treatment of you, for which with my dying Breath I most heartily ask pardon. I had indeed acted the Brother's part much better in making a handsome settlement for you while living, than after my decease; and can plead nothing in excuse, but that the Love of Money, which I have emphatically known to be the root of all evil, was too predominant over me. Though I hope I have made some amends for that odious sin of covetousness, in my disposition of those worldly goods, which it pleased the great Dispenser of Providence to bless me with.

"It will be a great Comfort to me, if departed souls have any sense of sublunary affairs, to know that your management of what I have bequeathed you for life shall be so laid out as to pave the way for you to a glorious immortality, by acts of goodness and charity: since you will thereby be furnished with means of subsisting yourself, and of giving support to your indigent neighbour, whom you are commanded by the Gospel to love as yourself.

"Your sister [Mrs Hannah Redshaw] is under a necessity of being at much greater expenses than yourself: I have therefore left her a double portion, being well assured, that it will create no misunderstanding between you, from that uninterrupted affection which you have hitherto had for her, and which she has reciprocally shewn to you; since £500 per annum will enable you to live as handsomely and comfortably as £1,000 per annum will her.

"I have made the same disproportion between my Nephews, with the same Hopes of their living amicably together; and desire you to let them know, that I conjure them to live as Brethren that are of the same Household of Faith, and of the same Blood.

"I have nothing further, than to beseech the Divine Being, who is the God of the Living, to prosper you, and all my Relations, with good and unblameable Lives, that when you shall change the world you are now in for a better, we may all meet together in glory, and enjoy those ineffable delights which are promised to all that love Christ's coming. Till then, my dear, dear Milly, take this as a last farewell from

"Your most affectionate, and
"Dying Brother,
"J. RADCLIFFE."

"N.B.—The Jewels and Rings in my Gilt Cabinet, by my Great Scritoire, not mentioned in my Will, I hereby bequeath to you."

The year of Radcliffe's birth, 1650, deserves notice also as having witnessed the last execution under a rude law, which had long been in force within the manor of Wakefield. Of the three malefactors who thus suffered, on the last day of April in that year, two—Abraham Wilkinson and Anthony Mitchel—lost their lives for an offence committed near Wakefield; being charged by John Cusforth of Durker, within the parish of Sandal, with having stolen a black colt belonging to him from Durker Green.[14] The law or

---

(14) Wright's *Antiquities of the town of Halifax* (1738), from which the particulars that follow are taken.

custom in question applied only to such criminals as were apprehended within the Forest of Hardwicke; a wide tract of country, extending from a small rivulet below Halifax Church on the East, to the borders of Lancashire on the West, and from the parish of Bradford on the North, to the Calder on the South. If a felon were captured within these limits, "with goods stolen out or within the liberty or precincts of the said forest, either *Handhabend, Backberon'd,* or *Confession'd,* to the value of thirteen pence halfpeny," he was kept for a week or so in the Manor Bailiff's prison at Halifax, and then beheaded by the gibbet. For this purpose "there was a peculiar Engine framed, the figure whereof may be seen in Bishop Gibson's *Camden's Britannia.* In this engine, the ax (which is yet to be seen at the Bailiff's house,)[15] was drawn up by a Pulley, and fastened with a Pin at the side of the Scaffold. If it were an Horse, or an Ox, or any other Creature that was stolen, it was brought along to the Gibbet, and fastened to the Cord by a Pin that stayed the Block; so that, when the time of Execution came, which was known by the Jurors holding up one of their fingers, the Bailiff or his servant whipping the Beast, the Pin was plucked out and Execution done: but if it was not done by a Beast, the Bailiff or his servant cuts the rope." The well-known petition in the Beggars' Litany, "From Hell, Hull, and Halifax, &c.," probably owed its mention of the last-named town to the aversion such a mode of punishment would naturally inspire.

---

(15) It is still kept in the Office of Messrs. Lumb, of Wakefield, solicitors to the Lord of the Manor.

RICHARD BENTLEY.

Richard Bentley, "the greatest of English critics in this, or possibly any other age," as he is called by Hallam,[1] was a native of Oulton, a village in the parish of Rothwell, about five miles north of Wakefield. His forefathers, yeomen of the higher class, had been settled for several generations at Heptonstall, in the neighbourhood of Halifax, where they possessed some property. During the civil wars they suffered severely. James Bentley, a captain in the royal army, was taken prisoner by the Parliamentarians, and died in Pontefract Castle. His son Thomas, who owned a small estate at Woodlesford, married in 1661 Sarah, daughter of Richard Willie, a stonemason of Oulton; he being then a widower considerably advanced in life, while she was only eighteen. Their first child, the subject of this sketch, was born Jan. 27th, 1662. Like many others, he owed his earliest instruction, even in classical learning, to his mother. By her he was taught the elements of Latin, and then sent to a day-school in Methley; from which, when old enough, he was

---

(1) *Literature of Europe* (1854), vol. iii., p. 251.—The account which follows is chiefly abridged from Monk's *Life of Richard Bentley* (1830); a truly "masterly performance," as it is styled by Derwent Coleridge.

removed to the Wakefield Grammar School.[2] For this scene of his early training Bentley retained through life a warm affection, and was always ready to assist with his patronage those who afterwards came from it. At the age of thirteen he lost his father; and as the estate at Woodlesford passed to a son of his by a former marriage, Richard was left to the care of his maternal grandfather. This person, who seems to have been a man of higher standing than his calling would lead us to expect, and whom Cumberland[3] alleges to have formerly been a Major in the royalist forces, was much attached to his young charge, and determined to send him to the University. Accordingly, at the age of fourteen Richard Bentley left Wakefield, and was entered at St. John's College, Cambridge, May 24th, 1676. The University was at that time very full of students, and St. John's the most crowded college. Among those who went up in the same year were Samuel Garth, author of the *Dispensary*, and John Dennis, the comedian, who thought his plays

---

(2) Two masters divide the merit of his education here;— Jeremiah Boulton, who resigned April 2nd, 1672, "being admitted Parson of Acquoth" (*Kennett's MSS.*, vol. 39), and John Baskerville, M.A., of Emmanuel College, Cambridge, who was elected May 1st in that year, and held the office till his death in 1681. The school is all but devoid of memorials of this her greatest scholar. A portion of an oak panel, discovered at the re-wainscoting of the old building, and now in the possession of the Head Master, bears his name; but there is no date attached to authenticate it. A copy of Horace in the school library is inscribed with the same name; but this appears, from the date, to have been the signature of Richard Bentley of Nailston, nephew to the preceding.

(3) Grandson of Richard Bentley.—Monk states that many of the corrections and additions in Kippis's edition of the *Biographia Britannica*, under this heading, were from his pen.

had so mortally aggrieved France as to necessitate a stipulation for his own safety in the treaty of Utrecht. Of Bentley's college studies we have few traces. Some English verses have been preserved, written by him at this period; but they are only noticeable as being in the forced and artificial style of Cowley.

In 1680 he took his degree of Bachelor of Arts, on which occasion his name appeared sixth in the list of mathematical honours. But, as a custom then prevailed for the Vice-Chancellor and the two Proctors to nominate each one an honorary member of the Tripos, whose names were inserted next after that of the first man in the year, Bentley's place really corresponded to that of third Wrangler at the present day. Owing to a regulation being then in force, which restricted the number of Fellows from any one county to two, he did not obtain a Fellowship at St. John's; but his college shewed the high sense entertained of his abilities, by presenting him to the Head Mastership of Spalding school, which he entered upon after just completing his twentieth year. In this capacity he did not remain long. After twelve months, he accepted the office of domestic tutor to the son of Dr. Stillingfleet, dean of St. Paul's; an office in which he enjoyed the benefit of one of the best private libraries in the kingdom, as well as the society of its learned possessor. Nor was his industry less than his opportunities. Before he was twenty-four, "he wrote" (as he himself tells us) "a sort of Hexapla; a thick volume in quarto; in the first column of which he inserted every word of the Hebrew Bible alphabetically; and, in five other columns, all the various interpretations of those words in the Chaldee, Syriac, Vulgate Latin, Septuagint, and Aquila, Symmachus and Theodotion, that occur in the whole Bible. This he made for his own use, to know the Hebrew, not from the late Rabbins, but from the ancient Versions; when, bating Arabic, Persic, and Aethiopic, he read over the whole Polyglott."

In July 1683 he took his degree of Master of Arts. He had all along been looking forward to taking Holy Orders; but in 1685, when he completed his twenty-third year, James ii. came to the throne; and his hostility to the Church of England made Bentley pause a while in his intention. Four years later, when Stillingfleet was consecrated Bishop of Worcester, his son was entered at Wadham College, Oxford, whither his tutor accompanied him. Thereupon the latter was incorporated an M.A. of Oxford, and for a time could revel in the treasures of the Bodleian. Here too he made the acquaintance of several eminent men; among them, Dr. John Mill and Dr. Edward Bernard. Being ordained deacon at length, in 1690, he received the appointment of chaplain to the Bishop of Worcester. Meanwhile he did not neglect his classical studies. We find him busily employed in constructing indexes for his own use, preparing Hesychius for the press, and contemplating an edition of the fragments of the Greek poets; works of the difficulty of which the scholar of the present day, surrounded by aids of every kind, can hardly form a just conception. What first brought him into general notice was his *Epistle to Dr. Mill*, of which it will be well to give a brief account.

Among the manuscripts in the Bodleian he had found a copy of an old historical work, written in Greek, about the beginning of the ninth century, by John Malelas of Antioch. This was one of those chronicles of events from the time of Adam downwards, such as Christian writers had compiled in numbers, and which derive their chief value from the remains preserved in them of ancient works now lost. In Charles the First's time an attempt had been made to publish the manuscript in question, by John Gregory, a man of great learning; but the commotions of the civil war had prevented him. After him Edmund Chilmead had undertaken the task, but the Parliamentarians expelled him from Christ Church before his book was sent to the press. Meanwhile the old chronicler was lying neglected. Now, however, the work was to be carried through, under the superintendence of Dr. Mill; and Bentley was asked to write an appendix of remarks upon the author. This he did, and threw his observations into the shape of an epistle to Dr. Mill, which was published in June 1691.

It would be out of place here to enter into any discussion as to the merits of this performance. Suffice it to say that the various and accurate learning displayed, the sagacity brought to bear in detecting verses of ancient poets embedded in the chronicler's prose, and the boldness and self-reliance of his style, drew the attention of all Scholars to the Appendix, and marked the author out for (what Monk tells us Grævius and Spanheim pronounced him) "the rising constellation of literature."

We come now to the events which first connected

him with the name of Boyle. In the latter part of 1691 died the Hon. Robert Boyle; a man, whose name in science still needs no testimonial, and whose treatises on Hydrostatics and Pneumatics had given him a rank then second only to Newton's. He was, moreover, exceedingly zealous for the spread of Christianity. For this object he annually spent the sum of £1000, and, on his death, left an endowment of £50 a year to maintain a lectureship for the defence of revealed religion against infidelity. Bentley was the first chosen to fill this office; and the manner in which he discharged his commission even surpassed expectation. At that day the opinions of Spinoza and Hobbes were widely spread: writers, whose philosophic tone, and assumption of calm, dispassionate reasoning, made them dangerous antagonists; while the replies of Cudworth and Bishop Cumberland were but little read. Here was a noble field for Bentley's efforts. Choosing for his subject "A confutation of Atheism," he showed, in his first lecture, the folly of it even with respect to this present life; whilst in those which followed, he confuted it by arguments drawn from the faculties of the soul, the structure of human bodies, and the origin and frame of the world. For the seventh and eighth lectures in his course he made use of the recent discoveries of Newton. The *Principia* had been published about six years, but was as yet little understood; and to Bentley belongs the credit of first presenting it to the public in an inviting form. Evelyn was in St. Martin's Church when the second of these addresses was delivered; and the high opinion he there formed of the author's merits led to a warm friendship between them. Bentley's *Boyle Lectures*, of which there is a good edition by Dyce, still amply repay perusal. The varied learning; the vigour of style, which was said by Dr. Johnson to resemble South's; and above all that rare elasticity, which prevents the reader from becoming weary, even on the most difficult topics; combine to save them from the general fate of controversial writings.

In the autumn of 1692 he was made Prebendary of Worcester; and in the following year, on the death of Henry de Justel, he was appointed keeper of the royal library at St. James's. Whilst in this capacity, he became involved in a dispute, about which perhaps as much has been said and written as about any literary controversy of modern times. I allude, of course, to that on the *Epistles of Phalaris;* with which Macaulay's Essay on Sir William Temple has made the reader so familiar, that, but for the completeness of my subject, I should leave untouched such well-trodden ground.

The foolish dispute as to the rival pretensions of ancient and modern authors had its origin in France, where, about the year 1688, Fontenelle, in a dissertation at the end of his Pastoral poetry, asserted the general superiority of the latter over the former. He was followed by Perrault, who, in his "Parallel between the ancients and moderns," went so far as to match individual French writers against the several masters of classical antiquity; pitting Balzac against Cicero, Boileau against Horace, Voiture against Pliny, and Corneille against Aeschylus, Sophocles, and Euripides combined. Against such extravagant assertions Sir William Temple came forth to do battle. Quitting the retirement in which he was spending the autumn of a busy life, he published in 1692 his *Essay upon the Ancient and Modern Learning*. With a style that was polished and elegant, but in a manner far too dogmatical and one-sided, he assails the position of Fontenelle and Perrault; and, rushing into the opposite extreme, asserts the intellectual superiority of the ancients in every department of literature. Whatever were the faults of this performance, it successfully turned the tide of public opinion: it was translated into French, praised by Boileau and Racine, and extorted a recantation from the champion of the moderns.

Now it so happened, that among his arguments for proving the decay of human learning, Sir William had ventured the assertion, that the oldest books we possessed were still the best in their kind; as instances of which he quoted what were considered by him to be the two oldest works by profane authors extant, "Aesop's Fables," and the "Epistles of Phalaris." The passage, moreover, in which this opinion was expressed, was one of such eloquence as to attract the reader's attention; and such a panegyric, so pronounced, naturally raised a wish in the minds of many, to know something more of the less familiar of the two authors above-mentioned. Accordingly, Dean Aldrich of Christ Church, whose custom it was to present an edition of some classical author every new-year's day, prepared by one of their number, to the members of his college, requested the Hon. Charles Boyle to gratify public curiosity by an edition of the "Epistles of Phalaris." This young gentleman, a brother of the Earl of Orrery, and a scholar of promising abilities, turned his attention to the task about the middle of 1693; having for his coadjutor Dr. Freind, the afterwards celebrated physician. In preparing this edition, it was judged advisable to collate a manuscript in the library at St. James's; and Mr. Boyle applied to Bentley, as librarian, for permission to use it. Leave was courteously given, though Bentley had no sympathy with the projected undertaking, as it was his own declared opinion that the Epistles in question were only a clumsy forgery, the work of a much later period. Bennett the bookseller, who was Boyle's agent in this transaction, neglected his task in a way which need not here be detailed; and, after delaying to send for the manuscript till it was too late for the collator to finish his work, excused himself to his employer by throwing the blame on Bentley. It thus happened that, when Boyle's edition of *Phalaris* appeared, the Preface contained the following charge :—" that a partial collation only of the manuscript in the royal library had been made, because the librarian, *in accordance with his usual distinguished courtesy*, had refused any further use of it."[4] Bentley upon this wrote to inform the editor of the true facts of the case; but received merely the cold reply, that his account did not agree with the bookseller's. In this unsatisfactory state matters remained for nearly three years; when Bentley, in fulfilment of a promise made before the above-mentioned work had appeared, published a "Dissertation on the Epistles of the Ancients," as an appendix

---

(4) "Epistolas . . . collatas etiam curavi usque ad Epist. 40 cum MS° in Bibliothecâ Regiâ, cujus mihi copiam ulteriorem Bibliothecarius pro singulari suâ humanitate negavit."

to a work by his early friend Wotton. In this he censures the false principles of Temple's criticism, and declares that neither the "Epistles of Phalaris," nor "Aesop's Fables," are genuine. This produced in reply the famous "Examination of Bentley's Dissertation;" nominally indeed the work of Boyle, but in reality a joint production of Dean Aldrich, Atterbury, King, Freind, and in short all the choicest wits of that University.[5] So little, in fact, had Boyle to do with it, that "in Atterbury's correspondence is a letter, where, with equal anger and dignity, Atterbury avows his having 'written about half, and planned the whole' of Boyle's attack upon Bentley."[6] Swift, as might have been expected, sided with the allies of his patron Sir William Temple, and in his "Battle of the Books" describes Boyle as "clad in a suit of armour given him by all the gods." Garth followed on the same side; and one of the few vigorous couplets in the *Dispensary* is

"So Diamonds take a Lustre from their Foyle,
And to a Bentley 'tis we owe a Boyle."

---

(5) "Before I leave this subject, I will just tell you what Mr. Pope told me, who had been let into the secret, concerning the Oxford performance:—That Boyle wrote only the narrative of what passed between him and the Bookseller, which too was corrected for him; that Freind, the Master of Westminster, and Atterbury, wrote the body of the criticisms; and that Dr. King of the Commons wrote the droll argument to prove Dr. Bentley was not the author of the Dissertation on Phalaris, and the Index. And a powerful cabal gave it a surprising run."—Warburton's *Letters*, No. 5.

(6) D'Israeli's *Miscellanies of Literature* (1840).—D'Israeli calls one of Boyle's coadjutors in this work Dr. *John* Freind, who was the physician: Warburton, by describing him as Master of Westminster school, implies that it was *Robert* Freind, elder brother of the former. Both were at Christ Church, and nearly at the same time.

The appearance of the Oxford book was hailed with a general shout of triumph. The parade of learning, which was plausible enough to impose on all but deeply-read scholars; the polished account given of the manuscript transaction through which the quarrel had arisen; above all, the happy way in which Bentley's Wolseyan manner and diction were hit off,[7]—all conspired to strengthen the impression that the proud Cambridge scholar must hide his head for the future. Endless were the *jeux d'esprit* to which this presumed victory gave rise. The tyrant Phalaris had caused a brazen bull to be made, in which to roast his criminals to death; that the sound of their cries, passing through pipes in the interior, might make music to his ear. Accordingly, in the windows of the print-shops appeared a representation of Bentley creeping into Phalaris's bull, with the words "I had rather be *roasted* than

---

(7) "Bentley happened to say ''Twas a surprise to find that *our MS.* was not perused.'—'*Our* manuscript' (they proceed); 'that is, His Majesty's and mine!'.........It has been said that Bentley used the same Wolseyan egotism on Pope's publications:—'This man is always abusing *me* or *the King.*'"—D'Israeli's *Miscellanies* as above.

Pope's satire is well known :—

"Before them march'd that awful Aristarch :
Plough'd was his front with many a deep remark :
His hat, which never vail'd to human pride,
Walker with rev'rence took, and laid aside. . . ."

And then, at the conclusion of his speech,

"'Walker our hat!'—nor more he deign'd to say :
But, stern as Ajax' spectre, strode away."

(*Dunciad*, bk. iv.)

The origin of Pope's dislike is mentioned in the following passage from a letter of George Hardinge's, dated June 29th, 1714 (quoted in Nichols' *Literary Illustrations*) :—" I am not sure if it has ever been published, that he (Bentley) said of Pope, 'I said that his *Iliad* was not Homer; and the *portentous cub* never forgives.'"

Boyled!" In fine, as D'Israeli remarks, "wit, ridicule, and invective, by cabal and stratagem, obtained a seeming triumph over a single individual, but who, like the Farnese Hercules, personified the force and resistance of incomparable strength. 'The bees of Christ Church,' as this conspiracy of wits has been called, so musical and so angry, rushed in a dark swarm about him; but only left their fine stings in the flesh they could not wound."

Bentley now rejoined, by his enlarged "Dissertation on Phalaris," a volume of lasting value to the lovers of ancient literature. The loudness of the outcry raised against him made him write cautiously, and therefore well. In the words of Macaulay:[8]—"His spirit, daring even to rashness, self-confident even to negligence, and proud even to insolent ferocity, was awed for the first and last time; awed, not into meanness or cowardice, but into wariness and sobriety. For once he ran no risks, he left no crevice unguarded, he wantoned in no paradoxes; above all, he returned no railing for the railing of his enemies. In almost everything that he has written we can discover proofs of genius and learning. But it is only here that his genius and learning appear to have been constantly under the guidance of good sense and good temper." Of the singular power and command of resources shewn in this work, it would be out of place here to speak at length. Step by step does he dislodge his opponents from their positions, and establish his own rules upon the vacant ground; and that too with an absorbing

---

(8) *Essay on Sir William Temple.*

appearance of ease and certainty, which carries even the chance reader along with him. "The arms of Boyle, in Swift's language, were given him by all the gods: but his antagonist stood forward in no such figurative strength; master of a learning to which nothing parallel had been known in England, and that directed by an understanding prompt, discriminating, not idly sceptical, but still further removed from trust in authority; sagacious in perceiving corruptions of language, and ingenious, at least, in removing them; with a style rapid, concise, amusing, and superior to Boyle in that which he had chiefly to boast, a sarcastic wit."[9]

The first and immediate effect of the "Dissertation" was, that it silenced the clique of Oxford writers. After an empty vaunt that they would publish a book against him every month, till he succumbed, they fairly left him in possession of the field. As to its more enduring effect, it may not be too much to assert, that, as Bentley himself may be considered the "progenitor of the great and enlightened philologers of Germany," so the *Phalaris* in particular "paved the way for Niebuhr's History of Rome."[10]

On the deanery of Durham falling vacant, in the latter part of 1699, Dr. John Montague, Master of Trinity College, was elected to fill that office; and Bentley was then unanimously recommended by the royal commissioners to supply his place in the University. He was installed in the Mastership early in

---

(9) Hallam, *Literature of Europe*, as above.
(10) Article in the *Biographical Dictionary*, edited by Hugh James Rose (1857.)

the following year. It had been intended that the young Duke of Gloucester, on whom the hopes of the nation then rested, should be educated under the immediate superintendence of the new Master; but this design was frustrated by the death of the former, July 29th, 1700. From this period the history of Bentley's life becomes little more than a chronicle of never ending quarrels and litigations. In some matters indeed, especially at first, he made a beneficial use of his newly acquired authority. Being made Vice-chancellor of the University in 1700, he put a stop to the unwarrantable custom of candidates for Fellowships keeping· open house at some tavern, while the examination lasted : and it was to his care and energy that the University Press owed its supply of new types, and general restoration to a state befitting the seat·of learning in which it stood. But within his own college walls the Master of Trinity was an unmingled tyrant. To obtain funds for the repair of his Lodge, he did not scruple to employ the most arbitrary modes of coercion upon the bursar and the other Fellows. Towards the latter indeed he seems to have behaved "as a Norman lord to Saxon boors; to have treated their perquisites and privileges, as if they were mere conditional concessions, voluntary and temporary abatements of his prerogative, dependent upon good behaviour. But, worse than all, he did not associate with them, he would not be 'one of us' among them; and of all crimes which any man can commit against mess, common-room, corporation, or coterie, of which he is an enrolled member, this is the most grievous, and the more grievous in proportion to his admitted superiority."[11] These college dissensions, over which we must pass rapidly, may for convenience be divided into three periods. The first open rupture took place in 1709, when a charge was brought by the Fellows against their Master, for violating the statutes and wasting the revenues of the college. Their leader was Miller, a lay Fellow and rising barrister; and the immediate cause of the revolt was Bentley's scheme for a new system of distributing the college funds. After long delays, occasioned chiefly by the difficulty of ascertaining with whom the visitatorial power was lodged, the Bishop of Ely was declared visitor, and the cause came on at Ely House in May, 1714. The articles of accusation were fifty-four in number, some of which, at this distance of time, have a rather ludicrous sound. In one, for instance, it was asked—"Why did you use scurrilous words and language to several of the Fellows, particularly by calling Mr Eden an ass, and Mr. Rashleigh the college dog; by telling Mr. Cock *he would die in his shoes*, and calling many others *fools* and *sots*, and other scurrilous names?" In another:—"Why have you, for many years past, wasted the college bread, ale, beer, coals, wood, turf, sedge, charcoal, linen, pewter, corn, flour, brawn, and bran; viz., 40,000 penny loaves, 60,000 half-penny loaves, 14,000 gallons of ale, 20,000 gallons of beer, 600 chaldrons of coals, 60,000 billets of wood, 1,000 hundreds of turf, 100 load of sedge, 500 bushel of charcoal, 100 ells of Holland, 400 ells of diaper and other linen, 5,000 ounces of pewter, 200 bushels of

---

(11) *Lives of Northern Worthies*, by Hartley Coleridge (1852), vol. i., p. 140.

corn, 400 bushels of flour, 300 bushels of bran, and other goods to the value of £3,000, or other great sum, in expending the same, not only on yourself, but upon your wife, children and boarders, and that in a very extravagant manner, by causing your servants to make whole meals upon the said college bread and beer only, (you not allowing them either flesh, cheese, or butter, with the same,) and by many other ways?" Bishop Moore, considering the charges substantiated, prepared a sentence of ejectment against Bentley; but died before he could pronounce it. Queen Anne died Aug. 1st., 1714, and Moore the day before.

As Fleetwood, who succeeded him in the see of Ely, refused to stir in the matter, Bentley remained comparatively unmolested till 1717, when a fresh period of litigations began. On the 1st of May, in that year, by a series of manœuvres worthy of the subtlest electioneering agent, Bentley had procured himself to be chosen Regius Professor of Divinity. Having to preside, in this capacity, at the admission of a number of persons to the degree of D.D., on the occasion of a royal visit in the October following, he insisted on receiving from each one the unusual fee of four guineas.[12] This sum one of the number, Conyers Middleton—"*fiddling* Conyers," as Bentley contemptuously called him—paid under protest; and shortly afterwards, when the money was not refunded,

---

(12) Hartley Coleridge *(Northern Worthies, &c.*, as above) offers some palliation for this conduct. Considering the trouble and expense to which Bentley was put by this visit of George i., and the easy terms on which the new Doctors of Divinity, owing to the same event, obtained their degree, he thinks the latter might have paid the fee with a good grace.

procured a warrant from the Vice-Chancellor to arrest him for the amount. Clarke, an esquire-bedell, was sent to execute the warrant; but got nothing for his pains but a locking-up of several hours in the Master's Lodge, with no opportunity of serving the writ. On this act of contumacy, a grace of the Senate was passed, Oct. 17th, 1718, by virtue of which Bentley was deprived of all his degrees, and reduced to the rank of an undergraduate. Against this he petitioned the King, as supreme Visitor; and after the matter had lain in abeyance for more than five years, a *mandamus* was sent down from the court of King's Bench, Feb. 14th, 1724, compelling the University to restore him to his degrees. Meanwhile he had successfully prosecuted his old enemies Middleton and Colbatch for libels; and, in short, had come off victorious from six law-suits within three years.

The third period commences with a declaration by Bishop Greene, Fleetwood's successor in the see of Ely, of his readiness to act as Visitor, if his right were legally confirmed. This point being settled by the opinions of the Attorney-General and four other leading counsel, proceedings were once more instituted against Bentley, and on April 1st, 1729, he was cited to appear at Ely House. Without attempting to relate the expedients by which Bentley staved off a decision from year to year, suffice it to say, that on April 27th, 1734, the Bishop pronounced him guilty, both of dilapidating the goods of his college and of violating its statutes, and thereupon sentenced him to be deprived of his Mastership. By the 40th statute, (the very one, by the way, which from its careless wording had left the visitatorial office in doubt,) the execution of this sentence was entrusted to the Vice-Master. Hacket, who at present occupied that post, not liking the task entrusted to him, resigned in favour of Richard Walker, an old and tried friend of Bentley's: and he, on the plea of not being the Vice-Master mentioned in the writ, declined to enforce the ejectment altogether. Greene does not seem to have taken any active steps to compel the execution of his own sentence. Perhaps after all, as Hartley Coleridge suggests, "the prelate was satisfied with having done what *he* could call his best, and was not anxious to drive the famous old man from his home. There is something in dauntless perseverance, however exercised, that overawes the weak, and gains the respect of the noble." Colbatch, Bentley's most inveterate foe, did indeed obtain three *mandamuses* against Walker; but they were all quashed. Bishop Greene's death, May 28th, 1738, put a final stop to the proceedings. "And thus did Bentley, by his firmness and ingenuity, hold out for twenty-eight years against all right and law, despising alike ecclesiastical authority, and the censures of the University."[13]

In the midst of all these turmoils, he found time to prosecute his literary undertakings with unabated ardour. It was noted that "whenever the tide of accusation was strongest against him, he was sure to come out with some book, which turned the public attention from his delinquencies to his abilities, and indisposed the world to believe that so much learning could lack honesty."[14] In 1711 he published his edi-

---

(13) Article in Rose's *Biographical Dictionary*, quoted above.
(14) Hartley Coleridge; who quotes a squib of Arbuthnot,

tion of Horace; in 1713 his answer to the *Discourse of Free-thinking* of Anthony Collins, for which he received the thanks of the University; in 1720 he put forth a prospectus of an edition of the Greek Testament, for which he had been collecting materials since 1716, and which he promised should exhibit the very text that was read at the time of the council of Nice; in 1726 he hurried through the press an edition of Terence, to supplant one by Bishop Hare, in which Bentley's suggestions had been used without acknowledgment; and, still more effectually to forestall his rival, who was announcing an edition of *Phædrus*, appended to his Terence an edition of that author as well, which must have been prepared with almost breathless haste. That works so undertaken should contain, notwithstanding many blemishes, treasures of unexcelled scholarship, is a testimony to Bentley's genius. Passing over his other writings, we will only mention what, in some respects, is the worst that he has left,—his edition of Milton.[15] Little acquainted with the early English poets, entirely ignorant of the Italian and romantic schools, and devoid of real poetic taste, he exhibits here his defects of style and character in unrelieved prominence. As some excuse for attempting a task that lay beyond his province, he is said to have undertaken it at the request of Queen Caroline.

---

written in the manner of Swift, which relates how Bullum, the Emperor's Library-keeper in Lilliput, "whenever he thought himself affronted, immediately *flung a great book at his adversary*, and, if he could, felled him to the earth."

(15) "His *mad* edition of Milton," as it is called by Buckle: *History of Civilization in England* (1857), vol. i, p. 744, n.

In his domestic relations Bentley was pre-eminently happy. He married, Jan. 4th, 1701, Joanna, daughter of Sir John Bernard of Brampton in Huntingdonshire; and during the forty years that she shared his joys and sorrows, her gentle manners, and excellence of disposition, did much to smooth his frequently rugged path. She died in 1740, leaving three surviving children. Of these, Richard, who showed such early promise that he was made a Fellow of Trinity College at fifteen, became in after life the friend of Horace Walpole, and designed the plates which accompanied Walpole's edition of Gray. He suffered from the effects of a too desultory education. Of the other two, who were daughters, Elizabeth, the elder, married for her first husband Humphrey Ridge, Esq., a Hampshire gentleman, and for her second the Rev. James Favell: the younger one, Joanna,[16] *(Jug* Bentley, as her father called his favourite child) married the Rev. Dennison Cumberland, and became mother of Richard Cumberland, the well-known dramatic writer of the last century.

In his *Memoirs of Richard Cumberland, written by himself*,[17] this last-named writer has left us a pleasing

---

(16) In her honour, when a beautiful girl of eleven, Byrom (then a B.A. of Trinity College,) wrote the little pastoral poem found in No. 603 of the *Spectator*:—

"My time, O ye Muses, was happily spent,
When Phœbe went with me wherever I went;
Ten thousand sweet pleasures I felt in my breast:
Sure never fond shepherd like Colin was blest," &c.

(17) I quote from the Philadelphia edition of 1856.—Cumberland is there describing his grandfather's old age, when probably much of his sternness of disposition had softened down. Of his manners at an earlier period we have an accidental notice pre-

picture of his maternal grandfather, and one contrasting strongly with the description given by Pope and Swift. After denying the truth of the accounts which represented him as boisterous and unfeeling, he continues:—"I have broken in upon him many a time in his hours of study, when he would put his book aside, ring his hand-bell for his servant, and be led to his shelves to take down a picture-book for my amusement. I do not say that his good-nature always gained its object, as the pictures which his books generally supplied me with were anatomical drawings of dissected bodies, very little calculated to communicate delight: but he had nothing better to produce; and surely such an effort on his part, however unsuccessful, was no feature of a cynic: a cynic should be made of sterner stuff. I have had from him, at times, whilst standing at his elbow, a complete and entertaining narrative of his school-boy days, with the characters of his different masters very humourously displayed, and the punishments described which they at times would wrongfully inflict upon him for seeming to be idle and regardless of his task, 'when the dunces,' he would say, 'could not discover that I was pondering it in my mind, and fixing it more firmly in my memory, than if I had been bawling it out amongst the rest of my schoolfellows.' Once, and only once, I recollect his giving me a gentle rebuke for making a most outrageous noise in the room over his library and

---

served in a letter of Benjamin Smith, half-nephew to Sir Isaac Newton.—(Nichols' *Literary Illustrations*, vol. iv, p. 33). The writer says "that Dr. Bentley was, when in town, frequently at Sir Isaac's table; and that his behaviour was singularly haughty and inattentive to every one but Newton himself."

disturbing him in his studies : I had no apprehension of anger from him, and confidently answered that I could not help it, as I had been at battledore and shuttlecock with Master Gooch, the Bishop of Ely's son. 'And I have been at this sport with his father,' he replied, 'but thine has been the more amusing game, so there is no harm done.'"

Richard Bentley died, in possession of his Mastership, July 14th, 1742, of a brain fever, or (as others say) of a pleuritic fever. He had completed his eightieth year in the preceding January, and had thus reached the age which he had declared "long enough to read everything worth reading." A better Master of a college might be readily found; a more energetic man not easily; a more consummate classical scholar it is probably not reserved for our generation to behold. [18]

---

(18) The letters of this eminent man, under the title of *The Correspondence of Richard Bentley*, have been edited by the Rev. Chr. Wordsworth, and were published in 1842, in 2 vols. 8 vo.

JOSEPH BINGHAM.

This learned author, who has been truly called "one of the most illustrious scholars produced by the English church,"[1] was born in September 1668 at Wakefield, where his father, Francis Bingham, held a respectable position. After being educated at the Grammar School, under the care of Mr. Edward Clarke, he proceeded to Oxford, and was entered at University College, May 26th, 1684. Whilst there, he applied himself industriously to the studies of the place: but, though giving a full share of attention to the classical authors, he manifested all along a stronger liking for the works of the early Fathers of the church. With their opinions he laboured to make himself conversant; and at an early age could quote from them explanations of difficult or disputed passages of Scripture. In 1688 he took his degree of Bachelor of Arts, and on July 1st of the year following was elected a Fellow of his college, "with," as we are told, "some flattering marks

---

(1) Article in H. J. Rose's *Biographical Dictionary.*—In Nichols' *Literary Illustrations*, vol. i, p. 748, our author is called *John* Bingham; as also in the short sketch found in vol. ii of Zouch's Works: but this is a mistake.—The account given above is derived, in the main, from the *Life* prefixed to the edition of Bingham's Works, in 10 vols. (Oxford 1855), by his lineal descendant the Rev. Richard Bingham of Gosport.

of distinction." He took his degree of Master of Arts in June 1691, and was shortly afterwards appointed Tutor. In this capacity he had an opportunity of directing the studies of a young fellow-townsman, afterwards Archbishop of Canterbury. This was John Potter, who obtained a scholarship at University College about the same time that Bingham was elected Fellow. To the turn thus given to Potter's reading we owe not improbably his valuable *Discourse of Church Government*.

Towards the end of the seventeenth century, controversies were running high among learned men with regard to that great article of our faith, the doctrine of the Trinity. Samuel Clarke's work, which called forth the able defence of Waterland, did not indeed appear till 1712; but already there were warm discussions at Oxford as to the sense in which this doctrine had been understood by the early writers of the church, and the meaning attached by them to the terms *ousia* and *substantia*. Bingham, in his turn, being called on to preach before the University in St. Mary's, and having heard from that pulpit what he considered to be very erroneous teaching on the subject in question, thought himself bound to seize the opportunity thus presented of applying the knowledge he had acquired from his study of the Fathers. Accordingly, on Oct. 28th, 1695, he preached a long and elaborate sermon on 1 St. John, v. 7, 8; which, though containing nothing more than a careful and complete exposition of Patristic teaching on the points in dispute, drew on him a heavy censure from the ruling body of the University. The charge was taken up by writers outside the academic world, and Bingham had for a while to bear accusations as false, as ignorantly made, of Arianism, Tritheism, and the heresy of Valentine Gentilis.[2] So strongly for a time did the current of popular opinion set against him, that he found it necessary to withdraw from the University, and resigned his Fellowship Nov. 23rd, 1695. How unjust these imputations were, is shewn, not only by the whole tenour of his writings, but also by the fact that as soon afterwards as 1697 he was again chosen to preach the University sermon. Unfortunately for the state of our information on the subject, these transactions took place during Anthony a Wood's last illness, and we thus miss the light which the author of the *Athenæ* would have thrown upon them. At any rate there is no record extant of any official censure passed upon Bingham.

Immediately on resigning his Fellowship, he found a friend in Dr. John Radcliffe, then in the height of his reputation. He, unsolicited, presented his fellow-townsman to the rectory of Headbourne-Worthy, near Winchester, which offered an income of about £100 a year. Here Bingham led a quiet, retired life; and one offering but few prominent points for a biographer to notice. His proximity to Winchester was in one respect of advantage to him, as it gave him access to the well-stored Cathedral library. After he had been there about six years, he married Dorothea, one of the daughters of the Rev. Richard Pococke (grandfather of the well-known Eastern traveller), who was at that

---

(2) A Neapolitan, who suffered death at Berne in the year 1566. He adopted the Arian hypothesis.—See Mosheim's *Ecclesiastical History* (1790), vol. iv, p. 493.

time rector of Colmere in Hampshire. He now saw a numerous family rising about him; and before any preferment came, had two sons and eight daughters dependent upon him. "Good Richard Hooker, when called from a coze with his old pupils to rock the cradle, is not the only quiet man who has sighed in 'the thorny wilderness of a busy world' for the peaceful tranquility and independence of a college-life, and found it ill exchanged for 'the corroding cares that attend a married priest and a country parsonage.'" So writes a *Quarterly Reviewer*, in a passage of no ordinary eloquence,[3] and one might think he had Joseph Bingham specially in his mind. But the latter allowed neither the scantiness of his means, nor the cares of a large family to interfere with his literary toils. Besides many separate publications, such as *The French Church's Apology for the Church of England*, in 1706; the *Scholastical History of Baptism by Laymen*,[4] in 1712-4; and the *Dissertation on the eighth Nicene Canon*, between 1715 and 1719; he was enabled to complete that most learned and laborious work, the *Origines Ecclesiasticæ*, of which the first volume saw the light in 1708, the tenth and last in 1722.

---

(3) Vol. lxxiii., p. 92.

(4) This was called forth by a controversy that arose in 1711, the origin of which was as follows:—"Mr. Lawrence, a learned layman, baptized and bred among the dissenters, was not satisfied concerning the validity of his own baptism, and was baptized by a clergyman of the church of England; and wrote the following ingenious tracts in defence of what he had done: one intitled *Lay-Baptism invalid*, 1711; a *Defence* of it in the same year; and in 1712 a tract intituled *Dissenters' Baptism null and void.*" —Nichols' *Literary Anecdotes*, vol. iv., p. 227, n.

Bingham, whilst admitting that, as a rule, baptism by laymen was not considered lawful in the primitive church, maintained

Of the importance and utility of such a work it would be presumptuous here to speak. "No book," it has been justly remarked,[5] "either here or abroad has yet appeared which can supersede his *Origines*, which should be found in every clergyman's library." Of the difficulties with which he had to contend, in carrying through this great undertaking, the author speaks, in several parts of his work, in terms which cannot fail to move our sympathy. Besides the drawback of a weak and sickly constitution, he had to labour under a disadvantage from comparative scarcity of books. To one excellent library he had indeed access: without the aid of it his *Origines* could never have been written at all. But this was deficient in many necessary authors. One little circumstance shows well the straitness of his finances. The editor of his works above referred to mentions that he has in his possession a copy of *Pearson on the Creed* (the folio of 1669), in which there are eight missing pages neatly supplied in manuscript by Bingham's own hand; and this, though a new copy might have been purchased for a few shillings. Yet notwithstanding these hindrances, if the reader turn to the *Index Auctorum* at the end of the *Origines*, he will find a list of more than eight hundred authors quoted or referred to; many of them being writers whose works fill ponderous folios. The words in which Gibbon records his feelings at finishing the last page of his History have been often admired. The following passage from Bingham's preface to the

---

the validity of it in exceptional cases, and the consequent impropriety of re-baptism.

(5) *Quarterly Review*, No. cl.

last two volumes of his work, though far less striking, contains an expression of just and modest pride in which we shall readily sympathise :—" I bless God that I have lived to confute the objection " (that such undertakings are beyond the power of a single individual) "and give the world a proof that great and laborious works are not always so frightful as sometimes they are imagined. I have given a little specimen of what the industry of a single person may do, in whom there is neither the greatest capacity nor the strongest constitution."

Of such importance have Bingham's works been esteemed abroad, that they have all been translated into Latin by Grischovius, a learned German, who published the first volume of the *Origines* at Halle in 1724. This mark of appreciation the author did not live to see. Death came upon him, not even resting after his great achievement, but busily preparing for fresh undertakings, on the 17th of August, 1723. Though only in his fifty-fifth year, he might be said to have died of old age ; so worn and enfeebled was he in body by unceasing application to study. He was buried in the churchyard at Headbourne-Worthy, where a plain slab of stone records his name, his age, and the year of his death. An inscription for a monument was contributed by his old schoolmaster, Edward Clarke, but not made use of. The concluding lines of it allude to the scanty acknowledgement of his services, which the author in his lifetime received :—

VÆ SÆCULO MERITORUM IMMEMORI
ET INGRATO,
CUM QUI PATRIARCHATUM IN ECCLESIA
MERUIT
NON NISI HEADBOURN-WORTHY ET AVANTI IN AGRO HANTON.
PAROCHUS OBIIT.

Though a writer, as another *Quarterly Reviewer*[6] justly styles him, "who does equal honour to the English clergy and to the English nation, and whose learning is only to be equalled by his moderation and impartiality," he met with but small patronage, and that not till late in life. It was not till 1712 that he was collated to the rectory of Havant, near Portsmouth, on the nomination of Sir John Trelawney, Bishop of Winchester. Dr. Trimwell, Trelawney's successor, declared his intention of bestowing the first vacant prebend in his cathedral upon Bingham: but this was, so to speak, doubly frustrated by death; as Bingham and he both died on the same day. Even the slender provision for his family which this late preferment, joined to the proceeds of his pen, enabled him to make, was suddenly taken away, by the loss of nearly all his savings in the bursting of the South-sea Bubble in 1720. Yet such was his pious and resigned temper, that he did not allow the news of his loss to interrupt his studies for a single day; and continued to labour, without intermission, up to the very close of his life.

At the time of his death, his widow and six surviving children were left in straitened circumstances. Mrs. Bingham died in 1755, at an advanced age, in Bishop Warner's College at Bromley in Kent. The elder of the two sons, Richard, was educated at Winchester College, Oxford; and, when of age to enter Priest's Orders, was instituted by Bishop Willis to the rectory of Havant. The respect for Bingham's memory, which procured this mark of favour to his son, was afterwards assigned by Lowth as a reason for con-

---

(6) No. liv.

ferring preferment upon his grandson. "I venerate" (he writes in a letter conveying the presentation) "the memory of your excellent grandfather, my father's particular and most intimate friend. He was not rewarded as he ought to have been: I therefore give you this living, as a small recompense for his great and inestimable merits."[7]

Joseph, the younger son, was entered at Corpus Christi College, Oxford; and there gave promise of much ability. The *Theban Story*, a series of five Greek plays, had been prepared by him for the press, and printed, all but the title-page and preface, when death closed his career at the early age of twenty-two. To him Byron's verses on Henry Kirke White might be well applied.

Of the daughters, one married a Hampshire gentleman of the name of Mant; and their grandson rose to eminence as Bishop of Killaloe: the other three died single.

In the same year in which Bingham was born, died a physician of some eminence, named Henry Power. He was buried in the middle chancel of the Parish Church, where a brass plate bearing a Latin inscription[8] was formerly to be seen. Of the place of his birth I am ignorant; but the connection, though slight, which the fact of his interment there gives him with Wakefield, may justify a passing notice. Wright, in his *Antiquities of the Town of Halifax*, speaks of him as

---

(7) Quoted in Nichols' *Literary Anecdotes*, vol. i, p. 191. n.
(8) Quoted in Sisson's *Historic Sketch*, p. 40.

residing in that town about the year 1657, from which "he afterwards removed to New Hall, nigh Ealand, where he died." He was the author of a work, published in 1663, entitled *Experimental Philosophy, in three books, containing new experiments Microscopical, Mercurial, Magnetical.* Owing to the discoveries made in natural philosophy since his time, the value of the work, in a scientific point of view, is probably not great: but the style is lively and picturesque, as an extract or two, taken almost at random, will suffice to shew:—

"Look at the backside of a nettle-leaf, and you shall see it all full of needles, or rather long, sharp, transparent pikes, and every needle hath a crystal pummel; so that it looks like a sword-cutler's shop, full of glittering swords, tucks, and daggers: so that here you may autoptically see the causes, as well as you have formerly felt the effects, of their nettling."—*p.* 51.

"He" (referring to a common enemy of mankind) "has also a very long neck, jemmar'd[9] like the tail of a lobster, which he could nimbly move any way: his head, body, and limbs also be all of blackish armour-work, shining and polished, with jemmars most excellently contrived for the nimble motion of all the parts; nature having armed him thus *cap-a-pe* like a Curiazier in warr, that he might not be hurt by the great leaps he takes; to which purpose also he hath so excellent an eye, the better to look before he leap: to which add this advantageous contrivance of the joynts of his hinder legs, which bend backwards towards his belly,

---

(9) *i.e.* creased *or* scolloped.

and the knees or flexure of his forelegs forwards (as in most quadrupeds), that he might thereby take a better rise when he leaps. His feet are slit into claws or talons, that he might the better stick to what he lights upon: he hath also two pointers before, which grow out of the forehead, by which he tryes and feels all objects, whether they be edible or no. His neck, body, and limbs are also all beset with hairs and bristles, like so many turnpikes, as if his armour was palysadoed about by them. At his snout is fixed a proboscis, or hollow trunk or probe, by which he both punches the skin and sucks the blood through it, leaving that central spot in the middle of the flea-biting, where the probe entered."—*p.* 2.

The author's own copy of the work is in the library of the British Museum, containing many manuscript notes and additions. He died Dec. 23rd, 1668, at the age of forty-five.

JOHN POTTER.

John Potter was born at Wakefield about the year 1674; but as there is no entry of his baptism in the parish registers, the exact date is not known. His father Thomas kept a linen-draper's shop in the Market-place. Being sent to the Grammar-school of his native town, he made remarkable progress under the tuition of Mr. Edward Clarke, especially in Greek literature. At the age of fourteen he proceeded to Oxford; and in Lent term 1688 was entered as a servitor[1] at University College. Here he had the example and encouragement of his fellow-townsman Bingham, who had just graduated with distinction. In January 1692 he took his degree of Bachelor of Arts, and in the following year published an edition of Plutarch's treatise *De audiendis Poetis*, accompanied by the *Oratio ad Juvenes* of Basilius Magnus. This task was undertaken at the request, and under the superintendence, of Dr. Arthur Charlett. In 1694 he was elected a Fellow of Lincoln College, and was for some time engaged in private tuition. But, whilst

---

(1) Wood's *Athenæ Oxonienses*, vol. iv.; from which, and from the article in the *Biographia Britannica*, the particulars which follow are mainly derived.

directing the studies of others, his own pen was not idle; for in 1697 appeared his folio edition[2] of Lycophron's obscure poem, the *Alexandra* or *Cassandra*, and also the first volume of his well-known *Archæologia Græca*, or Antiquities of Greece. The second volume, completing the work, was published the year after.

This work, though now superseded by more elaborate compilations, enjoyed a long term of popularity, and established the author's reputation at an age when most scholars are but just emerging from pupilage. It was incorporated, immediately on its appearance, into the *Thesaurus* of Gronovius; "whose warm eulogies," says Hallam, "attest its merits." Its defects are not unfairly stated by a correspondent of the *Gentleman's Magazine*:[3]—"The *Grecian Antiquities* of Mr. Potter, afterwards Archbishop of Canterbury, are confessedly a learned and elaborate work; and the more to be admired, when it is considered as the production of a youth of about twenty-two years of age at the utmost. It must be allowed, however, to be an ill-digested book; loaded in many respects with needless prolixity and length of quotation; and in other respects not sufficiently ample, in point of reference to authors, for the elucidation of several matters which sometimes seem to need a fuller confirmation."

In 1704 Potter was appointed chaplain to Archbishop Tenison, having taken Orders in 1698; and thereupon removed to Lambeth. Two years afterwards

---

(2) Called by Harless (1812) a "plenissima et splendida editio." Harwood's description is still more flattering.

(3) Vol. lxvi., p. 644.

he took his degree of Doctor of Divinity, and was at the same time made chaplain in ordinary to Queen Anne. In 1707 he published his *Discourse of Church Government*, "wherein" (as the title-page runs) "the rights of the Church and the supremacy of Christian princes are vindicated and adjusted." Early in 1708 he was chosen to succeed Dr. Jane as Regius Professor of Divinity at Oxford, and Canon of Christ Church; and, as he was occupying this chair in 1717, when Bentley was elected to the same post at Cambridge, the Grammar School of Wakefield enjoyed "the singular distinction of having produced two scholars, who held the office of Regius Professor of Divinity in their respective Universities at the same time."[4] This honour was obtained for Potter by the interest of the Duke of Marlborough; though it is but fair to add, that his abilities rendered him worthy of it, independently of any external influence. Dr. Smalridge, the friend of Atterbury, and then Prebendary of Lichfield, seemed to have a special claim to the appointment, as he had for some time been acting as Dr. Jane's deputy; but the Whig, or Marlborough, faction having taken alarm at the way in which the sees of Exeter and Chester had lately been filled up, determined to try their strength in disputing the election of another political opponent to the Professorship at Oxford. Accordingly Marlborough wrote "a very moving letter" to the Queen, and, being seconded by the Duchess, obtained his end. By the same interest, added to his own merits, Potter was raised to the see of

---

(4) Monk: *Life of Richard Bentley*, as above.

Oxford in 1715. Shortly before this, event he had published an edition of *Clemens Alexandrinus*.[5] He still continued to discharge the duties of Regius Professor; seldom failing to preside at the Divinity Acts in the Schools.

Up to this time Potter had kept clear of polemics; but he now became involved in a controversy with the Bishop of Bangor. That prelate, in a work published in 1717, "took occasion to recommend a union among the different religious sects, upon the ground that all held the same fundamental doctrines of belief, and, if sincere in the principles they professed, would all obtain the divine favour."[6] Hence arose the well-known Bangorian controversy, as it is generally called, in which Hoadly was assailed by Sherlock, Hare, Law, and others. In the charge delivered at his triennial visitation in 1718, Bishop Potter took occasion to animadvert upon the doctrines of Hoadly, though without mentioning him by name. But, as the allusion was too plain to be misunderstood, the latter published a reply to the charge; and the dispute was carried on with considerable warmth on both sides. As a testimonial to the Bishop of Oxford's ability, "it deserves to be remarked, that Bishop Hoadly in his answer declares, that he was more concerned on account of this adversary than of any other with whom he had been engaged."[7]

---

(5) Harless speaks of it as a superior edition. The typographical errors which disfigure it are accounted for by the fact that the author was suffering from a disorder in the eyes, at the time that it was going through the press.

(6) *Life of Dr. John Potter*, prefixed to the 1st vol. of the *Antiquities of Greece* (1813), p. ix.

(7) *Life*, as above, p. x.

He soon afterwards grew into favour with the Princess of Wales, subsequently Queen Caroline; and, on the accession of George the Second, the office of preaching the coronation sermon was assigned to him. These marks of approbation at court did not tempt him to exchange the work of his episcopate for the more exciting pursuits of politics. Retiring to his diocese of Oxford, he continued to occupy himself in the assiduous discharge of his duties, till the death of Archbishop Wake, in January 1737, left the primacy vacant. Potter, then in the 64th year of his age, was chosen to succeed him; and thus the Wakefield tradesman's son became Archbishop of Canterbury. "This arduous post," we are told, "he filled ten years with great reputation, wholly attentive to the duties of his ecclesiastical function, without engaging too busily in the secular affairs of that high office."[8] From a contemporary writer, however, we have a different and less favourable picture. The ingenious, but eccentric, Whiston has left us the following description in his *Memoirs:*[9]—"I have some reason to speak my mind freely of him, and of the most unhappy change this great exaltation made in him: because the late queen (Caroline), when consultation was had who should be made Archbishop, asked me about his character, and the book[10] he had written against the Erastians, or for the ecclesiastical authority as distinct from the state. For his character at that time was with me one

---

(8) *Biographia Britannica.*
(9) *Memoirs of the Life and Writings of Mr. William Whiston, by himself* (1749), vol. i, p. 359.
(10) The *Discourse of Church Government* above referred to.

of great piety, learning, and moderation; and an excellent pastor of a parish, as I heard afterwards, without any marks of pride or vanity: whom I accordingly recommended to her Majesty, as one proper to be Archbishop, which I then sincerely wished he might be. . . . I then little dreamed that this Dr. Potter, by going to Lambeth, would take high and pontifical state upon him; . . . . that he would procure half-a-dozen footmen to walk bareheaded by him, when he was in his coach, three of a side, besides his train-bearer, at such his appearances." Probably the above account is to be taken with some little modification, as Whiston was not one to be over scrupulous in his language. Thus, a little further on in the same passage, he brings as another charge against the Archbishop, "that horrid cursing of Christians in the Athanasian Creed, which he still supported in his own chapel at Lambeth, and everywhere else."

After filling the see of Canterbury for ten years, Potter died of a lingering disorder, Oct. 10th, 1747. He was buried in the chancel of Croydon Church, where a plain slab bears the following inscription:—
"Here lieth the body of the most reverend John Potter, D.D., Archbishop of Canterbury, who died Oct. 10th, 1747, in the 74th year of his age."[11]

By his wife, whom Wood believes to have been a Miss Venner, granddaughter of Thomas Venner the Fifth-monarchy man,[12] he had a numerous family of

---

(11) Quoted in Wood's *Athenæ* from Lysons' *Environs of London*, vol. i, p. 185.

(12) "Thomas Venner, a wine-cooper, who acquired a competent estate by his trade, was reputed a man of sense and religion, before his understanding was bewildered by enthusiasm. He

children, of whom only two sons and three daughters survived him. The latter were married, respectively, to Drs. Sayer, Archdeacon of Durham, Tanner, prebendary of Canterbury, and Milles, dean of Exeter. A fourth daughter is mentioned as having been married to Dr. Tenison, grandfather of the Archbishop of that name, and as having died in childbed in 1730. Of the sons, John, the elder, was born in 1713, and entered at Christ Church, Oxford, in 1727. After his father's elevation, he was made dean of Canterbury, and received various pieces of preferment; but incurring the Archbishop's displeasure, by marrying one of his maid-servants, he had no share in the personal property left by the Primate at his death, which amounted to the large sum of £70,000, or, as some say, £90,000.[13] We might have supposed that Potter's own parentage was of a nature to preclude any such display of family pride. But, though "a learned and exemplary divine," we are told,[14] he was "of a character by no means amiable; being strongly

---

was so strongly possessed with the notions of the Millenarians, or Fifth-monarchy men, that he strongly expected that Christ was coming to reign upon the earth, and that all human government, except that of the saints, was presently to cease. He looked upon Cromwell and Charles ii. as usurpers upon Christ's dominion, and persuaded his *weak brethren* that it was their duty to rise and seize upon the Kingdom in his name. Accordingly, a rabble of them, with Venner at their head, assembled in the street and proclaimed King Jesus. They were attacked by a party of the militia, whom they resolutely engaged, as many of them believed themselves to be invulnerable. They were at length overpowered by numbers, and their leader, with twelve of his followers, was executed in January, 1660-1."—Granger's *Biographical History*, vol. iv, p. 206.

(13) Nichols' *Literary Illustrations*, vol. iii., p. 691, n.
(14) Nichols' *Literary Anecdotes*, vol. i., p. 178.

tinctured with a kind of haughtiness and severity of manners. It may be added too, though not to his credit, that he disinherited his eldest son, because he mortified his ambition, by marrying below his dignity. He got for him, however, £2,000 a year in church preferments; as if a man might be very deserving of that, who was not fit to receive his private fortune. The younger son, the favourite Jacob, whom he thought more worthy of his estate, was highly exceptionable in his moral character, however distinguished by his abilities; and, in particular, his behaviour both before and after marriage to his first lady (Miss Manningham), whom his father obliged him to marry, is well known and remembered."

This younger son, Thomas, was bred a barrister of the Inner Temple; but after acquiring a moderate knowledge of his profession, turned his attention entirely to politics. He was successively appointed Recorder of Bath, joint Vice-treasurer of Ireland, Paymaster to the forces, member of Parliament for Aylesbury in 1754, and afterwards for Oakhampton. He died June 17th, 1759.[15]

In a letter from Lady Harvey to the Rev. Edward Marsh, dated Nov. 21st, 1747,[16] we find his first appearance in the House thus described:—"Mr. Potter the lawyer is a second Pitt, I hear, for fluency of words: he spoke well and bitterly, but with so perfect an assurance, so unconcerned, so much master of himself, though the first session of his being in Parliament, and the first time of his opening his mouth there,

---

(15) *Literary Illustrations*, as above, vol. iii, p. 687, n.
(16) *Ib.* vol. 4, p. 888. n.

that it disgusted more than pleased. Mr. Potter was then Secretary to Frederick, Prince of Wales, who was then in the most decided opposition to his father's government; and Mr. Potter's speech was, for those days, extremely violent. Mr. Pelham, offended by a portrait of a Minister which Potter was drawing, called the young gentleman to order; but the interruption, as usual, only made the matter worse; for Mr. Potter turned the interruption into an appropriation of the picture, and acknowledgement of the likeness." This Thomas Potter must not be confused with one of the same name, also of the Inner Temple, and one of the Common Pleaders of the City of London, who committed suicide, in a fit of mental derangement, April 7th, 1741. Owing to the identity of name, the news of this event caused great uneasiness in the Archbishop's family, until all the particulars were known.[17]

I should have added that, besides the works above-mentioned, a collection of Potter's theological writings was published after his death, in 3 vols. 8vo, 1753.

---

(17) *Ib.* p. 337.

THOMAS BRADBURY.

Even if the life of Thomas Bradbury did not succeed to the foregoing in chronological order, a notice of an Archbishop of the Church of England would not be inaptly followed by one of "the patriarch of the dissenters of the same kingdom."[1] The early part of his story cannot be better told than in the words of Bogue and Bennett:[2]—"Mr. Bradbury was one of those men ot ardent temperament, who will always procure distinction among their contemporaries, and, when born for eventful times, will seldom fail to acquire for themselves a posthumous celebrity. He entered on the stage of life in 1677,[3] at Wakefield in Yorkshire. His father was a member of the church at Alverthorpe, of which Mr. Peter Naylor, an ejected minister, was pastor. Under his care, and at the free school at Leeds, Thomas Bradbury received the first rudiments

---

(1) "Mr. Granger saw a friendly letter from Archbishop Wake to him (Bradbury), which was part of a correspondence between the metropolitan of all England, and the patriarch of the dissenters of the same kingdom."—Granger's *Biographical History* (Noble's *Continuation*, vol. iii., p. 159).

(2) History of Dissenters (1833), vol. ii, p. 401.

(3) Noble says he died in 1759, aged 86; which would make him to have been born in 1673.

L

of learning. His memory was so tenacious, that Mr. Naylor and his father used to send him to a public-house in Wakefield, where one newspaper was read aloud for the public, to hear and report to them, before he himself understood that a man-of-war meant a ship." He was afterwards sent to an academy kept by Mr. Jollie, at Attercliffe, where he is said to have distinguished himself chiefly by his satirical wit and eccentric conduct. About 1696, when he was but eighteen, he began to preach. His youthful look and manner not unnaturally caused him to be received at times with but slight attention. This want of respect he overcame by his energy and abilities, and was afterwards heard to declare that "from that hour he had never known the fear of man." Leaving the academy soon after, he went to reside with Dr. Whitaker, whose sober judgment tempered his youthful ardour. After being stationed successively at Beverley, and at Newcastle-upon-Tyne, at which latter place he enjoyed "almost unbounded popularity," he removed to Stepney; and in 1707 was chosen Pastor of a congregation meeting in Fetter Lane, of which Mr. Benoni Rowe had previously been the leader. Here he laboured successfully for twenty years, when a quarrel arose between him and his congregation, on what account is not stated. It ended in a separation; and he was at once invited to succeed the noted Daniel Burgess[4]

---

(4) The son of an ejected minister; born at Staines in 1645, died in 1713. At his chapel in Brydges Street, Covent Garden, "he became distinguished for the broad humour and drollery that he introduced into his sermons, which in consequence attracted as many auditors for amusement as for edification."

in a meeting at New-court, Carey-street. So completely did he tread in the steps of his predecessor here, that, as his biographer informs us, "the pulpit a second time presented a phenomenon as rare as it is beneficial; wit consecrated to the service of serious and eternal truth." A correspondent of Dr. Doddridge, however, gives a less flattering account. In a letter dated Nov. 3rd, 1749, Nathaniel Neal[5] writes:—"I have seen Mr. Bradbury's Sermons, just published; the nonsense and buffoonery of which would make one laugh, if his impious insults over the pious dead did not make one tremble."

Against Dr. Watts's hymns, in particular, he seems to have loved to direct his sarcasm; and we are told that whenever he gave one of them out to be sung, he introduced it with "Let us sing one of Dr. Watts's *whims.*" He engaged in a controversy with that divine on the subject of the Trinity, in which he shewed himself an advocate of the orthodox opinion with more zeal than liberality.[6] His sermons are called by Noble "tedious in the extreme;" whilst of his published writings generally, another author[7] says

---

Some of the examples preserved would now be thought in bad taste: the following is, perhaps, a favourable specimen. Being, like his successor Bradbury, a great admirer of William iii, he assigned a new reason for the descendants of Jacob being called Israelites:—"because God did not choose that *His* people should be called Jacobites."—Gorton's *Biographical Dictionary* (1828).

(5) Son of the author of the *History of the Puritans.*—See *Doddridge's Letters* (1790), p. 388.

(6) "He [Viscount Barrington] had formerly been an attendant on Mr. Thomas Bradbury, but quitted that gentleman on account of his bigoted zeal for imposing unscriptural terms upon the article of the Trinity."—Nichols' *Literary Anecdotes,* vol. vi, p. 449.

(7) Chalmers' *Biographical Dictionary* (1812).

that they "amply justify the character usually given of him, that, with much zeal, he was totally destitute of judgment, and regardless of the dignity of his sacred calling; dwelling perpetually on political topics, and enforcing them in a strain of ridicule totally unfit for the place in which he stood." It has been remarked indeed, with regard to his admiration of the Prince of Orange, that "from the great number of sacred texts applied to the occasion, one would imagine the Bible was written only to confirm, by Divine authority, the benefits accruing to this nation from the accession of William iii."[8]

In private life Bradbury was a pleasant, jovial companion. He had a strong voice; and was supposed to sing "The roast beef of old England" better than any other man in the country. He grew rich, and divided his wealth more liberally than his fellow-townsman Archbishop Potter; giving to one daughter, Mrs. Winter, a portion of £6,000, and to his other children on a similar scale. He died Sep. 9th, 1759; leaving behind him a character, which in its last-mentioned feature, at any rate, was probably a deserved one, of "brave old Tom Bradbury, a good preacher and a facetious companion."

In a letter dated July 24th, 1787, written by Thomas Christie, a native of Montrose,[9] mention is made of a learned and ingenious, but singularly whimsical man,—

---

(8) Quoted in Chalmers, as above.—See, for example, a sermon of his on *The Nature of Faith*, preached Nov. 5th, 1721.

(9) Nichols' *Literary Anecdotes*, vol. ix, p. 379.

Thomas Amory. Describing a tour through various parts of England, the writer says:—"Thence I proceeded to Wakefield, where dwelleth the Rev. Mr. Turner, a man profoundly skilled in the Law and in the Prophets, and in the Hebrew language, and in the history of the ancient people of God. But, behold, I found him encompassed with gay young friends, who had come there from different parts on a visit, and amongst whom the old man was to me quite lost. For instead of Philosophy and Theology, we talked of I scarce can tell thee what; and we spake of Matlock and of Buxton, and of what smart ladies and of what dashing youths were there; and of the Lords and Dukes, and of their equipages, and of their horses, and of their lacquies, and of their dogs. Now, though I believe he spake rightly, who said *Dulce est desipere in loco*, yet thou wilt grant it was not here *in loco* to me. For I neither profited aught from the wisdom of the old man; neither saw I Mr. Amory, the author of *John Buncle*, nor his son Dr. Amory, M.D., nor the Rev. Mr. Michel, Rector of Thornhill, whose name thou hast often seen in the *Philosophical Transactions*."

To the author of *John Buncle*, Wakefield can lay but little stronger claim than Naples to Virgil,—the plea of *Tenet nunc Parthenope*. Still, the fact that he lies buried in the Vicarage Croft,[10] while the place of his birth is not recorded, may warrant some notice of him here.

According to a letter[11] written by his son, the Dr.

---

(10) The inscription on his tomb-stone is given in Sisson's *Historic Sketch*, p. 73: it is now, I believe, illegible.

(11) *Gentleman's Magazine*, vol. lviii, p. 1062.—The letter is dated Nov. 19th, 1788.

Amory above-mentioned, who at the time of his father's death had been practising as a physician in Wakefield for more than twenty-seven years, their family traced its descent from Amory de Montford, who married the sister of Henry ii., and was created Earl of Leicester. He states that his grandfather, Counsellor Amory, attended King William on his expedition to Ireland, and was appointed secretary for the forfeited estates in that Kingdom, and was possessed of very extensive property in the County of Clare.[12] He married Elizabeth, daughter of Patrick Fitz-Maurice, Baron of Kerry.[13] Their son, with whom we are now concerned, is described as of Brunatty Castle, though Dr. Amory asserts that he was not a native of Ireland. Probably some portion of his early life was spent there. If we are to infer that his own history is pourtrayed in *John Buncle*, he received a University education. He is also said to have been bred to the study of medicine, but never to have followed it as a profession. By his

---

(12) In vol. lix, p. 107, of the *Gentleman's Magazine*, a writer signing himself Louis Renas disputes these statements of Dr. Amory. But from an abstract of a Deed, which I owe to the kindness of Mr. T. N. Ince, it appears that "in 1723, Thomas Amory of Brunatty, co. Clare, Ireland, Esq. was seized of the town and lands of Brunatty; when he made a Deed, declaring the uses of a Recovery which he had lately suffered."

(13) In vol. lx, p. 325 of the *Gentleman's Magazine*, Louis Renas states that Elizabeth Fitz-Maurice, third daughter of Patrick, 19th Baron of Kerry, married a Mr. Thomas Amory, one of the Victuallers of the navy under Sir Dennis Gauden; and by him, who died in 1667, had a son Thomas of Bunratty. If he died in 1667, he could not be the father of our author, who was born in 1691. Yet Dr. Amory states that his grandfather, the author's father, married a daughter of Fitz-Maurice, Earl of Kerry. Either, therefore, there is some mistake, or both Dr.

wife, a near relation of the Earls of Orrery, he had several children; of whom Robert, the Wakefield physician before alluded to, alone survived him. He resided chiefly at Milbank, Westminster; and came to this town probably in order to end his days with his son. An article in the *St. James's Chronicle*, published a few weeks before his death, thus describes his manners and appearance :—Mr. Amory was a man of very peculiar look and aspect, though at the same time he bore quite the appearance of a gentleman. He read much, and scarce ever stirred out, but, like a bat, in the dark of the evening, and then he would take his usual walk, but seemed always to be ruminating on speculative subjects, even while passing along the most crowded streets."

Such was Thomas Amory, as he appeared to the eye of the passer by. We will now try to survey him as delineated in his writings; the chief of which are *Memoirs of several Ladies of Great Britain* (1755), and *The Life of John Buncle*, of which the first volume was published in 1756, and the second in 1766. The *Memoirs* were intended to fill eight volumes; but no more than the first ever appeared, though a second was advertised, containing memorials of Swift and Mrs. Grierson. *John Buncle*, in fact, forms a continuation of the *Memoirs*. As to the merits of these two works, it will not be easy to enable the reader to form an opinion, from the scanty extracts to which our space will limit us; nor indeed is it easy for one with

---

Amory's grandfather and great-grandfather married daughters of that house.

the volumes before him to estimate at its proper value the strange medley of learning, love-making, and theology, which they contain. One writer[14] does not scruple to call them "two of the most extraordinary productions of British intellect." Defending the author from the imputations of heterodoxy and mental derangement cast upon him,[15] he says:—"If a deep veneration for the New Testament, an intense conviction of its truth, and an incessant labour to spread abroad its glorious precepts and promises, constitute an Infidel, then Mr. Amory was an infidel. If a vivacious temperament, a social heart, great erudition, and acute reasoning powers, united in one by sect a Unitarian, denote insanity, then too was Mr. Amory insane. Insane, indeed! we would a thousand times rather be gifted with the insanity that produced this book, than with such faculties as made the discovery of his being so." Even William Hazlitt,[16] whose criticisms demand respect, does not hesitate to set our romancer on a level with the author of *Gargantua and Pantagruel*. "John Buncle," according to him, "is the English Rabelais..... The soul of Francis Rabelais

---

(14) *Retrospective Review* (1822), vol. vi, p. 101.

(15) As, for example, in the article in Chalmers' *Biographical Dictionary* (a passage, by the way, repeated almost *verbatim* in *Notes and Queries*, vol. x, p. 30):—"The author of this work is the eccentric Thomas Amory, who appears to have travelled in search of Socinians, as Don Quixote in search of chivalrous adventures, and probably from a similar degree of insanity."

See also *Notes and Queries*, vol. x, p. 388; where an extract from *John Buncle* is dismissed with the short comment:—"The writer of this Rhodomontade was evidently a duly qualified candidate for a lunatic asylum."

(16) *Round Table* (1841), ch. x.

passed into Thomas Amory, the author of the *Life and Adventures of John Buncle.* Both were physicians, and enemies of too much gravity. Their great business was to enjoy life. Rabelais indulged his spirit of sensuality in wine, in dried neat's tongues, in Bologna sausages, in Botargos. John Buncle shews the same symptoms of inordinate satisfaction in tea and bread-and-butter. While Rabelais roared with Friar John and the monks, John Buncle gossiped with the ladies, and with equal and uncontrolled gaiety. These two authors possessed all the insolence of health, so that their works give a fillip to the constitution; but they carried off the exuberance of their natural spirits in different ways. The title of one of Rabelais' chapters (and the contents answer to the title), is, 'How they chirped over their cup.' The title of a corresponding chapter in *John Buncle* would run thus :—' The author is invited to spend the evening with the divine Miss Hawkins, and goes accordingly; with the delightful conversation that ensued.' "

But it is time to give the reader some opportunity of forming a notion of these works for himself, so far, at least, as a few brief specimens will enable him. Premising that the scene of his adventures is laid chiefly in the part of Yorkshire called Richmondshire, let us see how the author (or his hero) makes the acquaintance of one of the beauties he celebrates :—

"As I travelled once, in the month of September, over a wild part of Yorkshire, and fansyed in the afternoon that I was near the place I intended to rest at, it appeared from a great water we came to, that we had for half a day been going wrong, and were many a mile from any village. This was vexatious; and, to perplex it higher, the winds began to blow outrageously, the clouds gathered, and, as the evening advanced, the rain came down like waterspouts from the heavens. All the good that offered was the ruins of a nunnery within a few yards of the water, and—among the walls once sacred to devotion—a part of an arch that was enough to shelter us and our beasts from the floods and tempest."[17]

He then descries a little pleasure-boat moored on the lake; and after rowing about in it for two hours, in hopes of finding some house on the banks, he reaches a mansion occupied by a widow lady, where he knocks, tells his tale, and is admitted.

"In a few minutes I was shewn into a parlour. I continued alone about a quarter of an hour, and then entered a lady who struck me into amazement. She was a beauty, of whom I had been passionately fond, when she was fourteen and I was sixteen years of age. I saw her first in a French family of distinction, where my father had lodged me for the same reason that her parents placed her there, that is, for the sake of the purity of the French tongue; and, as she had a rational generosity of heart, and an understanding that was surprisingly luminous for her years, could construe an Ode of Horace in a manner the most delightful, and read a chapter in the Greek Testament with great ease every

---

(17) *Memoirs of several Ladies of Great Britain* (1755), Dedication, p. viii.—This work was first published anonymously, and by some attributed (as was *John Buncle*), to Archdeacon Blackburne, a native of Richmond, and noted controversialist of his day. See *Gentleman's Magazine*, vol. lxviii, p. 490.

morning, she soon became my heart's fond idol."

The way in which he enjoys the society of his idols is as original as the mode of his introduction to them. Here is a specimen from *John Buncle:*[18]—

"Upon this Mr. Noel brought me into his house, and the lovely Harriot made tea for me, and had such plenty of fine cream, and extraordinary bread and butter set before me, that I breakfasted with uncommon pleasure."—And what is the discourse with which they flavour the repast? She asks him of "the primævity and sacred prerogatives of the Hebrew language!" So it is throughout; except that the light badinage of the pair sometimes plays, instead, round such topics as the Differential Calculus, or the Longevity of the Antediluvians. To quote Hazlitt once more:—"Natural philosophers are said to extract sunbeams from ice: our author has performed the same feat upon the cold, quaint subtleties of theology. His constitutional alacrity overcomes every obstacle. He converts the thorns and briars of controversial divinity into a bed of roses. He leads the most refined and virtuous of their sex through the mazes of inextricable problems, with the air of a man walking a minuet in a drawing-room; mixes up in the most natural and careless manner the academy of compliments with the rudiments of algebra; or passes with rapturous indifference from the 1st of St. John .... to the no less metaphysical doctrines of the principle of self-preservation, or the continuation of the species."

---

(18) *The Life of John Buncle, Esq.*, a new edition (1770), vol. i, p. 35.

This is no exaggeration. For instance, in one passage of *John Buncle*[19] we have "an account of ten extraordinary country girls," who "could not only add, subtract, multiply, divide, find a fourth proportional, and extract roots of every kind, with exactness and readiness, and apply them upon all common occasions; but were perfect in fractions vulgar and decimal. They had even gone as far in algebra as the resolution of simple equations."—In another place [20] he apostrophizes the "Admirable Maria,"—Miss Spence, namely, now in her twenty-fourth year, and who afterwards becomes one of the eight wives whom the hero marries, and is bereaved of, in quick succession. Is the fair reader curious to learn the secret of his admiration? Maria was skilled in finding "not only the fluxions of flowing or determinate quantities . . . . but from given fluxions could find the fluents, and was ready in drawing tangents to curves, in the solution of problems *de maximis et minimis*, . . . in the invention of points of inflection and retrogression, in finding the *evoluta* of a given curve, in finding the caustic curves by reflection and refraction,"— and much more. As for the author's Unitarianism, to which allusion has been made, it appears in almost every page. Thus it is not enough that one of his ladies "equalled the Medicean Venus in every charm of body;" that "all that is just in society, or lovely in our system, whatever is decent in company, or beautiful in arts, Belvidera Dellon was mistress of:"—"she was likewise of my own religion" (he adds), "a pure

---

(19) Vol. ii, p. 10.
(20) Vol. iv, p. 24.

theist."[21] Indeed such expressions as "wretched tritheist," "destructive theology of Athanasius," meet the eye at every turn.

If it were easier to tell when the author is relating matter-of-fact, and when only speaking "in character," we might regret that the second volume of his *Memoirs*, with its promised account of Swift, never appeared. For, in a sort of *Introduction* to the first volume, he professes to have had great opportunities of personal intercourse with the Dean. "I had him often to myself," he writes, "in his rides and walks, and have studied his soul when he little thought what I was about. As I lodged for a year within a few doors of him, I knew his times of going out to a minute, and generally nicked the opportunity. He was fond of company on these occasions, and glad to have any rational to talk to: for, whatever was the meaning of it, he rarely had any of his friends attending him at his exercises .... we talked generally of factions and religion, states, revolutions, leaders, and pieties." Perhaps the following passage[22] may be taken as conveying a true account, due allowance made, of the author's younger days. After stating that he was born in London,[23] and carried, when still an infant, into Ireland, where he remained till he had learned the native language, he proceeds :—" I was in the days of

---

(21) *Memoirs*, p. 143.

(22) Preface to *John Buncle*, p. viii.—The Preface is dated from the Barbican in London, Aug. 1st, 1756.

(23) This, of course, would settle the question of Amory's birth-place, if we could be *certain* that, in the character of John Buncle, he was speaking of himself.

my youth one of the most active men in the world at every exercise; and to a degree of rashness often venturous, when there was no necessity for running any hazards: *in diebus illis* I have descended headforemost from a high cliff into the ocean, to swim; when I could, and ought to have gone off a rock not a yard from the surface of the deep. I have swam near a mile and a half out into the sea, to a ship that lay off; went on board, got clothes from the mate of the vessel, and proceeded with them to the next port; while my companions I left on the beach concluded me drowned, and related my sad fate in the town. I have taken a cool thrust over a bottle, without the least animosity on either side, but both of us depending on our skill in the small sword for preservation from mischief." Yet what are we to say of such reminiscences as the following, told with an equal air of reality?—" Gallaspy .... drank seven in a hand; that is, seven glasses so placed between the fingers of his right hand, that, in drinking, the liquor fell into the next glasses, and thereby he drank out of the first glass seven glasses at once. This was a common thing, I find from a book in my possession, in the reign of Charles ii."[24]

But the reader has probably had enough of Thomas Amory, and may be ready to acquiesce in the epitaph which he desired for himself, though not perhaps in the sense intended. After defining, in one place, in

---

(24) To the Swift-like air of sincerity about this last sentence an amusing testimony is borne by a correspondent of *Notes and Queries* (vol. x, p. 388), who gravely writes to ask whether the statement has any foundation in fact.

what *oddness* consisted ; namely, "in spirit, freedom of thought, and a zeal for the divine unity ; in a taste for what is natural, romantic," and the like ; he adds :— "May it be written on my stone, HERE LIES AN ODD MAN."

Before entering on the eighteenth century, within which the birth of the next of our Worthies has to be placed, one little event deserves to be noticed, from its influence upon the trade and prosperity of the town. This was the rendering of the Calder navigable as far as Wakefield, which was accomplished in 1698.

In 1760 the passage was extended to Elland, near Halifax. By this means the coal, and other produce of Wakefield, was rendered capable of being conveyed along the joint stream of the Aire and Calder into the Ouse, and so, either up that river to York, or down the Humber to Kingston-upon-Hull.[25] This was not effected without opposition. In Ingledew's *History of Northallerton*[26] there is quoted a petition of the inhabitants of that town, in the year 1697, against making the Ayre and Calder navigable ; as it would "drain the Ouse," and so spoil their export of lead, butter, &c., by way of Burrough Briggs.

---

(25) See Bigland's *Beauties of England and Wales* (1812), vol. xvi, p. 805.
(26) p. 130.

JOHN CLARKE

was born at Kirby-Misperton, sometimes called Kirby-over-Car, in the North Riding of Yorkshire, May 3rd, 1706.[1] His father, an honest and hard-working mechanic, was anxious to give him the benefit of a liberal education; and as the rector of the parish, the Rev. Peter Dubordieu, had discerned many signs of promise in the lad, he was placed in the village school of Thornton, from which he subsequently obtained a small exhibition, to enable him to proceed to the University. This school had been founded by Elizabeth, Viscountess Lumley, in 1657, and endowed with £40 a year, to be divided among ten poor scholars at Oxford or Cambridge. After being well grounded here in the rudiments of learning, he was removed to Wakefield Grammar School, the head of which at that time was Thomas Clark, a teacher of considerable celebrity.[2] Under his charge, first at

---

[1] See *The good Schoolmaster exemplified in the character of the Rev. John Clarke, M.A.*, by Thomas Zouch (1798); of which this account is little more than an abridgement.

[2] At his instance the Library adjoining the old school was erected. The proposals for raising it by subscription are given in Kennett's *MSS.*, vol. xxxix, fol. 56. He was of Jesus College, Cambridge; B.A. 1696, M.A. 1700.

Wakefield, then at Kirkleatham, he remained till 1723, when he entered as a sizar at Trinity College, Cambridge. Here he graduated at the usual time, and in 1729 was made a Fellow of his college. As the emoluments of a junior Fellowship at that day were seldom adequate of themselves to maintain a student, he had to cast about for some additional means of subsistence; and on a vacant mastership presenting itself in Shipton school, near York, he offered himself as a candidate, and was elected. Shortly afterwards, having been ordained, he was presented to the perpetual curacy of Nunmonkton; and as the joint stipends of these two offices amounted to £56, he felt himself rich enough to marry. He accordingly resigned his Fellowship, and took for his wife a Mrs. Meek, a widow with four children. In 1735 the Mayor and Aldermen of Beverley elected him head master of the Grammar School in their town, whither he was followed by many of his pupils at Shipton: and in 1751 he was solicited to accept the mastership of Wakefield Grammar School, then rendered vacant by the promotion of Benjamin Wilson, "one of the first Greek scholars of the age," to the vicarage of the same town. During the eight years in which he occupied this post, he was very successful as a teacher. In scholarship he was behind few of his contemporaries. The name of "Little Aristophanes,"—for he was small in stature —had long ago been given to him, from the praise bestowed upon him for his acquaintance with that author by one well able to judge. A page of the Greek poet had been given him to translate, on his entrance examination at Trinity College; and so well

M

did he acquit himself, that the Master, Richard Bentley, presented him with a handsome edition of the plays of Aristophanes; telling him at the same time, in characteristic language, that "no scholar in Europe understood them better, *one* person only excepted." Like Henry Dodwell, who is said to have generally carried in his pocket, along with other matters, the Hebrew Bible in four volumes, the Greek Testament, and the Book of Common Prayer, he made a practice of having his favourite authors constantly about him; and, as he recommended this custom to his pupils, he made a point of presenting to his head boys, as they left the school, an *Elzevir*, or some such small edition of a classical author, to facilitate the acquisition of the habit. His zeal for the spread of learning made him embrace every opportunity of enriching the school-libraries of Beverley and Wakefield with well-selected books; and, to this assiduity on his part, each of the above places is indebted for many a well-stored shelf. The corporation of Beverley expressed their sense of his merits in this respect, by erecting a marble tablet in his honour.

One feature in his mode of teaching deserves special notice; and that is, the attention which he gave to the study of the Scriptures in Greek. About the beginning of this century, the Bishop of Meath published some remarks on the neglect of Christian instruction in our public schools. This was replied to by Dr. Vincent, who makes particular mention of the system at Rugby, Manchester, and Wakefield. A writer in the *Gentleman's Magazine*,[3] referring to this controversy, says:—

---

(3) Vol. lxxii., p. 122.—The letter is dated Feb. 8th, 1802.

"With regard to the last (Wakefield), I beg leave to recommend the plan pursued by the Rev. John Clarke, who for many years was master of the school. Among other respectable persons educated under him was Bennet Langton, Esq.,[4] the friend of Dr. Johnson, whose recent death is sincerely regretted by every good man. It was one of the rules established by Mr. Clarke in his school, to begin the mornings of the three first days in each week with explaining to his scholars one select portion in the version of the Septuagint, and another in the Greek Testament."

So well, in fact, did he discharge the duties of this office, that his acknowledged ability was made the ground of denying him ecclesiastical preferment. The Duke of Newcasle, when prime minister, had been solicited by several influential friends of John Clarke, to bestow some patronage upon him; but he replied that "to comply with their request would be to deprive the public of a good schoolmaster." At length he was presented to a small vicarage in Essex by Mr. Jolliffe, who had married his step-daughter, Miss Meek. But by this time he was growing too infirm to enter on a fresh sphere of employment, and so remained at Wakefield. The failure of his bodily strength was hastened moreover by mental anxiety. He had fancied himself secure from want; but, on examining into the state of his accounts one day, he found it to answer his expectations so little, that he fairly burst into tears, as

---

(4) For a pleasing description of this amiable scholar, and his friend Topham Beauclerc, see Forster's *Life and Adventures of Oliver Goldsmith* (1848), p. 280.

the thought arose that sickness or old age might yet leave him a beggar. Though of late years in possession of a good income, he was too easy-tempered and accommodating to others to grow rich. The depression of spirits caused by this discovery was too much for a frame naturally delicate, and enfeebled by ceaseless study; and a circumstance which occurred in 1758 hastened his end. Having been desired by a sick clergyman, one day in that year, to supply his place at Rothwell, he entered a cold church, when overheated by a long walk on a frosty morning; and a damp surplice settled the matter. The day following he was seized with an apoplectic stroke, from which he never wholly rallied. A second attack, in the beginning of the year after, rendered him unable to discharge any longer his duties in school, and he resigned; the Governors presenting to him, unsolicited, a donation of fifty guineas. The evening of his life was a sad contrast to the bright promise of its morning. His reason was shattered; and it was only in brief intervals that, like Lord Grenville,[5] he could amuse himself with his Theophrastus. After resigning his mastership, he removed to Tadcaster, and thence to the house of his brother Francis at Scarborough, where he died; sur-

---

(5) "After having been occupied incessantly in politics for nearly thirty years, he was seized by illness, and confined to his arm-chair a great part of the remainder of his life. In this state I always found him," (says Sir Henry Halford: Preface to his *Nugæ Metricæ*, 1848) "not tranquil and cheerful only, as I might have expected from his habitual piety; but amused: and on my asking him the secret of this happy peculiarity, he answered, 'I go to my classics, Sir.'"—Quoted in the *Christian Remembrancer*, vol. xiv, No. 57.

viving his wife, by whom he had no issue, about eleven months. He was buried at Kirby-Misperton, Feb. 11th, 1761.

At a meeting called by advertisement in Wakefield, Aug. 29th, 1793, a number of his old pupils consulted about some mode of commemorating their former master. As the readiest way of doing so, they resolved to erect a monument, with an English inscription, in the church of Kirby-Misperton; and also to place a marble tablet in each of the schools over which he presided. The Latin inscription on this latter, which has been much admired for its elegance, was from the pen of Thomas Zouch, Clarke's pupil and biographer.[6]

---

(6) Truth compels me to admit, that the marble tablet in the old School was, in spite of its good Latinity, chiefly used as a mark for tennis-balls. But the mention of it leads me to make a suggestion, if I may be excused for doing so; which is, that the names of eminent scholars of former days should be painted on labels (or otherwise), round the Hall of the new School. It is not every place of education that can shew such a list.

THE "VICAR OF WAKEFIELD."

In the preceding article mention was made of the Rev. Benjamin Wilson, of whose personal history I know nothing more, than that he was successively master of the Wakefield Grammar School and Vicar of Wakefield, which last office he held from 1750 till his death, Sep. 16th, 1764;[1] and that he is called by Zouch, "one of the first Greek scholars of the age." But as he is the embodiment of all the claim which our town can make, to have supplied not only the name, but the principal character, of Goldsmith's delightful tale, this seems the fitting place to throw together a few particulars relating to the original of Dr. Primrose. It is now pretty generally agreed, that the one who sat for the portrait was the author's own father, the Rev. Charles Goldsmith, incumbent of Pallasmore, in the county of Longford, Ireland. The name of his Vicarage may have been chosen from mere caprice, or from some such reason as made Sir Walter Scott select *Ivanhoe* as the title of his romance; but it is not improbable, after all, that Goldsmith had

---

(1) See the list of Vicars, extracted from Torre's *Archdeaconry of York*, quoted in Whitaker.

seen Wakefield, which was then a clean and cheerful-looking country town. "The origin of the tale," says Prior,[2] "or rather the reason for fixing the scene near Wakefield, is said to have arisen from an excursion into Yorkshire about the period at which it was written, with what view we are unacquainted; but there is reason to believe he spent some months in that county at some previous period." Cradock indeed, in his *Memoirs*,[3] goes so far as to declare that Goldsmith expressly mentioned such a journey into Yorkshire, and connected it with the title of his story. Speaking of the little ballad of *The Hermit*, he says:—"I knew he had been offered £10 for the copy; and it was introduced into the *Vicar of Wakefield*, to which he applied himself entirely for a fortnight, to pay a journey to Wakefield. 'As my business then lay there,' said he, 'that was my reason for fixing on Wakefield as the field of action.'" Both Prior and Forster discredit this account; the former considering the assertion to be vaguely made, and the latter calling it "a confused and quite incredible statement of Mr. Cradock's."[4] Still, though inaccurate in details, it may be thought to lend additional support to the opinion that Goldsmith did, on some occasion, travel into this part of Yorkshire.

Prior's judgment is, that "the name of the Vicarage is probably fanciful;" but he yet mentions one or two coincidences that, to say the least, are very singular.

---

(2) *Life of Goldsmith* (1837), vol. ii, p. 115.

(3) *Literary and Miscellaneous Memoirs*, by J. Cradock, Esq. (1828), vol. iv, p. 286.

(4) *Life and times of Oliver Goldsmith* (1854), vol. ii, p. 9.

The *Vicar of Wakefield* was published in 1766, having been written some time before; and "it has been ascertained from contemporary statements," he says, "that the daughter of the actual Vicar of Wakefield, the Rev. Dr. W., married about this period a Captain M. of the militia, without, as is said, having previously obtained the parental sanction: hence rumour induced a suspicion, unfounded no doubt, that, with such additions as imagination supplied, he had touched upon circumstances in real life." With regard to the names of the characters in the story, he adds:—"Another coincidence may be mentioned. The Vicar's wife is made to speak of the family of the Blenkinsops, known for a physical peculiarity of which the name is indicative. Yet a family so called, though it is scarcely necessary to say not distinguished in the manner described in the novel, lived in this part of the country; and in some of its descendants, Miss Jane, Anna Maria, Sir Robert Kerr, and Dr. Ogilvie Porter, of Bristol, have exhibited talents of a high order."[5]

Forster quotes an extract from the *Journal* of an American loyalist refugee,[6] who visited Wakefield three years after Goldsmith's death, which indicates what was the impression prevailing in the town itself on this subject. Unfortunately, the last sentence shews that

---

(5) If the argument from similarity of names were worth much, the list of them might readily be extended. My fellow-townsman, Mr. J. Hewitt, points out the existence of a "Thornhill House," and "Thornhill Street," in Wakefield.—See p. 69 of the *History and Topography of the Parish of Wakefield and its environs*, which, under many difficulties, he is now publishing in sheets.

(6) Curwen's *Journal and Letters* (1842), p. 131.

the writer's judgment is not to be much relied on. Under date May 30th, 1777, is the entry :—" Departed in a stage-coach from Sheffield, and arrived at Black Barnsley, through a delightful, though uneven road. Here we took post-chaises, and in two hours alighted at Wakefield, a clothing town, where appeared evident tokens of taste in building and of wealth : the avenues to it delightful, the roads like a carpet-walk, on one side a raised terrace-walk for foot-passengers, flagged for more than two miles : the land hereabout excellent, and under the most improved cultivation. The Westgate-street has the noblest appearance of any I ever saw out of London ; its pavement in the best order, its length near half a mile, and width ten rods. Were it not for some old, low buildings, London could not boast of a more magnificent street. It has a very large episcopal church, with a remarkably lofty tower and spire. The principal character in the novel called the *Vicar of Wakefield* was taken from the late Vicar of this church, named Johnson, whose peculiarly odd and singular humour has exposed his memory to the ridicule of that satire."

As we have seen that Benjamin Wilson was Vicar from 1750 to 1764, and as he was succeeded by Dr. Michael Bacon, who held the office till 1805, we may safely conclude that the name of *Johnson*, given above, is a mere mistake for *Wilson*. It is almost provoking, indeed, to notice how vague or self-confuting are the passages, in which the pretensions of our town to be the Wakefield of Dr. Primrose seem to be countenanced. The same fatality of blundering has attended the writer of the following letter in the *Gentleman's Maga-*

zine :[7]—" Vicar of Wakefield is a name of renown, rendered famous by the pen of that elegant poet, Goldsmith, whose much admired novel is thus intituled; and could I hope that any work or production of the person who, (although he did nót sit for the picture,) is generally supposed to be sketched out in that character, would be agreeable to the literary world, having several of his MSS. in my possession, I have it in my power to oblige them. By the number of places he delivered his discourses at, he seems to have had several other cures for souls besides Wakefield,[8] and to have been a popular preacher in those parts. I have a sufficient number of them to make one volume. As a specimen of his style and manner, I take the liberty to inclose you a quotation or two, which to me seems to evince the honest simplicity of the man, as drawn by the above writer.... He concludes one of his discourses thus: 'Whoever therefore can take a view of Nature in her deep and solemn scenes, with the same pleasure as in her most gay and delightsome ones, indicates a mind duly considerate and composed. By this means I can improve myself with the objects which others consider with terror. When I look upon the tombs of the great, every emotion of envy dies in me; when I read the epitaphs of the beautiful, every inordinate desire goes out: when I meet with the grief of parents upon a tombstone, my heart melts with compassion; when I see the tomb of the parents them-

---

(7) Vol. lxx, p. 842.—The letter is dated Sep. 15th, 1800, and signed T. O. De Britain.

(8) "Wragby, Horbury, Hartshead, in 1754. He appears to have been a pastor here 30 years or more:"—note *ib.*

selves, I consider the vanity of grieving for those whom we must shortly follow. When I see kings lying by those who deposed them; when I consider rival wits lay side by side; and the holy men who divided the world by their contests and disputes; I reflect with sorrow and astonishment on the little competitions, factions, and debates of mankind.'" &c.[9]

Whatever be thought of the claim of our town to be the ideal Wakefield of Oliver Goldsmith, the following passage[10] will shew, I think, that the real aspect of the place was not wholly out of harmony with that of the parish "with three strange wants." It is part of a letter from the philanthropic James Nield, the inspector of prisons, to Dr. Lettsom; and is dated "Wakefield, Sunday evening, Aug. 15th, 1802." The writer says:—
"It is scarcely possible to form a greater contrast than between the two places I have just been visiting. Before I got into the chaise this morning, I thought I would take another peep into the gaol at Sheffield, to see how they spent their Sunday. I found the Low-Court debtors as black as chimney-sweepers, and as busy as bees, sifting cinders, to make up the ashes two loads, which are to be fetched away to-morrow morning. I arrived at this place (Wakefield) just as divine service had begun; and was surprised not even to see a single beggar, or vagrant, or even an idle lounger, about the streets. The church was filled within, and

---

(9) I am ashamed to own, that, when I first contributed this to the *Wakefield Journal and Examiner*, of Dec. 9th, 1859, I had not perceived that the passage thus singled out is neither more nor less than the concluding paragraph of No. 26 of the *Spectator*.

(10) *Gentleman's Magazine* for 1805, p. 304.

peace and order dwelt without. I was pleased to be informed this was not a casual circumstance, but that I should always find it so whenever I visited it on the Sabbath day."

Whether Goldsmith ever saw Wakefield or not, there is no doubt that the author of a book, which has been almost as great a favourite with boys as the *Vicar of Wakefield* with men, found in that town the "gentle lady of the West," for whom he sighed. The brave, good, simple-minded author[11] of *Sandford and Merton*, when roaming, in his younger days, in the West of England, gave utterance to his longings for such a partner as his imagination pourtrayed, in a little poem, of which the following stanzas are a part :—

"O gentle lady of the West,
 Whose charms on this sequester'd shore
With love can fire a stranger's breast,—
 A breast that never lov'd before!

"O tell me in what silent vale,
 To hail the balmy breath of May,
Thy tresses floating on the gale,
 All simply neat thou deign'st to stray!

"Not such thy look, not such thy air,
 Not such thy unaffected grace,
As, 'mid the town's deceitful glare,
 Marks the proud nymph's disdainful face.

"Health's rosy bloom upon thy cheek,
 Eyes that with artless lustre roll,

---

(11) Mr. Thomas Day was born in Wellclose Square, London, June 22nd, 1748; and died, by a fall from his horse, Sep. 28th, 1789. The first part of *Sandford and Merton* was published in 1783, the third in 1789: it was probably meant to be continued. He wrote also several other works, chiefly pamphlets.

>   More eloquent than words to speak
>   The genuine feelings of the soul;
> "Such be thy form! thy noble mind
>   By no false culture led astray,
>   By native sense alone refin'd
>   In reason's plain and simple way;
> "Indifferent if the eye of Fame
>   Thy merit unobserving see,
>   And heedless of the praise or blame
>   Of all mankind,—of all but me;
> "O gentle lady of the West!
>   To find thee be my only task:
>   When found, I'll clasp thee to my breast!
>   No haughty birth or dower I ask.
> "Sequester'd in some secret glade,
>   With thee unnotic'd would I live;
>   And, if content adorn the shade,
>   What more can Heav'n or Nature give?
> "Too long deceiv'd by pomp's false glare,
>   'Tis thou must soothe my soul to rest;
>   'Tis thou must soften every care,
>   O gentle lady of the West!"

"Among the number whom fortune threw in his way," says his biographer,[12] "there was one young lady who never failed to attract particular notice. A friend of his, more advanced in years, knowing his wish to settle himself in marriage, could not help expressing his surprise that he did not shew more serious attentions with regard to her. His answer was truly characteristic:—'He knew and felt her merit; and nothing but her large fortune prevented him from wishing that he had it in his power to effect such an union; for the plan of life which he had laid down for himself was too remote from common opinions, to

---

(12) *An account of the Life and Writings of Thomas Day, Esq.*, by James Keir (1791); at p. 43 of which the above stanzas are quoted.

admit of flattering himself with the expectation of so much conformity from a person of her affluent circumstances.' It was in vain that his friend urged that there appeared a security for that young lady's conduct, which few had an opportunity of giving : young, and mistress of herself and of her fortune, her prudence had been proved ; although admired by men, she was nevertheless beloved by her own sex ; that, in the generous and humane use she had made of an ample income, she had shewn a heart no less liberal than his own ;"—and the like. It was not till chance again threw her in his way, and he had found, from her own lips, that her tastes were akin to his own, that he sought and won a lady who proved a true and congenial helpmate to him, and whose character is probably reflected in the Miss Sukey ("for so she had the misfortune to be called"), as that of the author himself is, first in the brave little Sandford, and afterwards in the Sophron, of his whimsical but charming tale.

On the 7th of August,[13] 1778, "Mr. Day was married to Miss Esther Milnes, of Wakefield, in Yorkshire."

---

(13) This is the date given by Keir; who dedicates his book to Mrs. Day. In the *Biographia Britannica* it is the 10th of August.

THOMAS ZOUCH.

This writer, whose name has already been mentioned, was born at Sandal, near Wakefield, Sep. 12th, 1737. His family was probably a branch of the Zouches, Barons of Harrington[1]; more than one of whom have been distinguished in English history. After receiving some elementary instruction from his father, the Vicar of Sandal, he was sent to the Wakefield Grammar School, where he remained up to the age of twenty. He was a promising pupil of an able master; and in his time the literary studies of the place, if we may judge from one slight trace that has been preserved,[2] were carried to as high a point as they have ever attained. In 1754 he lost his father; but his elder brother Henry seems to have supplied a father's place to him. In 1757[3] he entered as a Pen-

---

(1) *Works of the Rev. Thomas Zouch, D.D., F.L.S. &c.*, by the Rev. Francis Wrangham (1820), vol. i; from which, and from Nichols' *Literary Anecdotes*, vol. vii, the above account is principally derived.

(2) "If I mistake not, Bennet Langton, the friend of Dr. Johnson, told me more than twenty years ago, that Mr. Clarke once read with his scholars the very difficult poem of *Lycophron.*" —*Letter* to Dr. Zouch from "an illustrious scholar," quoted by Wrangham.

(3) So in the *Literary Anecdotes*. Wrangham says July, 1756.

sioner at Trinity College, Cambridge. Of his manner of life here no memorial has been left, beyond the indications of diligent and successful study which the annals of the University contain. There his name stands prominently. The year after his entrance, he was elected a Scholar of Trinity College; in 1760 he obtained one of the Craven Scholarships, along with Joah Bates of Halifax, afterwards the celebrated musician; in 1761 he took the degree of third, or (as he himself always declared) second Wrangler[4]; in the year following he was elected Fellow of his college; in 1763 he gained one of the Members' Prizes; and in 1765 the Seatonian Prize for his poem on *The Crucifixion*. With the exception of the Chancellor's medal, and the Battie Scholarship (for which he was precluded from trying), he had thus won all that the University had to offer as encouragements to learning. But the "dusky bays" of the academy wither as fast as any other laurels; and one more comment upon the "Vanity of vanities" of the Preacher may be found in the following sentences, written by Zouch on the back of a Latin letter in which his election to a Fellowship was announced:—

> "O the misery of life!
> O the vanity of fame!
> O the folly of learning!
> O the madness of ambition!
> O the plague of wealth!
> O the distress of want!
> O the pageantry of pleasure!
> O the emptiness of pride!
> O the wretchedness of suspense!"

---

(4) In the list his name appears third; but the custom of granting honorary degrees, alluded to in the Life of Bentley, had (I believe) not yet been abolished.

In 1763 he was appointed assistant-tutor in his college; an office which he discharged with great reputation. But finding that his health was becoming impaired, he resigned in 1770, and was then presented by the college to the rectory of Wycliff, in the North Riding of Yorkshire. This village, situated in a pleasant and picturesque country, is famous as being the birth-place of the great Reformer, who took his name from it; and here Zouch continued till 1793, diligent in his calling, and at the same time improving his health, and gaining an acquaintance with natural history, by long botanical excursions. The study of plants was a favourite one with him, and in 1788 he was elected a Fellow of the Linnean Society. The same year he was appointed chaplain to the Right Honourable Sir Richard Pepper Arden, afterwards Lord Alvanley, then Master of the Rolls, who had been a pupil of his. In 1791 he was made Deputy-commissary for the archdeaconry of Richmond; and in 1793 he quitted Wycliff for the rectory of Scrayingham in the East Riding. By the death of his brother Henry, in 1795, he succeeded to an estate at Sandal; and on the demise of his brother's widow in the year following, he removed to his native village, where he remained till the end of his life. His usefulness was somewhat impeded by a deafness, to which he had always been subject, and which was not lessened by advancing age. It was said that he once began his sermon in St. Mary's, at Cambridge, before the organ had ceased playing. An affection of the heart, to which he was liable, also prevented him from ever preaching in Sandal Church; for, with this infirmity, he dared not trust himself to stand in the pulpit which his father had occupied so long. This little trait shews at once the filial regard, and the susceptible nature of the man.

In 1798 Mr. Pitt had an intention of appointing him to the Mastership of Trinity College, then vacant by the death of Dr. Postlethwaite; but ultimately decided in favour of Mansel, afterwards Bishop of Bristol. The same Premier however bestowed upon him the second prebend in Durham Cathedral, in 1805; on which occasion he took his degree of Doctor of Divinity. In 1808 the vacant see of Carlisle was offered to him by the Duke of Portland; but his advanced age and retiring habits made him decline the office. The *nolo episcopari* was from his lips both becoming and sincere. Thus in peaceful seclusion at Sandal he continued to spend the evening of his days, till death quietly took him, Dec. 17th, 1815.

Though twice married he left no children. His first wife was Isabella, daughter of the Rev. John Emerson, rector of Winston in Durham; his second, whom he married in 1807, was Margaret Brooke, whose brother was formerly Somerset Herald.

It is not of course intended to represent Thomas Zouch as a man of striking character or conspicuous ability. But he was considerably more than what is generally meant by an amiable and well-read country clergyman. "A valued friend," whose contribution Wrangham inserts,[5] says of him, that "though, as a divine, he conscientiously deemed it to be his duty, no

---

(5) *Introductory Memoir*, p. lviii.

less than it was his delight, to devote the greatest part of his time to the Hebrew Scriptures, with which he mingled a certain portion of Chaldee and Arabic learning, few possessed a more elegant taste for classic literature, or a happier talent, in consequence of his extraordinary memory, of applying passages from the ancient poets and historians, both to the important and familiar incidents of the day. With the French and Italian languages also he was intimately acquainted, and occasionally drew largely upon them for the amusement of his leisure hours." His works, which are numerous rather than lengthy, indicate a prevailing taste for biography. Besides one or two which have been already alluded to, he wrote *An attempt to illustrate some of the Prophecies of the Old and New Testaments; Memoirs of the Life and Writings of Sir Philip Sidney; Memoir of John Sudbury, Dean of Durham; Memoir of Sir George Wheeler; Attica Eboracensis, or Sketches of Yorkshire Biography;*[6] and various shorter pieces.

---

(6) This was left unfinished by the author, and was published, with some additions, by Wrangham. I believe mention has been made, in the earlier part of this book, of all the Wakefield names which it contains, of a date previous to Zouch. Joseph Watkinson must be excepted; of whom I know nothing more than is told by the following inscription in the chapel of Merton College, Oxford. If he deserved his epitaph, this passing notice is at least his due:—

"Hic situs est Josephus Watkinson, A.M.
Ex antiquâ familiâ apud Wakefield
In comitatu Eboracensi oriundus;
A scholâ Westmonasteriensi
Collegii hujusce Portionista,
Deinde Socius ascitus.
Vir ad normam a Mertonâ statutam
Probus, humilis, pacificus;

He also edited, with notes, Izaak Walton's *Lives*, and the *Love and Truth* of the same author; and, along with his old friend and schoolfellow, Dr. Swire, rector of Melsonby,[7] he published a pamphlet written by a solicitor of Middleton Tyas, named Sampson George, entitled *Reflexions of a Layman on the Divinity of Christ, &c.* He was moreover a frequent contributor to the anonymous literature of his time.

> Omnium virtutum choro societatem
> Recreavit domi,
> Foras honestavit.
> In humanioribus literis varius et elegans,
> In theologiâ doctus et disertus.
> Quas a Deo dotes feliciter expendit
> In instituendâ juventute
> Assiduus aliquando tutor,
> In Parochiæ curâ
> Pastor ad extremum vigilantissimus.
> Obiit Anno Domini MDCCXX, Aetatis suæ XXXVII."

(7) I regret that I cannot recover many particulars of one with whom Zouch is said to have "walked hand in hand through life." Carlisle, in his *Endowed Grammar Schools* (1818), vol. ii, p. 912, after mentioning Bentley, Potter, and other Wakefield scholars, for whom "the world is indebted to this eminent seminary," adds:—"And in conclusion the author may be pardoned the expression of his sorrow and esteem, in recording the name of a friend, whom death permitted him so shortly to know, the Rev. Dr. Swyre, late Rector of Melsonby near Richmond."—From Whitaker's *Richmondshire* (1823), vol. i, p. 219, it appears that he was instituted to the rectory of Melsonby, July 19th, 1787. His death is thus noticed in the *Gentleman's Magazine* for 1816: —"Died, April 1816, aged 76, Samuel Swire, D.D., rector of Melsonby and Barningham." And the arms of his family, as exhibited on the north side of the Hall in University College, Oxford, are described as follows in Wood's *History, &c. of Oxford* (1786), vol. iii:—"Azure, three swans' Heads couped arg. Roger Swire, Esq; Samuel Swire, M.A. Fellow: Rector of Melsonby, Yorkshire."

THOMAS ROBINSON.

Thomas Robinson, the author of the well-known *Scripture Characters*, was born at Wakefield, Sep. 10th, 1749.[1] He was the fourth son of Mr. James Robinson, a respectable hosier, who occupied a house in the market-place next to that in which Archbishop Potter was born. As soon as he could read, he was sent to the Grammar School of his native town, where he remained under the tuition, first of Mr. Brookes, and afterwards of the Rev. Christopher Atkinson,[2] till the time came for proceeding to the University. At this juncture a difficulty arose. His own tastes were decidedly for a college life, and an attempt of his father to place him in business at the age of fourteen had proved ineffectual: but, though his ability in school gave promise of future distinction, the means of supporting him at Oxford or Cambridge were wanting. The

---

(1) In Vaughan's *Some account of the Rev. Thomas Robinson, &c.* (1815), from which the above is chiefly derived, the date is given in Old Style, Aug. 29th, 1749.—The author, Rev. E. T. Vaughan, was vicar of St. Martin's and All Saints, Leicester, and preached Robinson's funeral sermon.

(2) He was Head Master of the Grammar School for thirty-seven years, and afternoon lecturer at the Parish Church for twenty-two. He died on New-Year's day, 1793, aged 63.—See his epitaph at p. 31 of Sisson's *Historic Sketch.*

yearly value of an exhibition from the Grammar School was at that time not more than £20, which was inadequate to a student's maintenance. At last, on the motion of Mr. Smyth[3] of Heath, one of the Governors, a double exhibition was granted him; and he entered as a sizar at Trinity College, Cambridge, in 1768. One or two incidents, which are related by his biographer as having occurred about this period, seem to have made a lasting impression on his mind. One was a dream, in which, with awful distinctness, he beheld the Parish Church enveloped in flames. The other was his meeting with a poor shoemaker of Wakefield, who, on hearing that Robinson was about to proceed to the University, asked him if it were true that he was going to be a clergyman. Being answered in the affirmative, "Then, Sir," he said, "I hope you will study your Bible, that you may be able to feed the flock of Christ with spiritual food."

The great strictness and precision of his behaviour, while at Cambridge, appears to have attracted notice, and to have gained for him, though not ill-naturedly, the nicknames of "His Holiness," and "The Pope." He was one of the few who dared to make light of University prejudices so far, as to own the acquain-

---

(3) This was the Right Hon. John Smyth, the most distinguished of the family. He was M.P. for Pontefract twenty-five years; Lord of the Admiralty and Treasury; Master of the Mint; and one of His Majesty's Privy Council. He was born Feb. 12th, 1748, and died on the same day of the month in 1811. The one who, by his purchase of Heath Hall, first brought the family into permament connection with Wakefield, was John Smyth, Esq., who died on Christmas-day, 1729, aged 76, and was buried in the Parish Church, where there is a monument of white marble to his memory.—Burke's *Landed Gentry* (1852).

tance of a young undergraduate of St. John's College, then in disfavour with his contemporaries, but afterwards a distinguished man, Rowland Hill. In academical studies he made the progress which had been expected of him. In April, 1771, he was elected a Scholar of his college; in December of the same year he gained one of Dr. Hooper's medals for the best English declamation; in the Tripos list of 1772, he stood as seventh Wrangler; in October of the same year he was elected Fellow of his College; and in 1773 he obtained one of the Members' Prizes for a Latin essay. For the Chancellor's medal, then the chief test of classical proficiency, he did not contend. The wide range of his knowledge, to which several of his contemporaries have borne witness, was attested by one well able to form an opinion,—his tutor, Dr. Postlethwaite; who, in comparing him with others of his numerous pupils, was heard to say :—" I have known many, probably, who excelled him in separate branches of knowledge; but none who outstripped him in the whole compass of academical information." The influence of his character on his fellow-students is shewn by a little circumstance which befel him during his undergraduate course. An attempt was made by some young men to procure the setting aside of subscription to the Thirty-Nine Articles. On canvassing Trinity College, the first question asked of them was, " Has Robinson signed the petition?" and on learning that he had not, most of those applied to declined to share in the movement. Robinson was in vain plied with the flattering argument, that, if he would join the petitioners, all the undergraduates in his college would follow: he showed himself already animated by the same spirit, which made him, many years later, oppose with all his energy the repeal of the Corporation and Test Acts.

Soon after taking his Bachelor's degree, he entered upon the joint curacies of Witcham and Wichford, in the Isle of Ely. The stipend of both united was then very small. Here he began a course of ministerial activity, which, in that rather sleepy generation, soon produced visible effects. His churches were filled, and more room had to be provided. The success of his labours at Witcham was attended, as is often the case, with some amount of envy and misrepresentation. His youthful appearance was found fault with by some, his readiness to visit the families in his district by others: "he would go anywhere," they said, "for a cup of tea." Like many energetic men, he probably treated too lightly the opinions and prejudices of those around him; and this made his conduct pretty freely discussed, both in Ely Chapter-house and Cambridge Combination-rooms. Why he left his curacy is not clearly stated: one reason appears to have been his dislike of the prevalent mode of singing in churches; a matter which led him into disputes on subsequent occasions.

The place to which he now proceeded, and where he was to spend the remainder of his life, was one that he would not of his own accord have chosen. On passing through Leicester a few years before, he had been very unfavourably impressed with the aspect of the town, then in an uproar at what was long remembered as Coote and Grey's contested election. He went there now, however, on the invitation of one of the Leicester clergy, Mr. Haines, who was in want of a curate, and who overcame Robinson's dislike to the place by urging what was with him a cogent argument: —"Where should a man go but where he is most needed?" The state of the town, as it appeared on fuller acquaintance, did not materially alter the opinion he had conceived of it before. The latter part of the eighteenth century is no very bright period in the religious annals of our country; and the condition of Leicester was probably much like that of other provincial towns at the time. That is to say, there was abundance of idleness, luxury, and frivolous dissipation among the richer people; and much coarseness and sensuality among the poorer. Religion was a sickly plant, developing itself chiefly in formality and outward show. In such a state of things there was ample room for the exertions of a zealous and devout man; and there can be no question that Thomas Robinson, though not exempt from the failings of his school, did a great work there. At first, as had been the case at Witcham, he had many severe criticisms to encounter. On one bench of loungers in particular, a seat placed near a well-frequented shop, which had gained the appellation of "the seat of the scornful," his merits and demerits were unsparingly discussed. But the keenest of the scorners, a remarkable and somewhat eccentric character, William Ludlam,[4] soon became

---

(4) He was a son of Dr. Richard Ludlam, an eminent physician of Leicester. After graduating at Cambridge, he was elected a Fellow of St. John's College; and was the author of *The Rudiments of Mathematicks*, and several other mathematical works.

one of Robinson's supporters; and for a time was a steadfast and cordial friend. He summed up the results of the new curate's teaching curtly enough, by remarking "that the ladies could not now go home from church to their card-tables with as easy minds as before."

In 1778 a weekly lecture at St. Mary's Church was endowed by Mr. Joseph Wheatley, a wealthy manufacturer in the town, and Robinson was the first chosen to discharge the office. He had previously been afternoon lecturer at All Saints' Church, and chaplain to the Infirmary. Shortly afterwards he was raised to the incumbency of St. Mary's, which was in the gift of the Lord Chancellor; and here it was he preached those discourses, which, after being inserted in the *Theological Miscellany*, edited by De Coetlogon, were published under the title of *Scripture Characters*.[5] This is his best-known work, and one which has enjoyed a large measure of popularity, as shewn by the number of editions it has gone through. Some of the opinions contained in it were attacked by the Rev. Thomas Ludlam,[6] in a treatise published in 1797.

He had the reputation of being one of the cleverest mechanists of his day; and was so addicted to his favourite pursuit, that he would sometimes come into church on Sundays, with arms and knees in a state that betrayed his recent occupation.—See Nichols' *Literary Anecdotes*, vol. ix, p. 87; *Literary Illustrations*, vol. v, p. 349; and Vaughan's *Life*, above referred to.

(5) See the *Memoir* prefixed to the first volume of the *Scripture characters* (10th edition, 1815).

(6) Younger brother of the William Ludlam mentioned above. He was born in 1727, graduated from St. John's College, Cambridge, in 1745, and in 1791 was made Rector of Foston in Lincolnshire. The treatise referred to bore the title of *Four*

A copy of an early edition of the *Scripture Characters* is in the Grammar School library of his native town, with an inscription from the author's pen, expressive of his gratitude and attachment to the place of his early education.

Robinson's influence now began to be widely felt in the neighbourhood in which his lot was cast. Not that he succeeded in smoothing down all opposition. When first made incumbent of St. Mary's, he tried to alter the singing from "a ridiculous mode of conducting the musical part of the service," to what should "accord with the seriousness of devotion and the gravity of truth."[7] The churchwardens sided with the singers; and, as both parties were obstinate, the church was for a short period closed. This difficulty, however, soon gave way before the new incumbent's energy and

---

Essays on the ordinary and extraordinary operations of the Holy Spirit . . . in which the justness of the reasoning employed, and the propriety of the language adopted, in the Scripture characters *of the Rev. Thomas Robinson are fully considered.* The Essays themselves are reviewed in the *Gentleman's Magazine*, vol. lxvii., p. 984; where the writer says:—"This work is intended to expose and correct some errors, both of sentiment and language, adopted by that part of the clergy of the Church of England, who usually denominate themselves *Gospel Ministers;* a class of men deservedly respected for their piety and usefulness, but who too often injure their cause by opinions which are here shewn to be equally absurd and unscriptural, and by the harshness, if not uncharitableness, with which they treat those who differ from them. The points chiefly discussed in these essays, are, the claim to a sensible intercourse with the Deity, and the proof of religious truths from the personal experience of believers at the present time. . . . The third and fourth are a close and critical examination of many passages in the writings of Messrs. Robinson, Newton, Scott, &c.; in which both these doctrines are supported."

(7) Introductory *Memoir*, above cited, p. x.

good management; and in the establishment of schools, and other charitable institutions, he found a free and sufficient scope for his powers both of mind and body. Of such institutions in Leicester he is said to have been the acknowledged parent. Thus, in 1785, he procured the erection of a school which would hold more than a hundred children, to which he shortly afterwards added a smaller building for preparatory instruction. It is unnecessary to enter into details of the various ways in which he sought to improve the condition of those about him. The result of his labours was thus summed up by his old acquaintance Robert Hall, at a meeting of the *Leicester Auxiliary Bible Society*, held soon after Robinson's death:—" His residence in Leicester forms a most important epoch in the religious history of this county. From that time must be dated, and to his agency, under Providence, ascribed, a decided improvement in the moral and religious state of this town and its vicinity; an increase of religious light, together with a general diffusion of a taste and relish for the pure Word of God. It is only now and then in an age, that an individual is permitted to confer such benefits on a town, as this ancient and respectable borough has derived from the labours of Mr. Robinson; and the revolution which Baxter accomplished at Kidderminster, our deceased friend accomplished at Leicester. It was the boast of Augustus, that he found the city of Rome built with brick, and that he left it built with marble. Mr. Robinson might say without arrogance, that he had been the instrument of effecting a far more beneficial and momentous change. He came to this place while it was sunk in vice and irreligion; he left it eminently distinguished by sobriety of manners, and the practice of warm, serious, and enlightened piety. He did not add aqueducts and palaces, nor increase the splendour of its public edifices; but he embellished it with undecaying ornaments: he renovated the minds of its inhabitants, and turned a large portion of them from darkness to light, and from the power of Satan to God."[8]

Thus employed, Robinson passed many useful years. In his political principles he never varied. He was always a staunch Church and State man. In 1788 we find him opposing a vigorous agitation that was being made in the midland counties for the repeal of the Corporation and Test Acts,[9] and one of the last public

---

(8) Quoted at p. xx of the *Memoir* above referred to.

(9) Before censuring this as a proof of narrow-mindedness in Robinson, we must remember how very slowly these and other bulwarks of the Established Church, as they were once thought, have been surrendered.—At the assizes held at Newcastle, Aug. 7th, 1683, the Grand Jury for the county of Northumberland made a presentment, "that all persons who keep ale-houses, or other publicke-houses within this country, shall bring a certificate under the hand of the parson of the parish where hee or shee dwelleth, at the same tyme they come to renue their lycences, that they have duly repaired to their parish churches, and received the Sacrament according to Law."—*Depositions from the Castle of York* before referred to : Preface, p. xxvi., n.

An instance of the same spirit at an earlier period, as it affected our own neighbourhood, is to be met with in a letter from Lord President Sheffield to His Majesty's Justices of the Peace for the West Riding, dated from York, Jan. 7th, 1617, to the effect that they should "levy moneys for absence from church, xiid per Sunday, according to the Statute, and apply their best endeavours thereunto, whereby God may receive glory, the People benefitt, and the Statute that right it may expect at their hands."—Copied in Kennett's MSS., vol. xxxviii, fol. 48.

acts of his life was to join in a petition to parliament against repealing the remaining restrictions upon Popery.

The seventh of March, 1813, was the thirty-ninth anniversary of his connection with Leicester. He had lived to overcome all the prejudices that had met him at the outset, and had passed his grand climacteric with an amount of health and strength that seemed to promise a green old age, when a stroke of apoplexy seized him on the 24th of that month; and in a few hours he expired. "He fell," said Robert Hall, "like a noble tree after two or three strokes, with all his sap and verdure, with extended boughs and rich foliage, while thousands were reposing under his shadow and partaking of his fruits."

He was twice married; first, in 1774, to a lady whose name is not mentioned, and who died in 1791, leaving a family; secondly, in 1797, to the widow of Dr. Gerard, formerly Warden of Wadham College, Oxford. Besides his chief work, above-mentioned, he wrote *The Christian System Unfolded, or Essays on the Doctrines and Duties of Christianity*, in 3 vols., and two or three shorter pieces.

A few years after Robinson's birth, in 1758, was published the first volume (all that ever appeared) of the *Monasticon Eboracense;* of the author of which, Dr. John Burton, this will be a convenient place to say a few words. If we are to rely on Bigland's statement,[10]

---

(10) *Beauties of England and Wales*, above quoted; vol. xvi., p. 807, n :—" It ought to be remembered that the celebrated

he was a native of this town; but in Nichols' *Literary Illustrations*[11] and elsewhere, he is said to have been born at Ripon. Without clearer evidence, accordingly, I should not venture to place him among our Worthies. He was born in 1697; was educated at Christ Church, Oxford, but took his degree of M.B. at Cambridge, in 1733; settled at York, and became eminent as a medical author and practitioner; was with difficulty prevented by his friends from joining in the rebellion of 1745, being a strong Jacobite; and died Jan. 19th, 1771.[12] The immense collection of materials for a History of Yorkshire, which he had been accumulating for many years, he sold shortly before his death to William Constable, Esq., of Burton Constable, for an annuity to himself and his wife. In a letter to Dr. Ducarel, dated York, Jan. 24th, 1769,[13] he says of his collection, that "it cannot be equalled in Great Britain, either in public or private libraries; nor can such a number of original Charters, Grants, &c. be found or met with at this time." This opinion of his is borne out by another correspondent of Dr. Ducarel's[14] who says of the *Mon-*

John Burton, M.D., author of the *Monasticon Eboracense*, was a native of Wakefield."—His authority is followed by Leatham, in *Lectures delivered at Literary and Mechanics' Institutions* (1845), p. 143.

(11) Vol. iii, p. 375.—It is there admitted that "our accounts of him are very scanty."

(12) *Gentleman's Magazine* for 1771, and the volume of the *Illustrations* just quoted.

(13) *Illustrations*, vol. iii., p. 388.—In this year, if the coincidence is worth noting, the name of a Mr. Burton occurs in a list of contributors towards the repair of the old Rectory House at Wakefield.—See Sisson's *Historic Sketch*, p. 77.

(14) *Literary Illustrations*, vol. iv., p. 648.—The writer, Edward Hasted, dates from Canterbury, Feb. 18th, 1771.

asticon Eboracense that it "infinitely surpasses either of Sir William Dugdale's (volumes); and had not Mr. Burton unfortunately been misled, and involved in troubles and poverty, by his attachment to party, he would have given the world such a History of Yorkshire, as would have far surpassed any such work heretofore published. He had great abilities, and was withal indefatigable."

So much for one, whose works, had they been made accessible, would have rendered such attempts as the present either unnecessary, or better worth attention.

To another, and perhaps still more laborious, antiquary of earlier date, the neighbourhood of Wakefield has an undoubted claim. John Hopkinson, whose collections are still the great store-house for the Yorkshire topographer,[15] was a native of Lofthouse, near this town. He was a son of George Hopkinson of Lofthouse, by his second wife Judith, daughter of Mr. John Langley of Horbury.[16] The extent of his labours may be inferred from the following memorandum, made by one connected with the family, which states that, in 1815, "of his manuscript collections relating to the Antiquities of the county of York, forty volumes are preserved in the library of Miss Frances Mary Richardson-Currer, at North Bierley, who is great-great-great-grand-daughter to his sister; and about the same number . . . are now in the possession of John

---

(15) See James: *History and Topography of Bradford* (1841); Preface, p. viii.

(16) Nichols' *Literary Illustrations*, vol. iii., p. 366.—The first of the family, whose name is preserved, came out of Lincolnshire, and settled at Foleby, or Foldby, near Nostell Priory.

Henry Smyth, Esq.,[16] of Heath near Wakefield, M.P. for the University of Cambridge, who is descended from one of the daughters of Richard Richardson and Jane Hopkinson."[17]

---

(16) Son and heir of the Right Hon. John Smyth mentioned in a previous article, and father of the present possessor of Heath Hall, John George Smyth, Esq. He was born in 1780, and died Oct. 22nd, 1822. How he was descended from a daughter of Richard Richardson and Jane Hopkinson does not appear from the account of the family given in Burke ; but in the statement of the pedigree of Richardson of Finden (p. 1116 of *Landed Gentry*, 1852) it is mentioned that the third daughter of the said Richard Richardson and Jane Hopkinson was Judith, who was married to John Thornton, of Tyersall, in the parish of Calverley ; and that from this marriage the Smyths of Heath derive.

(17) Nichols' *Literary Illustrations*, vol. i., p. 225.—The compiler of the above account was Dorothy Richardson of Gargrave. From John, third son of the same Richard Richardson and Jane Hopkinson, sprung another man of some eminence, who was connected with Wakefield. This was Charles Naylor, son of William Naylor of Wakefield, and Anne, daughter of the above John Richardson. Charles Naylor was Dean of Winchester and Chancellor of Salisbury. He died unmarried, and was buried in the north aisle of Winchester Cathedral, where a monument is erected with the inscription:—" H. S. E. Carolus Naylor, Decanus Winton : 1739." An account of it may be seen in Milner's *History, &c., of Winchester* (1798)); appendix, p. 5.

C. S. VAN STRAUBENZEE.

In the north chancel of the Parish Church is a tablet, recording the death of Charles Spencer Van Straubenzee, Esq., who was born in 1750, and was for several years Governor of the West Riding House of Correction at Wakefield. "He was universally respected as a gentleman," says Sisson,[1] "and admired for his conduct under many afflicting circumstances. The history of his family, which had been involved in numerous misfortunes by the unrelenting anger of an offended parent, would form an affecting narrative. The cause of offence, and part of its calamitous consequences, have been detailed by the venerable Mr. Hutton of Birmingham, in one of his interesting Tours."

The tour referred to was one made by William Hutton to Redcar and Coatham in 1808, of which he published an account the same year. As the circumstances of Mr. Straubenzee's early life present much that is romantic, and have already been more than once made public,[2] it will not be out of place, or

---

(1) *Historic Sketch*, p. 55, n.

(2) Hutton's account was copied into the *Gentleman's Magazine* for 1810, and the *Trip* itself was reprinted in 1848.—A notice of the family of Turner will be found in Ingledew's *History of Northallerton*, p. 138.

intruding improperly on domestic matters, to quote an extract from the Birmingham historian.

"In our way from Northallerton to Stokesley," he writes, "we passed by Busby Hall, where resided a widow lady named Turner, who held the estate, which is large, in her own right. She had one daughter, whom she used to torture for her amusement: instead of kindness she bestowed pinches; and instead of smiles, pricked her with pins. The father of the present Sir Thomas Gascoigne, and several other baronets, would have offered her their hands; but the mother would not suffer it, for this cogent reason, that the daughter would have been a *Lady*, and she herself only *Mistress* Turner. The young lady afterwards placed her affections upon a Dutch officer of the name of Straubenzee, and married him. Perhaps this occurred in the year 1745, when the Dutch came over. The old lady was now so exasperated, that she would not see her daughter; forgetting that the daughter did not degrade herself to his rank, but elevated him to her own. The mother, however, could not be reconciled. This union produced two sons. The prospect before the family was poverty; not a ray of comfort could be seen. The mother had completely learned the arts of reproof and punishment, but had never learned that of forgiveness. No doubt, peace was as much a stranger to her mind as to her daughter's. The wind cannot make a rough sea, without being rough itself.

"By the interposition of some friends, the children were introduced to their grandmother, who took them into favour, consented to keep them, and leave them the estate, on one *trifling* condition; that the children should swear never to see the mother, and she should swear never to see them. This the children could not do, and the mother would not. The refusal of the daughter ought to have pleaded her forgiveness, as it displayed the laudable tenderness of parental affection; but what can soften a rock? The old woman, however, suffered the two boys to remain with her, and without goading or tweaking them; till maternal tenderness induced their mother, one Sunday morning, to steal a peep out of a window in Stokesley, to see her sons go to church: which dreadful crime coming to the knowledge of the old lady, she discarded them for ever.

"She then offered the reversion of her estate to a gentleman, who replied, 'If you leave it to me, I will give it to Mr. Straubenzee:'—thus he honourably cut himself off. She then offered it to several others; who declined it with thanks. She then advertised it, not for sale, but for gift. At length a gentleman, whose name I have forgotten, accepted the offer upon her own terms. This gentleman, I am informed, had five or six brothers; and, for fear that the property should in future revert to her own family, she entailed the estate upon every one of them, and their heirs, according to priority. Anxiety shortened the days of the daughter; and the heir-at-law keeps the House of Correction at Wakefield.

"I apprehend a parallel case cannot be found in the history of man; for the female breast is ever open to pity towards its offspring. We read of harsh fathers, but where can be found such a mother?"

A few particulars may be added, to complete and correct the above account. The Dutch officer, to whom Hutton alludes, was Philip William Casimir Straubenzee, who held the rank of captain in the Dutch Guards. His family was one of high standing in the Netherlands; and a younger brother of his, General A. Van Straubenzee, was Governor of Lutphen[3] in 1798. Captain Philip Straubenzee came to England about the year 174–; and, after being naturalized by Act of Parliament, married Jane, only daughter and heiress of Cholmley Turner, Esq., of Kirkleatham, in the county of York, by Jane, grand-daughter and sole heiress of Sir Henry Marwood, Bart., of Busby Hall. Charles Spencer was the third son whom that union produced; and therefore not, as Hutton says, "the heir-at-law," when, in April 1802, he was appointed Governor of the House of Correction. His eldest brother, John William, died in 1753; but the next, Marwood Turner, lived to inherit the estate at Spennithorne, which, as he died without surviving issue,[4] is now held by his grand-nephew, Henry Van Straubenzee, Esq.

Charles Spencer Van Straubenzee married Anne Theophila, daughter of the Rev. J. Davison, Rector

---

(3) So in Burke's *Landed Gentry* (1852), from which these particulars are taken. I may be wrong in supposing the word to be a misprint; but I can find no mention of Lutphen elsewhere, whilst there is a town called Zutphen, in Gelderland, on the Yssel.

(4) Col. Marwood Turner Van Straubenzee, as Mr. Cromek has pointed out to me, married two Wakefield ladies in succession: first, Henrietta Theresa, daughter of Dr. Cookson, April 28th, 1788; and, after her death in 1803, Miss Buckle, Jan. 19th, 1805, who died in 1825.—See *Gentleman's Magazine*, vol. lviii., p. 464, and lxxv., p. 84.

of Scruton, and grand-daughter of Sir George Vane of Raby, by whom he had a numerous family. The eldest of his sons, William, was a captain in the 24th regiment, and died of fatigue, after the siege of Ciudad Rodrigo, at Pinhel in Portugal, Feb. 13th, 1812. The third son, George, a lieutenant in the 40th regiment, was killed at Badajos, in May, 1811. Two sons more went down in the Saldanha frigate, that was wrecked off the coast of Ireland, about the close of the Peninsular war.[5] But though the familiar lines of Mrs. Hemans, on *A Household's Graves*, might be well applied to this family, its branches were so numerous as not to be sensibly thinned by these losses; and it is still flourishing and prosperous. Charles Spencer Van Straubenzee died at Wakefield, Nov. 22nd, 1816, at the age of sixty-six.

---

(5) For a knowledge of this fact I am indebted to the Rev. T. B. Clarkson, who also informs me that the family of Straubenzee always considered themselves related to Bentinck, afterwards Earl of Portland, who came over with William iii.

DANIEL CRESSWELL.

This writer, whose works had sufficient scientific merit to procure him the title of F.R.S., was born in 1775. His father, of the same name, was a native of Crowden-le-Booth, in Edale, in the county of Derby; and after residing many years at Newton, near Wakefield, died Feb. 28th, 1821, and was buried in St. John's Churchyard.[1] Daniel Cresswell was educated at the Wakefield Grammar School, and proceeded from it as an exhibitioner to Trinity College, Cambridge, of which he subsequently became a Fellow. In 1797 he took his Bachelor's degree, his name appearing seventh in the list of Wranglers; and in 1798 gained one of the Members' Prizes. He resided many years in the University, filling the office of Proctor in 1813, and Taxor in 1814.[2] In December 1822 he was presented to the vicarage of Enfield,[3] one of the most valuable livings in the gift of his college; and in the year following was successively appointed a Justice of the Peace for the county of

---

(1) For this, and several other particulars in the above account, I am indebted to the kindness of Mr. T. H. Cromek.
(2) Le Neve's *Fasti Anglicani*, vol. iii.
(3) *Annual Register* for 1822.

Middlesex,[4] and elected a Fellow of the Royal Society, along with Professor Barlow.[5] In this latter year, 1823, he also took his degree of Doctor of Divinity. He married a Miss Thompson, of Enfield, who survived him, but left no issue. He himself died March 21st, 1844, at the age of sixty-nine.

He is the author of a treatise on *Linear Perspective*, and of various mathematical works, chiefly geometrical. He published also, in 1833, *Three Sermons on the perpetual obligation of keeping the Seventh Day Holy*, to which was appended one on *The Sin of Drunkenness*.

---

(4) *Gentleman's Magazine* for 1823, pt. ii., p. 463.
(5) *Gentleman's Magazine* for 1824, pt. i., p. 63.

MISS MANGNALL.

"In ladies', in commercial, and in national schools," complains the author of *Cambridge Life in the seventeenth century*,[1] "the want of fresh, genial class-books is yet more grievous. Schoolmasters and governesses, spell-bound by custom, continue to consume edition after edition of books from which nothing can be learnt, and wilfully stick to the old *mumpsimus*, when even the booksellers feel scruples about enriching themselves by its blunders. Professor De Morgan has told us that the proverbial 'Cocker' was as far behind his predecessors in knowledge, as he surpassed them in lasting popularity. Nor can we boast ourselves better than our fathers; for the eighteenth edition of Mangnall's 'Questions' has just been added to the stores of the University library."

The venerable schoolmistress alluded to in the above passage, Richmal Mangnall, resided for many years at Crofton Hall, near Wakefield; but of the year of her birth I am ignorant. Few particulars of her personal history seem to have been preserved; and she survives chiefly in those redoubtable *Questions*,

---

(1) Part ii (1856); Preface, p. xvii, and *n*.

which have been the pride and terror of several generations of school-girls. The circulation of that work has been immense. In 1815 it had reached a twelfth edition; and an impression printed at New York in 1857 is stated to be taken "from the eighty-fourth London edition." The last I have seen is one of the year 1860, which contains an engraved portrait of the authoress, dedicated to Alderman and Sheriff Rose. The work itself is dedicated to Neville Maskelyne, D.D., Astronomer Royal. In 1815 Miss Mangnall also published a *Compendium of Geography;* and in a notice of her death, which appeared in the *Gentleman's Magazine* for 1820, she is said to have written a volume of Poems, entitled *Leisure Hours*.[2] "These publications," the writer of that notice says, "will always remain monuments of the acuteness of her understanding, the extent of her research, and the amiable and attractive nature of her piety."

She died at Crofton Hall, May 1st, 1820, and lies buried in the churchyard there. In the *Wakefield and Halifax Journal* of May 12th following appeared a eulogy upon her, but containing little information beyond what her publications disclose.[3]

---

(2) Of this production of her pen I can find no trace. A little volume of poems, called *Leisure Hours*, was published anonymously at Boston, U.S.; but the date of it is 1826.—The short notice in the *Gentleman's Magazine* appears to have been carelessly composed, as it calls the place of her residence Crafton Hill.

(3) Mr. Clarkson has informed me that she was of Irish parentage on both sides; and that her somewhat singular first name was the result of an attempt to combine the christian names of her father and mother, Richard and Mary.—From an article which appeared in the *Manchester Guardian* of Jan. 23rd, 1858,

JOHN WROE.

As a place has been given in this series to James Nayler of Ardsley, it would not be right to leave unnoticed one whose fanaticism in some respects resembled his, and who was, like him, connected by residence with this town.

On the death of Joanna Southcott, December 27th, 1814, it might have been expected that her followers would have been awakened from their delusion; and that, when unimpeachable medical testimony declared the circumstances attending it,[1] they would have abandoned at once all the hopes and expectations she had raised in them. But such was not the case. There still remained a number of persons who professed to look for the speedy coming of a Millennium,

---

on the death of James Coppock, the well-known Parliamentary agent (kindly communicated to me by Mr. Ince), I learn that Miss Mangnall had a brother James, partner with Sir Richard Welsh, an eminent solicitor in the City of London, and another brother, Col. Kay Mangnall, who fell in the East Indies. Matilda Mangnall, a sister, married a Mr. Coppock, of Stockport, Cheshire, father to the James Coppock above-mentioned; while another sister, Eliza Mangnall (as Mr. Cromek informs me), died unmarried in London, April 5th, 1821. She had previously resided at Crofton Hall.

(1) See the *Sunday Monitor* of Jan. 1st, 1815; the *Times* of Jan. 2nd; and the *Morning Post* of Jan. 9th, in the same year.

and their acknowledged head was for a time George Turner. When he died, in the latter end of 1822, the subject of our present memoir succeeded in establishing his claim to be the recognised leader, or Prophet, of the sect calling themselves "Christian Israelites."

John Wroe was born at Bowling, a little village near Bradford, Sep. 19th, 1782, and baptized in the parish church of Bradford.[2] He was a weak sickly child, and for many years experienced unkind treatment from his father, a master collier and worsted stuff manufacturer. His grandfather, it was said, had predicted that "the Lord would raise up a priest of the fruit of his body;" and, in consequence, a younger brother, Thomas, had been named after his grandfather, and sent to various schools, with the intention that he should in time be ordained. But from the defects of speech to which he was subject, this design was abandoned. Meanwhile John received but little education. He attended a school at Bretton for a year, but made so little progress, that his master declared "he would learn nothing however long he stayed." Up to the age of twenty-four his father kept him hard at work in his own trade, refusing to admit him into partnership. At the end of that period he took a house for himself, and after five years more he married a daughter of Benjamin Appleby, of Farnley Mills, near Leeds. He was not very prosperous in business, the misconduct of an apprentice causing him severe losses. Towards

---

(2) *Divine Communications, &c., given to John Wroe* (Wakefield, 1834), from which the particulars that follow are principally taken.

the close of the year 1819, he was laid prostrate by a severe attack of fever, which reduced him to a mere skeleton. From this he recovered, so far as his bodily strength was concerned, but he did not regain his former cheerfulness of spirit. He tells us he was much agitated in mind. And one day, while rambling in a field, "a woman came unto me," he writes, "who tossed me up and down in the field. I strove to get hold of her, but got hold of nothing; therefore I knew it was a spirit. After this, being laid in my bed, I was struck blind and dumb. This was about two o'clock in the morning, Nov. 12th, 1819. The sun and the moon appeared to me: after that there appeared a very large piece of glass, and looking through it, I saw a very beautiful place, which I entered into...and there came an angel which was my guide, &c." After experiencing several of these trances, or visions (as he himself named them), he began to attend the meetings of the remnant before alluded to, as still adhering to the doctrines of Joanna Southcott. He did not, however, openly join himself to them, in consequence of an intimation given him in one of his visions, that "after travelling three years in England, he should be joined to the Lord's people," which people he at that time supposed to be the Jews.[3] During this interval he did not let his supposed gifts remain concealed. According to his own statement,[4] he stopped Queen Caroline, on her way from the House of Lords to Lady Hamilton's, Aug. 30th, 1820, and accosted her

---

(3) *An abridgement of John Wroe's Life and Travels* (Gravesend, 1851); vol. i, p. 13.

(4) *Divine Communications*, as above, p. 11.

as she was entering the residence of the latter. "I have a message unto thee, O Queen," his words were: "and she said, 'Unto me?'—throwing back her veil—and I said 'Aye!' And she walked aside into one of the passages, and I gave her a letter, and a copy of each of the books of visions: then I went away, and no one spoke to me."

On the death of George Turner, in 1822, he became recognised as the head of the Southcottians, though not without some little opposition. Hereupon he commenced a long course of travels in propagation of his doctrines. After holding a farewell meeting in Bradford, which began at midnight, and lasted thirty-six hours, he started for Gibraltar; and between that period, and the spring of 1824, when he returned to England, he visited many parts of Spain, Italy, and Germany. On Saturday, Aug. 30th, 1824, he was publicly baptized in the river Medlock, near Park Bridge, not far from Ashton; and again on Sunday Sep. 29th, in the Aire, a little above Apperley Bridge. On this latter occasion the newspapers stated that about 30,000 people were present. The crowd were inclined to handle Wroe and his companions very roughly, and cries of "Drown him!" were heard; but they managed to escape with no worse results than a few bruises from the stones flung at them. For some time after he led a vagrant sort of life, "subsisting," as he himself tells us, "for fourteen days on hips, nuts, blackberries, &c."

We need not attempt to follow him in his travels during the ensuing years. In 1827 we find him traversing Scotland, and in the year following,

Wales. On Sunday, April 10th, 1831, his meeting-house at Bradford was broken in upon by a mob, and he himself only escaped after having three ribs broken. In 1834 he resided chiefly at Wakefield, where he published the volume of *Divine Communications* already referred to. A copy of this book he sent to William the Fourth in the year following; and we also read of him, about the same time, forwarding his pamphlets to "friend Morpeth," and predicting the success of the latter in his contest for the West Riding against the Hon. J. Stuart Wortley. Subsequently he extended his travels to America and Australia, where he appears to have had better success than he had met with in Europe. Writing to his wife from Sydney, Dec. 12th, 1850, he says:—"When I landed at Geelong, it was said there were more spectators than there were at the Governor's arrival at Melbourne. A large body of friends, drest in their best clothing, were ready to receive me; and in the place where I stood up, there were hundreds who could not get in."

Becoming now advanced in years, he returned to England, and settled in his native county; and on Whitsunday, 1857, there was formally opened, in presence of a motley assemblage of his followers from all quarters, a large and handsome stone building, at Wrenthorpe near Wakefield, as a residence for the head of the "Christian Israelites."[6] Here he remained

---

(6) Some severe comments on this proceeding having appeared in the *Leeds Times* of June 6th and 20th, 1857, a *Copy of a Letter addressed to the Editor* was printed at Gravesend in 1858, in answer to those strictures. The letter was signed by Frederick Thomas, Thomas Gwynne, Daniel Milton, and Julius Wiele;

undisturbed, with the exception of a rival claimant appearing in the person of Daniel Milton,[7] until 1863, when he undertook another voyage to Australia, and died at Melbourne, in the spring of 1864. It was some time before his followers at home would admit the reality of his death.

Wroe's writings being mainly filled with prophecies and their alleged fulfilment, it is difficult to collect from them any clear summary of the opinions he held. Of the predictions themselves a single specimen will be considered enough. When preaching to a large congregation in a field at Ashton, April 18th, 1824, he declared that "a light should break forth out of that place where he stood, which should enlighten the whole town; with a light also to enlighten the Gentiles." "This actually occurred," he adds, "within some years after, by the erection of the gas-house, and part of an edifice connected therewith being converted into a Methodist chapel." The following outline of the tenets of the sect, taken from an authority acknowledged by themselves to be impartial,[8] may serve to complete this sketch. After stating that its members

---

and was dated New York, Sep. 25th, 1857. It commences with:—"On Whitsunday of 1857, a number of delegates and members from many nations assembled at Melbourne House, near Wakefield, Yorkshire, England, to celebrate the yearly festival according to the usages of the Christian Israelite Church."

(7) The same who signed the *Letter* above referred to.—He renewed his attempts soon after Wroe's death; and on Dec. 14th, 1863, was sentenced by the magistrates at Wakefield to fourteen days' imprisonment, for defacing the property of Melbourne House.—See the Wakefield *Journal and Examiner* of Dec. 18th, 1863.

(8) New York *Daily Times* of March 25th, 1854, quoted in the *Copy of a Letter* before-mentioned.

are literally circumcised, the writer says:—"The doctrines held by the Christian Israelites are, that the Scriptures of the Old and New Testaments are the revealed word of God: that there was a time when man enjoyed this earth in perfect felicity; the brute creation being in perfect harmony: that man transgressed and fell, but that a church has ever held the faith delivered to the Saints of the earth's regeneration: that, on the first and great transgression, woman alone charged it to Satan, and exonerated her God: therefore, the work of redemption was to be performed by God and the woman; and that the women were the first commissioned to preach a risen Saviour; and that it was revealed to Joel that woman should proclaim the truth in the latter days: . . . that the return of the Son of Man is yet future, but nigh at hand: . . . that the spirit of truth has yet its greatest work to perform, in preparing a church to meet the Lord at his coming, by unfolding those scriptures which are at present sealed from the understanding: that the spirit of prophecy still exists: that Jesus will come again, and reign a thousand years, accompanied by the resurrection of the pious dead and departed worthies: . . . that the church which shall meet the Lord at his coming, will be neither Jew nor Gentile, but the true Israel of God, the sealed church, the hundred and forty-four thousand; and that the world has been warned by a visitation from heaven, in prophecy, to prepare for Christ's second coming, ever since 1792;[9] . . . and that the revelations of John Wroe, in respect to the will of God, and the interpretation of his word, are of heavenly origin."

---

[9] The year in which Joanna Southcott "opened her commission" in Exeter.—See Fairbairn's *Life of Joanna Southcott.*

THOMAS D'OYLY.

This brave soldier, whose tragical end excited much interest and sympathy at the time, was born at "The Lodge" at Heath,[1] near Wakefield, July 12th, 1794. He was twin son with Edward of Edward D'Oyly, Esq., who had married Miss Hannah Marston, of Thorpe-on-the-Hill. Thomas D'Oyly, when he grew up, entered the East India Company's service, and became a captain in the Bengal artillery. About the year 1819, he married in India a relation by the father's side, Charlotte Williams. They lived for some years in the enjoyment of East Indian opulence, at Dumdum, near Calcutta, Captain D'Oyly holding several lucrative

---

(1) See *The Topographer and Genealogist* (1853), vol. ii, p. 21; from which these particulars are taken. The correction of "The Lodge" at Heath for "Newton Lodge" (which appears in the text) is given in a note on *p.* 89 of the *Supplement.*

A notice of the Heath, written at the time of D'Oyly's birth, shews us that it was then as now famed for its beauty. Dr. Aikin, in his *Description of the country from thirty to forty miles round Manchester* (1795), p. 580, speaks of "the village of Heath, reckoned one of the most beautiful in England . . . . The village is built by the side of a green, the houses being all of stone found on the spot. Of these the principal are those of the late Sir G. Dalston, now Mr. Dillon's, built in the reign of Queen Elizabeth; of John Smyth, Esq., one of the lords of the treasury; and of Mrs. Smith and Mrs. Hopkinson."—In Gough's *Camden* also (1789, vol. iii., p. 39) it is spoken of as "the delightful village of Heath, which, for situation, gives place to few in the kingdom."

employments. Towards the latter end of 1828, or the beginning of 1829, he sent his two elder boys to his brother-in-law, Mr. Bayley, to be educated in England. Not long after, finding that his health was suffering from the heat of the climate, he went with his wife and younger sons to Sydney in Australia. But hearing that the Delhi Magazine appointment had been bestowed upon him, he hastened to return to India; and unfortunately, in his desire to lose no time, took a passage with his family in the "Charles Eaton." That ill-fated ship never reached its destination. It was wrecked, in August, 1834, on a coral reef in Torres Straits; and the crew and passengers, including himself, his wife, and third son, were massacred by the savages inhabiting the islands there. For a long time their fate was unknown, and it might have remained so, but for the unremitting exertions of Mr. Bayley. His applications to Government being seconded by Sir Charles D'Oyly and Major Twemlow, in India, the schooner "Isabella" was dispatched in search of them. The rest of the narrative we will give in the words of a relation, William D'Oyly Bayley.[2] "To be brief, it was ascertained that the 'Charles Eaton' had been wrecked in the Torres Straits, in August, 1834; and that, with the exception of five sailors who escaped in a boat to Batavia, and the two boys presently mentioned, Captain D'Oyly, his wife and third son, with all the crew and passengers, had been murdered and devoured by the cannibal savages.

---

(2) *A Biographical Account of the house of D'Oyly* (1845), p. 155.

With the intention of adopting them, the wretches had spared from the general massacre a cabin boy named Ireland, and Captain D'Oyly's youngest child, an infant of three years of age: and these were discovered on Murray's Island in the Straits, having resided with the savages not less than two years. Both were of course ransomed, and eventually brought to England. Mrs. D'Oyly's skull was found adorning a temple of the savages on the island of Aureed in the Straits; and, with many similar relics, was conveyed to Sydney, Nov., 1836, where they received the rites of christian burial, and a monument was erected recording the event. Mr. Bayley employed the celebrated marine painter, Carmichael, to execute two very fine pictures; one of the wreck of the 'Charles Eaton,' and the other of the redemption of his nephew: both of which are now in his possession. Five narratives of the event were published: the first by the Rev. Thomas Wemyss; the second by Mr. Brockett, of Newcastle; the third by Captain Lewis; the fourth by John Ireland, the redeemed cabin-boy; and another in The *Dissenter* Magazine. . . . . Captain D'Oyly was forty years of age when his tragical end took place. He was a sensible and upright man, prudent from his earliest childhood; a clever artist; a fine soldier; and of a tall handsome person."[3]

---

(3) The history of several members of this family is an eventful one. Edward, twin brother to Captain D'Oyly, was drowned, at the age of thirteen, in the wreck of the "Jane, Duchess of Gordon," off the Isle of France. Their father, who had been brought up with his grandmother, Mrs. Black, at Lofthouse, was married, whilst still a minor, and an undergraduate of Trinity

EDWARD MOXON.

"Died, June 3rd, 1858, at Putney-heath, Surrey, Edw. Moxon, Esq."—Such is the brief memento in the *Gentleman's Magazine* of the death of one, with whom this series may fitly close, as being a fair specimen of those shrewd, energetic Yorkshiremen—those "masterly Yorkshiremen," as the Bishop of Oxford calls them,—who, with no advantages of birth or fortune, and but few of education, have made their way to wealth and influence, and sometimes to fame. As no better sketch of his career can be given, than one which appeared in the *Illustrated London News* of June 12th, 1858,[1] I will quote it at length:—

College, Cambridge, to Miss Hannah Marston, also a minor, to keep him from going to sea. Their grandfather, also named Edward D'Oyly, who had been successively purser, chief mate, and captain of an East Indiaman, eloped into Scotland with Anna Maria, daughter of Mr. Jonathan Black, a London brewer in large business. As she was in her minority, and expectant heiress to large property, this was much resented by her friends. The young couple were parted by force, and he sailed away to India. But on his wife proving with child, her parents changed their mind, and the two were re-married on D'Oyly's return from India, Oct. 5th, 1768, at St. Mary Magdalen's, Bermondsey. Old Mrs. Black, on her husband's death, settled at Lofthouse, and died there in March, 1795, aged 86.—See p. 137, &c. of the *Biographical Account* above quoted.

(1) Copied into the *Leeds Intelligencer* of June 19th; from which I extract it.

"Edward Moxon, of Dover Street, the poet's publisher, the Dodsley of his day, was buried on Wednesday last in Wimbledon churchyard. He was a clever man, and wrote good verses:—better than other poetic publishers, such as Humphrey of Moseley, of King Charles the First's time, and Robert Dodsley, of the Augustan age of George the Second. Mr. Moxon was a native of Wakefield in Yorkshire;[2] took to books when very young; and evinced early in life such a taste for the trade and the Row, that his father found means to give him the Harrow and Eton education of an apprenticeship under the great house of Messrs. Longman and Rees. He was soon actively noticed among his fellow apprentices; and not a few foretold what a great publisher was to be seen in the hard-working lad from Wakefield in Yorkshire. It was observed of him even thus early that he had a poetic tendency; that he had greater pleasure in selling Southey's *Thalaba* than Southey's *History of Brazil*. He caught the poetic fever at once; wrote sonnets, and imagined epics; and, before his time was out, was a poet in print. Leaving Longman's, he went to the house of Hurst and Co., where he formed the valuable acquaintance of Mr. Evans, of the deservedly well-known firm of Bradbury and Evans. Other advantages

---

(2) I do not know the exact year of his birth, but it was probably about 1800. The Rev. T. B. Clarkson has kindly ascertained for me, from Mr. Cryer, of Wakefield, who knew the family, that Edward Moxon, after being educated at the Green-coat school, was apprenticed to a bookseller in the town, named Smith; from whose service he proceeded to London. A brother of his also went to London, from the Wakefield Post-Office; whilst a third brother rose to be a barrister of standing, and enjoyed the friendship of S. T. Coleridge.

soon followed. Verse introduced him to Charles Lamb; a Dedication introduced him to Samuel Rogers. He was now on the pinnacle of success: others sought his acquaintance; and he became a publisher on his own account. He put small savings into a weekly paper, that should not have died in its sixth or seventh number, called *The Reflector;* and he threw other savings into a better speculation, that died too early, called *The Englishman's Magazine.* His Yorkshire caution was too great for him. He withdrew from both publications; and was more content with seeking hundreds from certainties, than thousands from uncertainties. In the case of the Magazine, he made a mistake; and he was magnanimous enough (for a publisher) to acknowledge his mistake. Charles Lamb and Samuel Rogers started him in business; and his first shop was in New Bond Street, over against (if we mistake not) the great shop of Giblet, the purveyor of unintellectual but most necessary food. Rogers removed his illustrated *Italy* from the long-established house in the Row, and gave it to the clever apprentice newly started in New Bond Street. Authors flocked about him: better still, at such a time, lords and ladies drew up at the door, and bought and paid. He was now an established publisher; gave occasional dinners; and found well-known writers to accept his invitations. His first remunerating author, after Rogers, was Sheridan Knowles, then in the full blaze of his well-earned reputation. A play by Knowles put money into Moxon's purse; and, forgetting his Yorkshire caution, he ventured on his great move in life, and left a shop in New Bond Street for a private house in Dover Street. His success dates from this period. Authors of name sought his acquaintance. The elder Disraeli carried his *Curiosities of Literature* to his house; Barry Cornwall carried his songs; Allan Cunningham went with a rustic epic; Fanny Burney, in Rogers's carriage, left her father's *Memoirs;* Rogers took his second illustrated volume; and Charles Lamb gave, with his own hand, his ward in wedlock to the poet-publisher. Others soon followed; of whom Forster, the able author of the *Life of Goldsmith*, and of two volumes of *Essays*, was a most valuable friend. Then came Tennyson, and Monckton Milnes; and ere long Dover-street was looked upon as a rival (which it never was) to the adjoining Albemarle-street."

To the above account nothing need be added, beyond a few particulars regarding his poems, and his connection with Charles Lamb. His first publication was *The Prospect, and other Poems*, which appeared in 1826, dedicated to Samuel Rogers. In the *Preface* to it he thus seeks to disarm the critic:—" In the first place, it is the production of a very young man, unlettered, self-taught, ignorant of every language except his native tongue, and even imperfect in that, as he is afraid the following production will too evidently prove. . . . From little more than twelve years of age, to the present time, it has been his lot to be daily occupied from morning until evening in laborious employment; nor has he received any instruction since that period. . . The only time, in which he could indulge in his favourite recreation, was on a Sunday morning, or during the still more solemn hours of midnight." The sonnet immediately following *The*

Prospect is headed, "To the Rev. J. L. S.,[3] with the foregoing Poem;" and begins thus:—

> "My worthy, reverend, trusty friend,
>   'Tis far from me to teaze ye;
> At least what now I greeting send,
>   I hope, in sooth, will please ye.
>
> "'Tis not a poem with learning fraught,
>   To that I ne'er pretended;
> Nor yet with Pope's fine touches wrought,
>   From that my time prevented."

The unconscious vanity, which betrays itself in this last line, afforded a good handle for a somewhat satirical review of the second edition of Moxon's sonnets, which appeared in the *Quarterly*.[4] "This is quite a dandy of a book," the writer begins:— "Some seventy pages of drawing-paper, fifty-five of which are impressed each with a single sonnet in all the luxury of type, while the rest are decked out with

---

(3) I believe I am not mistaken in supposing this to indicate the Rev. Joseph Lawson Sisson, D.D., an early friend and encourager of Moxon's, and my own precursor both in the second mastership of the Wakefield Grammar School, and in this attempt to illustrate the antiquities of Wakefield. From the Rev. T. B. Clarkson I learn that he was born at Leeds, and educated in the Grammar School there, from which he proceeded to Clare College, Cambridge. He took his degree of B.A. in 1810, M.A. in 1814, and D.D. in 1827. In 1824, when he published his *Historic Sketch of the Parish Church of Wakefield*, he was Sunday evening Reader at that Church, as well as second master in the Grammar School. About ten years afterwards, he became curate of Duntsbourn Abbotts, Cirencester; and in 1843 was appointed to the perpetual curacy of Coleford near Newland, in the diocese of Gloucester and Bristol. Besides the work above-mentioned, he has published, at various times, *An Anglo-Saxon Grammar; Questions in Divinity;* and *Questions on Confirmation.*—Should these pages meet his eye, I trust he will pardon this passing mention of him.

(4) Vol. lix., p. 209.

vignettes of nymphs in clouds and bowers, and cupids in rose-bushes and cockle-shells. And all these coxcombries are the appendages of, as it seems to us, as little intellect as the rings and brooches of the exquisite in a modern novel."

The Prospect, &c. was followed, in 1829, by *Christmas, a Poem*, dedicated to Charles Lamb; and in 1830 and 1835 appeared the first and second parts of his *Sonnets*, inscribed respectively to his brother William and to Wordsworth. In Lamb the poet found a kindlier critic. "Mary is of opinion with me," he writes in one of his letters to Moxon,[5] "that two of these sonnets are of a higher grade than any poetry you have done yet. The one to Emma is so pretty! I have only allowed myself to transpose a word in the third line. Sacred shall it be from any intermeddling of mine. But we jointly beg that you will make four lines in room of the four last. . . . The next best is *The Ocean*:—

> 'Ye gallant winds, if e'er your lusty cheeks
> Blew longing lover to his mistress' side,
> O! puff your loudest, spread the canvass wide,'

is spirited."

The Emma alluded to above was Emma Isola, the adopted daughter of Charles Lamb, with whose name every reader of his *Letters* is familiar. An attachment sprang up between her and Edward Moxon, and forms the subject of many of his sonnets. To a present of a watch, sent by him to Miss Isola, Lamb thus play-

---

(5) *Final Memorials of Charles Lamb*, by Talfourd (1848), vol. ii, p. 101.

fully alludes :[6]—"She has spoiled some of the movements. Between ourselves she has kissed away 'half-past twelve,' which I suppose to be the canonical hour in Hanover Square." They were married July 30th, 1833.

St. George's Church, Hanover Square, may seem an unusual resting-place at which to leave off the Life of Edward Moxon, after commencing with his epitaph; and still more unusual, that a book, whose beginning was "bald with dry antiquity," should presume to end, like the orthodox novel, with a wedding. But so it is:

"So runs the round of life from hour to hour."

A wedding is at any rate the half-way house on life's road; and at a half-way house of some kind or other the author must needs part company with his subject. For, whether he bring this book to a close a few pages sooner or later, he will be equally far from having come to an end of the Wakefield Worthies.

---

(6) *Final Memorials, &c.*, vol. ii, p. 95.

APPENDIX.

APPENDIX.

Page 1, Note 1.

[*Derivation of the Name Wakefield.*]

The etymology, referred to in the note, is one which would make Wakefield to have been so called from its being the place in which some *Wakes*, or feasts at the dedication of churches, had been anciently held. Whatever may be thought of this opinion, which is certainly ingenious, the credit of it is due to Mr. J. Hewitt, who has propounded it in his *History and Topography of the Parish of Wakefield*, p. 16. I shall content myself, therefore, with adducing a few authorities in support of it.

When Mellitus, afterwards Bishop of London and Primate, and who died in 624, was departing for this country, Gregory the Great addressed to him a letter of instructions, for his better success in spreading christianity among the Britons. In it he writes:—
"When therefore Almighty God shall bring you to the most reverend Bishop Augustine, our brother, tell him

what I have, upon mature deliberation on the affair of the English, determined upon; namely, that the temples of the idols in that nation ought not to be destroyed; but let the idols that are in them be destroyed; let holy water be made and sprinkled in the said temples; let altars be erected, and relics placed. For, if those temples are well built, it is requisite that they should be converted from the worship of devils to the service of the true God; that the nation, seeing that their temples are not destroyed, may remove error from their hearts, and, knowing and adoring the true God, may the more familiarly resort to the places to which they have been accustomed. And because they have been used to slaughter many oxen in the sacrifices to devils, some solemnity must be exchanged for them on this account; as that on the day of the dedication, or the nativities of holy martyrs, *they may build themselves huts of the boughs of trees, about those churches which have been turned to that use from temples*, and celebrate the solemnity with religious feasting, and no more offer beasts to the devil, but kill cattle to the praise of God in their eating, and return thanks to the Giver of all things for their sustenance; to the end that, whilst some gratifications are outwardly permitted them, they may the more easily consent to the inward consolations of the grace of God. For there is no doubt that it is impossible to efface everything at once from their obdurate minds." (Bede: *Ecclesiastical History*, translated by Dr. Giles, 1840, bk. i., ch. 30). The bearing of the words which I have put in Italics upon the origin of the name "Goody Bower," to which Mr. Hewitt calls attention, will be seen at once. To the same purpose is a passage quoted by Sir William Dugdale (*Antiquities of Warwickshire*, 1730, vol. ii., p. 681) from an old manuscript legend of St. John the Baptist; a fuller version of which is given in Strutt (*Horda Angel-Cynnan*, 1776, vol. iii., p. 178):—"And ye shall understond and know how the *Evyns* were first found in old time. In the beginning of holi Chirche it was so that the pepull cam to the chirch with candellys brennyng, and wold *wake*, and coome with light toward night to the chirche in their devocions; and aftir, they fell to lecherie and songs, daunses, harping, piping, and also to glotonye and sinne, and so turned the holinesse to cursydnes: wherefore holy faders ordeined the pepull to leve that *waking*, and to fast the *evyn*. But hit is callyd *Vigilia*, that is *waking* in English; and it is callyd the *evyn*, for at *evyn* they were wont to come to chirche." From this and other testimonies Dugdale concludes that "there is no doubt to be made, but that such solemnities of the church's dedication were no less antient than the primitive times of christianity" (p. 682).

These ceremonies, from which it is thought our town received its name, must not be confounded with the *lyke-wakes* or watches for the dead on the eve of burial. The latter also are very ancient, and are alluded to by Chaucer in his *Knight's Tale*, where, as Tyrwhitt observes, he seems to have confused them with the funeral games of the Greeks:—

> "Ne how Arcite is brent to ashen cold,
> Ne how the *liche-wake* was yhold
> All thilke night, ne how the Grekes play
> The *wake-plaies*, ne kepe I not to say."

The analogy of *Lichfield* may possibly lend some confirmation to this view of the derivation of *Wakefield*. For though authorities are not agreed on the meaning of the name (see Harwood's *History and Antiquities of Lichfield*, 1806, p. 1), still a comparison of *lich-gate* seems to support the derivation given by Johnson, and alluded to in the city's coat of arms, that it is "the field of the dead," so called from the christians martyred there.

Of course, this view of the matter supposes a church, or christian centre of some kind, to have been established on the spot, before it obtained the name of Wakefield; a presumption which (as far as I am aware) we have no evidence either for or against. If indeed the supposition (to be mentioned hereafter) that Low Hill is a Druidical remain, should ever receive confirmation, then it would be by no means incredible, that Paulinus, as he went along the valley of the Calder from Dewsbury, or some other early missionary of christianity, caused some temple in the neighbourhood to be converted into a church, and that a *wake* and its *wake-field* thus arose.

Page 19.

[*On the Italian origin of the Saviles.*]

The Italian family alluded to by Cooper is that of the Savelli; one of whom, singularly enough, I find to have held ecclesiastical preferment in Yorkshire, early in the fourteenth century. When Edward ii. wrote to

Pope Clement v., on the death of Archbishop Greenfield in 1315, to recommend William de Melton for the see of York, "his wishes were thwarted by some *attachés* of the papal court, among whom may be mentioned Pandulph de Savelli, George de Poregia, and Francis Gaetano, all of whom were beneficed in Yorkshire, and had some grudge, in all probability, against the archbishop elect."—Raine's edition of Dixon's *Fasti Eboracenses* (1863), vol. i, p. 400.

Cooper's opinion, however, is supported by that of Hunter :—"Writers of reputation have ventured to assert for the Saviles a descent from the Savelli, an Italian family; but this is, probably, little more than a piece of genealogical flattery. At any rate, no evidence has been given. The family, like most others of those which are now accounted the best and most ancient families in England, began early with small possessions, probably in the parish of Silkston."—*Antiquarian notices of Lupset, &c.* (1851), p. 14.

Page 23, n. 2.

[*Henry de Wakefield.*]

In the *Issue Roll of Thomas de Brantingham*, and in the *Issues of the Exchequer*, edited by Frederick Devon, in 1835 and 1837, frequent mention is made of Henry de Wakefeld, who is there described as "Keeper of the King's wardrobe." Beyond this fact, the entries supply no information about Bishop Wakefield's history, and so a single extract will suffice as a sample :—

"22nd September [48 Edward iii.]—To Henry de Wakefield, keeper of the King's wardrobe, by the hands of William Strete, the King's butler. In money paid to John Oetanebroke, for one cask of vinegar purchased from the said John, to be expended in the King's household, £2 13*s*. 4*d*."

Page 41, n. 3.

[*Collar of Esses.*]

Eccleston (*Introduction to English Antiquities*, 1847, p. 216) assigns a different origin to this symbol. Speaking of the reigns of Henry iv. and v., he says :— "The collar of S.S. is first seen on monuments of this period, and is traced, with some probability, to the initial letter of Henry ivth's motto,—*Souveraine.*"

Page 43, n. 6.

[*Low Hill.*]

About the meaning to be attached to the word "Low," most people, I suppose, are agreed. Thus Thoresby, when speaking of Harelow-hill, says that it is "another instance of the superfluous addition of *hill* to *low*, which is of the same signification: Hare-low, in the language of our Saxon predecessors, was the *Soldiers'-hill*, or the *Hill of the Army*, as Harewich an

Haven or *Bay* where an *army* might lie." (*Ducatus*, p. 143). And the writer of the article in the *Saturday Review* referred to, which (as I only saw it when correcting the proof-sheet) I had not space to quote at length, says that "even where the mound is no longer visible, the name 'Low,' from the Saxon *hlæw*, or barrow, shows that some notable cairn or artificial mound formerly existed." (p. 654). Taking this for granted, what now are we to suppose the origin of the mound in question to have been? Leland, as we see, had met with a tradition, in Henry viiith's time, that it was once the site of a castle; and in another passage he mentions it more particularly:—"A quarter of a mile withowte Wakefeld apperith an hille of erth caste up, wher sum say that one of Erles Warines began to build, and as fast as he buildid violence of winde defacid the work. This is like a fable. Sum say it was nothing but a wind-mille hille. The place is now caullid Lohille." (*Itinerary*, 1745, vol. i., p. 43.) On this Dr. Whitaker remarks,—"Traditions, however ancient, are rarely without a foundation; and though I agree with Leland, in the improbability that a castle begun by the Earl of Warren on this site was abandoned in consequence of its exposure to winds, I accept the report as evidence that a castle was once begun on this elevated ground; though, from its general appearance, corroborated by the tradition that it was the antagonist of the Saxon fort at Horbury" (of which remains are said to be still visible near the mill) "I should consider the earthwork of older date." (*Loidis and Elmete*, p. 292). Whitaker's opinion, it thus appears, is in favour of the mound having been raised for military purposes. And akin to this is the judgment formed by Watson. After alluding to the improbable tradition, that one of the batteries employed in the siege of Sandal Castle was stationed on it, he adds:—" This Lowe Hill may have originally been a work of the Romans, as the great military way between York and Manchester lay under it. At present it has the appearance of a Danish mount, surrounded with a double ditch, having also a piece of fortified ground, on that side where the approach was easiest. If a watch-tower has been here, it probably gave name to the adjoining town of Wakefield, called in Domesday Book Wachefeld." (*Memoirs of the Earls of Warren*, vol. ii., p. 21). The remaining notion, mentioned by Leland, that it was nothing but a wind-mill hill, scarcely deserves attention; for though a wind-mill may possibly have stood upon it, at some period of its existence, it is inconceivable that any one should have been at the pains of raising such an intrenched mound for this purpose, when there were natural eminences in the neighbourhood that would have served as well. A better-grounded opinion, in my judgment, than any of these, is one communicated to me by Mr. Thos. Taylor, of Wakefield. From an inspection of the extensive platform on the north-east of the hill, he considers it likely that it was used for Druidical ceremonies.

Having now set down all the conclusions, which I find others to have arrived at on the subject, I will, with much diffidence, offer a suggestion of my own, namely, that it is a sepulchral mound, and probably of British origin. In the first place, the name affords a presumption of this. Though a *Low-hill*, as the reader may have inferred from the passage of Thoresby above-quoted, does not necessarily imply a funeral mound, or barrow, yet there is no doubt that, in the great majority of instances, the name is found to be so applied. In a very interesting article on the *Notices of heathen interment in the Codex Diplomaticus*, by J. M. Kemble (*Archæological Journal*, vol. xiv., p. 124), it is said that "although the word *hlæw*, still called *low* in some parts of England, may have a more general sense of *hill*, or a slight rise in the surface of the soil, yet its usual and proper meaning is also that of a barrow for sepulchral purposes." He instances the frequent mention of *hlæws* in the Codex, for the purpose of marking the boundaries of estates, as in the case of Linchlade in Buckinghamshire, where the line in drawn "from the tree to the midmost low, along the street; from the low along the street to the seven lows; from the seven lows to the solitary low:" and adds, "it is very evident that this is a group of barrows, not by any means a set of natural hills, especially as they lie upon the side of a road or way." The researches carried on in all parts of the country, of late years, of which a record is preserved in the various publications of our antiquarian societies, have shewn the great extent to which this practice of barrow interment at some former period prevailed. That it is not to be ascribed to the Danes, is made apparent by the arguments of Douglas (*Nenia Britannica*, 1793, p. 153): for they, he says, "from the nature of their inroads into Britain, and from their sudden conversion to Christianity on their conquest of the island, would not have adopted such a general custom of interment on our waste lands, as we find the remains of at this day." That some of the barrows, at least, are older than the time of the Roman occupation of this country, is manifest from such circumstances as that pointed out by Sir R. C. Hoare (*Ancient Wiltshire*, vol. ii., p. 39), in the case of the Roman road at Lower Pertwood, which passes over the base of an ancient barrow. And King (*Munimenta Antiqua*, 1799, vol. i., p. 267), says distinctly that the Romans "do not seem to have raised any barrows at all; except in a few instances, after great battles." After shewing, from various authorities, that the Celtic race did practise such barrow-interment, this writer concludes that "there is very great reason to believe, that almost all (the barrows) that we have in this island are *British;* and that even those that were heaped up in Roman times, and where Roman insignia have been found, were the sepultures, not of Romans, but of British officers or chieftains in Roman service." Assuming now that the ancient Britons adopted this mode of burial, whilst in their pagan state, we might expect that some traces of such funeral mounds would exist in a district so fertile, and therefore so likely to be inhabited, as this part of the vale of the Calder. Nor, when Christianity was introduced, would the old custom be discontinued. "The earliest Christians," says Kemble, in the article before cited, "buried beyond a doubt, where the earliest Pagans had deposited the burnt remains of their dead. They still desired to rest among those whom they had loved, or from whom they were sprung." (*p.* 125.) When the Romans had departed, and the heathen Saxons were overrunning the country, they would naturally appropriate the burying-places found existing; and so it might easily come to pass, that a mound should become the last resting place of many generations, British and Anglo-Saxon, and be known as the *Low* of a neighbouring hamlet. This will be more readily assented to, when we remember that "nearly a century and a half elapsed, after the second introduction of Christianity into this island under the Saxons, before burial-places were made around the churches within towns. This was done under the authority of Cuthbert, Archbishop of Canterbury, in 742; though perhaps, in Northumbria, not till a somewhat later period." (*Archæological Journal*, vol. vi., p. 125). A case in point is that of Lamel-hill, near York, the excavation of which is described in the volume of the *Archæological Journal* just quoted. It appears to have been not dissimilar to Low-hill, as regards size, its base being about 375 feet in circumference, and the numerous remains which it contained shewed it to have been a perfect cemetery.

This note has already extended to an inordinate length, but I will insert one more extract from the article by Kemble above referred to. After describing what appears to have been a common mode of barrow interment (namely, burning the body first in a trough of loose stones), and inferring that "the Anglo-Saxons used the stone kists which they found erected by elder races, or which perhaps they erected themselves for this purpose," he subjoins :—" It is probable that they heated the stones with light burning wood, *especially thorn*, and that they placed the body in the kist, and so reduced it to ashes." It may be thought very fanciful to found any argument on the words which I have put in italics; but it is at least noticeable that Low-hill stands on the verge of a district where the wood in question would be found in abundance. For I suppose that the village of Thornes, after the analogy of the ancient Acanthus, took its name from the hawthorn (the *hæg-thorn* of the Anglo-Saxon); the former prevalence of which in that neighbourhood is testified by the relics still left standing.

Page 44.

[*Streets of Wakefield.*]

The statement in the text is probably too close a limitation of the extent of the town in Leland's time. Whitaker, speaking of the state of Leeds in the Conqueror's reign, says "Whatever streets do not bear the Saxon name of Gate, were then, if anything, lanes in the fields; and this rule restricts the original Leeds to Briggate, Kirkgate and Swinegate." (*Loidis and Elmete*, p. 6.) Conversely, we must suppose that such streets, at any rate, as now retain this name, were to be found in the period referred to. This will add Northgate, Southgate, and the little passage called Marygate, to the list. Hunter, in his *South Yorkshire*, vol. ii., p. 145, speaking of the branch of the Savile family by whom the Grammar School was established, describes them as "of North Gate head, or Haselden Hall in Wakefield." If that old burgage house, built in Elizabeth's time, was known also by the name of

North Gate Head," we may conclude that, in the previous period under consideration, no houses north of it had arisen.

Page 87.

[*Ejected Ministers.*]

After giving the names of those Nonconformist ministers in the neighbourhood of Wakefield, who suffered by the Act of 1662, it would scarcely be just to omit one who had been a previous sufferer on the other side. I allude to James Lister, who was appointed Vicar of Wakefield, Aug. 15th, 1625, and died in January, 1677. The following is the account given of him in Walker's *Sufferings of the Clergy* (1714), p. 300 :—" At the Restoration he was invited to return to his former station, from whence he was expelled before the Martyrdom, and the living afterwards usurped by Mr. W——. Mr Lister was often in danger of his life while he staid at Wakefield. The ordinances of Parliament at that time coming thick one after another, rendered his staying with his flock impossible, who loved him universally all the time of the anarchy. He was plundered, sequestered, and suffered all the hardships of a vagabond for some years. His temporal estate was good ; and, sequestered as it was, he made a shift to live without alms where he could privately, till it pleased God to inspire Colonel Bramley, that married my lady Hopton, to take him into the competent living of Leathley ; which yet was so little, that it tempted not the enemy to meddle with him he living very privately and sparingly all the time, till, with joy and satisfaction of the inhabitants of Wakefield, he was called home to his own.—' He was a man of excellent learning, exemplary piety, and a popular preacher.'"

Sisson (*Historic Sketch*, p. 80) quotes from the Parish Register of 1630 a licence, signed by Lister, authorising a person to eat meat during Lent, and at other times of fasting, "by reason of her olde age, and many yeares, and stubborne and long continued sicknesse."

Page 114.

[*Radcliffe's Bequests.*]

To the bequests of Dr. Radcliffe here cited, should be added that of the house in which he was born, alluded to in the beginning of the article. This, Mr. Clarkson informs me, was bequeathed in augmentation of the living of East Ardsley, to which it still belongs. Mr Thos. Taylor, of Wakefield, has also made known to me, that in 1801 the trustees under Dr. Radcliffe's will gave £1,000 to the trustees of St. John's Church.

Page 207.

[*John Burton, M.D.*]

Though not yet able to prove that this antiquary was, as Bigland asserts, a native of Wakefield, I have obtained several particulars which show him to have been closely connected with the neighbourhood.

From an obliging communication sent to me by the present Vicar of Warmfield, the Rev. John Pullein, I learn that Dr. Burton's mother was Margaret, daughter of the Rev. John Leake, many years Vicar of that parish. The Rector of All Saints, Colchester, kindly informs me, that in the register of that church is an entry of her burial there, Jan. 22nd, 1712; and also of the baptism of two children, Christopher and Elizabeth. Neither there nor at Kirkthorp is there any record preserved of the baptism of John Burton.; but Mr. Cryer assures me, (through the Rev. T. B. Clarkson,) that he was undoubtedly born at Heath. John Burton, sen., Esq., after his wife's death removed to York, where he died, but was buried at Kirkthorp, April 13th, 1743. On the death of his maternal grandfather, the Vicar of Warmfield, Dr. John Burton erected a monument to his memory in Kirkthorp church, the inscription on which is as follows :—

"Here lieth
the body of the ancient and venerable
clergyman, Mr. John Leake: after 56
years constant residence, he died upon
this his Vicarage, Feb. 10th, 1740,
in the 89th year of his age.
A long time to live, but longer
still to maintain so excellent a
reputation, as endeared him ever
to his flock,
who loved him when alive,
and now mourn him dead.
Tho' he boasted not that sort of merit
which leads to Preferment, he
abounded notwithstanding in all such
qualities as distinguished him for
an honest man and a good Christian.
John Burton, M.B., M.D.,
in memory of so worthy a person
as was this his grandfather,
caused this small monument
to be erected."

Page 215.

[Daniel Cresswell.]

Previous to this *Life* should have been inserted a notice of Richard Linnecar, whose name and writings were unknown to me, till pointed out by the kindness of Mr. Ince. He published by subscription, in 1789, a volume of miscellanies, containing two comedies, *The Lucky Escape* and *The Plotting Wives;* a tragedy, *The Generous Moor;* Strictures on Freemasonry; and a number of sonnets. The motive for his publication appears to be hinted at in the following lines:—

> "I've heard a certain author say
> He wrote to pass his time away;
> Then prythee, critic, let me use
> His very words, for my excuse.
>
> You might have wrote, I hear you cry,
> But wisely should have thrown them by.
> I own you're right;—but take this hint,
> 'Tis bread, not pastime, makes me print."—*p.* 266.

Mr. Thos. Taylor informs me that in 1763 he was elected one of the Coroners for Yorkshire, having previously filled the office of Postmaster at Wakefield. There is an allusion to his appointment in one of his songs, on *Calcavelle:*—

> "'A boon,' cry'd old Janus; 'thus lowly I bend;
> One pipe of this wine, to present to a friend:
> When I tell you for whom, the favour you'll yield;
> It is for the Crowner of merry Wakefield.'
>   Derry Down.
>
> "'That I will,' said great Jove, 'and straightway I'll send
> To an honest good mortal, and always my friend,
> Ten pipes to one Charnock I yearly will grant,
> That the Crowner may have what liquor he'll want.'
>   Derry Down."—*p.* 216.

At p. 246 he speaks of his having been for many

years Master of the Lodge of Unanimity, (then No. 238,) at Wakefield; and at p. 233 is a *Song* on the constitution of that Lodge of the Freemasons, beginning—

"What joy fills our hearts! what transports we share!
When thus, my dear Brethren, we meet on the *Square;*
Our light now shines forth, where darkness appear'd,
For the Lodge is revived, that at Wakefield was reared,
   Derry Down."

It is noticeable that in the *Roxburgh Songs and Ballads* (iii. 711), is a *Song on the constituting and revival of the Lodge 296, at Wakefield*, which is identical with Linnecar's, except that various coarse expressions in the broadside have been altered to a more becoming form. As the Roxburgh collection is professedly of ballads written between 1560 and 1700, we must conclude that this song has got inserted by mistake.

Richard Linnecar died, whilst holding an inquest at Swillington, in the year 1800. His portrait, painted by Singleton and engraved by T. Barrow, is now, I believe, in the possession of the present respected Coroner for this district.

Page 224.

[*John Wroe.*]

In the *Wakefield Journal and Examiner* of May 29th, 1863, appeared the following extract from the *Melbourne Review*, relating to Wroe's death a little while before in Melbourne:—"It will probably be a piece of perfectly novel intelligence to the bulk of our readers," the writer says, "to learn that the wretched old man who thus obscurely ended his career, was up till the very last looked upon by his deluded followers as an inspired personage ... able to bestow immortal life on all who believed in him.... Yet it is very certain that this man was nothing more nor less than a monomaniac.... There lies before us a volume of the *Life and Journal of John Wroe*, which contains many alleged 'divine communications revealed to him.'.... The book in fact is very like a monstrous and profane parody of the prophecies of Jeremiah and Ezekiel.... Mormonism is surely bad enough, but even Mormonism is rational and pure compared with the teachings of John Wroe.... The miserable maniac who died the other day at the 'Synagogue' in Fitzroy, steadily declared all his life that neither himself nor his followers could ever taste death, but that both they and he would be translated to Heaven as Elijah was! Indeed John Wroe's latest 'revelation,' delivered only a few days before his death, was that he should return to England within a few months. He had actually taken his passage by one of the Liverpool liners, in fulfilment of this prophecy, when the inevitable hand of death fell upon him. So ended the eighty years of hallucination and daring impiety of John Wroe. His duped followers, it is averred, are at this hour looking for his resurrection and reappearance amongst them."

In Horridge's *Wakefield Almanack* for 1864, it is stated that the recognised head of the sect at present is Mrs. Deane of Gravesend, whose daughter was married by one of Wroe's sons.

It should have been mentioned that Ashton-under-

Lyne was for some time their head-quarters. But here too a similar scene was enacted to that described at p. 223; and Mr. R. Micklethwaite, who was then residing in the neighbourhood, informs me that from that town also John Wroe barely escaped with his life.

Page 230, n. 2.

[*Edward Moxon.*]

In the register of the Wakefield Parish Church is an entry of the baptism of Edward, son of Michael and Ann Moxon, Dec. 12th, 1801. This Edward Moxon I presume to have been the one in question.

INDEX.

Altofts 4, 54.
Alverthorpe 2.
Amory Dr. 166.
Amory Thomas 165.
Ardsley 59, 91.
Atkinson Christopher 197.

Bacon Michael 185.
Barker Richard 19.
Barnaby Drunken 16.
Baskerville John 121.
Bate Richard 24.
Bawdwen William 9.
Bentley Richard 120.
Bentley Richard (of Nailston) 121.
Benton Jennet 82.
Bingham Joseph 142.
Black Mrs. 228.
Bland Sir Thomas 78.
Bolles Lady 67.
Bonnivant Col. 79.
Boulton Jeremiah 121.
Bradbury Thomas 161.
Bradeforde 44.
Brereton Sir W. 46.
Browne William 82.
Bunny Hall 82.
Burton Dr. John 206, 252.

Cair Loid Coit 3.
Calder 6, 175.
Camden Lady 88.
Camidge Rev. C. J. 12.

Castleford 4.
Cave Thomas 58.
Chapel on the Bridge 13.
Christie Thomas 164.
Clarke Edward 142, 152.
Clarke John 176.
Clarkson Rev. T. B. 214, 218, 230, 233, 252.
Clipping Coin 84.
Cloth Trade 85.
Coke Richard 47.
Cresswell Daniel 215.
Cressy Hugh Paulin 70.
Cromek T. H. 4, 53, 213, 215, 219.
Cromwell Oliver 61, 65.
Cryer John 230, 253.
Currer Miss 208.

Day Thomas 188.
Dewsbury 84.
Domesday Book 8.
Doughty Robert 95.
D'Oyly Edward 228.
D'Oyly Thomas 226.
Drayton 16, 33.

Edwin King 6.
Elmet 2, 5.

Fleming Richard 29.
Fleming Robert 31.
Fordyce Dr. 105.
Forman John 37.

INDEX.

Frobisher Sir Martin 53.
Fuller 62.

Garth Samuel 121, 129.
Goldsmith Oliver 182.
Goody Bower 240.
Goring General 77.
Grammar School 58, 79, 80, 104, 179.
Green Coat School 59.
Green George à 15.

Haigh Hall 90.
Halifax 119.
Hankyn Thomas 11.
Hatfelde 7.
Heath 226.
Hewitt John 184, 239.
Hill Edward 87.
Holdsworth Samuel 33.
Hoole Charles 95.
Hopkinson John 208.
Horbury 91.
Horridge: *Wakefield Almanack* 256.
Hoveden Roger de 18.
Hutton William 210.

Ilkley 5.
Ince T. N. 9, 104, 219, 254.
Isola Emma, 234.
Jackson Richard 82.
James John 3, 6, 44.

Kirby Joshua 88.
Kirkstall 44.
Kirkthorp 75, 253.
Kneller Sir Godfrey 111.
Knolles Thomas 47.
Knollys Robert 45.

Lamb Charles 231, 234.
Langton Bennet 179, 191.
Leake John 253.
Leatham W. H. 43, 95, 104.
Ledis 44.

Leeds 3.
Leeds Duke of 14.
Leland 41, 42.
Lingwell Gate 5.
Linnecar Richard 254.
Lister James 251.
Litestre Richard 36.
Lofthouse 208, 228.
Low Hill 43, 244.
Lyster Sir Richard 39.

Mangnall Miss 217.
Margaret Queen 32.
Marsden Jeremiah 87.
Maud John 19.
Micklethwaite R. 257.
Milton Daniel 223, 224.
Mortuary 26.
Moxon Edward 229, 257.
Moxon Joseph 97.

Nayler James 91.
Naylor Charles 209.
Naylor Joseph 65.
Naylor Peter 161.
Nennius 3.
Nevinson John 86.
Nield James 187.
Normanton 4, 58.
Northallerton 104, 175.
Nostell 8.

Oates Titus 101.
Oley Barnabas 75.
Oswald 7, 8.
Overton Col. 79.

Paulinus 6.
Pilkington Sir John 21.
Pilkington Sir Lyon 21.
Pindar William 100.
Pollard John 25.
Pontefract 76.
Potter Archbishop 143, 152.
Potter John 158.
Potter Thomas 159.

Power Henry 149.
Preston John 36.
Pukenills 32.
Pullein Rev. J. 253.

Quakers 89.

Radcliffe John 104, 144, 252.
Ramsey Abbey 49.
Robertson Thomas 50.
Robinson Thomas 197.
Rothwell 38.
Roxburgh Ballads 255.
Royston 38.

Sandal 13, 79, 86, 193.
Savile family 19, 242.
Savile George 59.
Savile Sir Henry 20.
Savile Sir John 57.
Savile William 59.
Sens Council of 30.
Shaw William 33.
Sisson Dr. 233.
Smyth Henry 209.
Smyth Right Hon. John 198.
Smyth John George 209.
Southcott Joanna 219.
SS. Collar of 41, 244.
Storie John 58.
Straubenzee C. S. Van 210.
Straubenzee Philip 213.
Swift Dean 129, 173.
Swire Samuel 196.

Taylor Thomas 246, 252, 254.
Tempest Sir R. 46.
Test Acts 205.
Thompson Richard 100.
Tobacco 85.

Torre James 10.
Turner George 222.
Turner Mrs. 211.
Tyas : *Battles of Wakefield* 78.
Venner Thomas 157.
Vicar of Wakefield 182, 184.

Wakes 241.
Wakefield 1, 239.
Wakefield Arms of 46.
Wakefield Battle of 32.
Wakefield Church 9.
Wakefield Henry de 22, 23, 243.
Wakefield *Journal and Examiner* 218, 555.
Wakefield Manor of 12.
Wakefield Peter de 18.
Wakefield Robert 48.
Wakefield Streets of 44, 250.
Wakefield taking of 78.
Walker Richard 137.
Warmfield 77.
Warren Earls of 10, 12.
Watkinson Joseph 195.
Went 7.
Wentworth Lord 57, 70.
Whiston William 156.
Whitaker Jeremiah 61.
Wilson Benjamin 177, 182.
Winwaed 7.
Witchcraft 82.
Wood Timothy 87.
Wrenthorp 223.
Wroe John 219, 255.

York Duke of 37.

Zouch Thomas 181, 191.

www.ingramcontent.com/pod-product-compliance
Lightning Source LLC
Chambersburg PA
CBHW032131230426
43672CB00011B/2304